FATHOMING THE HOLOCAUST

SOCIAL PROBLEMS AND SOCIAL ISSUES

An Aldine de Gruyter Series of Texts and Monographs

SERIES EDITOR

Joel Best, *University of Delaware*

FATHOMING THE HOLOCAUST

A SOCIAL PROBLEMS APPROACH

RONALD J. BERGER

ALDINE DE GRUYTER
NEW YORK

ABOUT THE AUTHOR

Ronald J. Berger, Professor of Sociology at the University of Wisconsin-Whitewater, has previously published six books and numerous articles and book chapters. His earlier book on the Holocaust was a sociological account of his father and uncle's survival experiences.

Copyright © 2002 Walter de Gruyter, Inc., New York

ALDINE DE GRUYTER
A division of Walter de Gruyter, Inc.
200 Saw Mill River Road
Hawthorne, New York 10532

This publication is printed on acid free paper ∞

Library of Congress Cataloging-in-Publication Data

Berger, Ronald J.
   Fathoming the Holocaust: a social problems approach / Ronald J. Berger
      p. cm.
   Includes bibliographical references (p.) and index.
   ISBN 0-202-30669-0 (cloth : alk. paper) — ISBN 0-202-30670-4 (pbk. : alk. paper)
   1. Holocaust, Jewish (1939–1945)—Historiography.   2. Holocaust, Jewish (1939–1945)—Causes.   3. Holocaust, Jewish (1939–1945)—Influence.
   4. Germany—Social conditions—1933–1945.   5. Germany—Ethnic relations.
   I. Title.

D804.348 .B47 2002
940.53'18—dc21   2001055317

Manufactured in the United States of America

10 9 8 7 6 5 4 3 2 1

For
Ruthy, Sarah, Corey, Chad, and Kristi

and my parents,
Michael and Mildred

Contents

Acknowledgments

There are, as always, many people to thank for the success of a project such as this. First of all, there are the students I have taught over the last twelve years, whose interest in the subject assures me that the Final Solution will never be forgotten. There is the support I received from my colleagues in the sociology department and the administration at the University of Wisconsin-Whitewater. I am especially grateful for the sabbatical I was awarded that gave me the time to complete this book. Along the way, Norman Denzin and James Holstein supported my work by giving me valuable feedback and publishing my articles in *Sociological Quarterly* and *Perspectives on Social Problems,* respectively. Portions of these articles are excerpted in modified form in this book: "The Banality of Evil Reframed: The Social Contruction of the Final Solution to the 'Jewish Problem,'" *Sociological Quarterly*, Vol. 34(4) 1993 © JAI Press/University of California Press; and "The Politics of Collective Memory in Israel and West Germany," *Perspectives on Social Problems*, Vol. 8, 1996, and "Altruism Amidst the Holocaust: An Integrated Social Theory," *Perspectives on Social Problems*, Vol. 10, 1998 © JAI Press/Elsevier Science. I am grateful as well to the staff at the University Press of Colorado for publishing *Constructing a Collective Memory of the Holocaust,* my first book on the Holocaust, which includes my father's testimony, portions of which are quoted in the pages that follow.

I also want to express my appreciation to Joel Best, editor of the Aldine de Gruyter series Social Problems and Social Issues, for his support and for bringing *Fathoming the Holocaust* to the attention of Richard Koffler, executive editor of Aldine de Gruyter. And one could not ask for a finer editor than Richard, whose knowledge of the Holocaust and constructive critique significantly improved the quality of the book. Thanks go as well to Aldine de Gruyter managing editor Jan Goldsworthy and copy editor Mike Sola for their work on the book.

Lastly, and most importantly, there are my wife Ruthy, whose love and friendship has sustained me throughout the years, and my daughter Sarah, who is the absolute joy of my life and the spirit that brightens the future.

Preface

Growing up in the 1950s and 1960s, I was exposed to very little about the Holocaust—what the Nazis called the Final Solution—even though my father was a survivor of the Nazi concentration camps. As far as I could tell, the only observable trace of that experience was the blue tattooed number on his arm. It was not until the late 1980s that he and I sat down together to recount his ordeal in any detail. This was a powerful and moving experience for us both, and it had the additional impact of transforming my interests as a sociologist. I subsequently began an intensive program of retraining to develop expertise on the subject, started teaching a course about it, and published several academic articles as well as a book about my father's (and uncle's) survival.

Fathoming the Holocaust represents the culmination of these efforts, and more specifically, is a unique attempt to explain the Final Solution to the "Jewish problem" in terms of a general theory of social problems construction. The book is comprehensive in scope, covering the origins and emergence of the Final Solution, the wartime reaction to it, and the postwar memory of the genocide.

Social problems constructionism is a perspective that treats social problems not as a *condition* but as an *activity* that identifies and defines problems, persuades others that something must be done about them, and generates practical programs of remedial action. As such, social problems have a "natural history," that is, they evolve through a sequence of stages that entail the development and unfolding of claims about problems and the formulation and implementation of solutions.

Chapter 1 opens the book by reviewing how historians have studied the subject and examining some issues and controversies they have raised about it. I then consider several avenues of sociological analysis, including the constructionist approach outlined above. I also suggest how a constructionist account of the postwar period would benefit from insights drawn from the literature on collective memory.

Chapter 2 focuses on Christian claims about the Jews that formed the historical foundation for anti-Semitism. I discuss the German variation on these claims as it was elaborated by German nationalists and given its racial characterization by the Nazis. The chapter then examines how Hitler and the Nazis appealed to the German population and garnered political and financial support. Upon their seizure of power, the Nazis began formulating solutions to the "Jewish problem" that gradually evolved through the legislative solution, the emigration/deportation solution, and eventually the Final Solution.

Chapter 3 looks at the organizational settings and processes that enabled the Nazis to implement the Final Solution. I discuss, among other things, the role of the railways, Order Police, medical establishment, and concentration/ extermination camps. I also look at how Nazi officials and their collaborators, including German and international businesses, profited from solutions to the "Jewish problem."

In Chapter 4 I note that social problems development does not proceed without resistance from those who organize to thwart or redirect the implementation process. Here I discuss efforts by Jews and gentiles, including Allied governments, to subvert the Final Solution.

Chapters 5 to 7 turn to the postwar legacy of the Holocaust. Chapter 5 examines how collective memories have been contested and negotiated in domestic and international context by two nations that best serve as reminders of the Holocaust: Israel as the symbolic if not political representative of the Jewish people, and the Federal Republic of Germany as the originating site of Nazism.

In Chapter 6 I show how the United States has moved to center stage with respect to postwar representations and activities regarding the genocide. Here I examine the popularization of the Holocaust through American films, the role of American historiography and the problem of Holocaust denial, the U.S. Holocaust Memorial Museum, and the politics of victimization and compensation claims.

Finally, in Chapter 7 I conclude by considering a set of interrelated issues that have emerged as significant problems in the postwar period: the problem of religious faith after the Holocaust, the problem of Jewish continuity and of Christian-Jewish reconciliation, and the general problem of "difference" that underlies various forms of exclusionary social practices.

1 Approaching the Holocaust

Not far from us, flames were leaping up from a ditch, gigantic flames. They were burning something. A lorry drew up at the pit and delivered its load—little children. Babies! Yes, I saw it—saw it with my own eyes . . . those children in flames.

I pinched my face. Was I still alive? Was I awake? I could not believe it. How could it be possible for them to burn people, children, and for the world to keep silent. No, none of this could be true. . . .

Never shall I forget that night, the first night in [Auschwitz concentration] camp, which has turned my life into one long night. . . . Never shall I forget the smoke. Never shall I forget the little faces of the children whose bodies I saw turned into wreaths of smoke beneath a silent blue sky. Never shall I forget those flames which consumed my faith forever . . . and turned my dreams to dust. (Wiesel)   —Elie Wiesel

These words, from Elie Wiesel's *Night,* give us but a proximate glimpse of the horrors that Wiesel and other victims of the Holocaust experienced over half a century ago. A prolific author and 1986 Nobel Peace Prize recipient, Wiesel is perhaps the most well-known Jewish survivor of the Holocaust. Like him, others who survived lived forever with their pain, with the burden of their memories. Some never recovered the psychological health they once enjoyed. Some lapsed into utter despair or sought relief through suicide. Yet most showed a remarkable capacity to move on, to establish productive work and family lives, to appreciate like no others "the infinite value of human life" (Lanzmann 1985:146; see also Davidson 1992; Helmreich 1992).

The Holocaust—the genocidal program of extermination that the Nazis called the "Final Solution"—took the lives of some six million Jews.[1] This amounted to about 60 percent of European Jewry and one-third of the world's Jewish population (Gutman & Rozett 1990). To be sure, other groups suffered at the hands of the Nazis as well. When one adds the murder of Gypsies,[2] Poles, Slavs, Soviet civilians and prisoners of war, gays, the disabled and mentally ill—among others—the number of innocent dead may be greater than fifteen million (Rubenstein & Roth 1987; Spielvogel 1996).[3]

Some analysts, therefore, argue against the common focus on the particularity of the Jewish experience during the Holocaust, noting that the Nazi assault on the Jews took place in the context of a more general attempt to construct a racial utopia in which persecution was extended to a wide range of "impure" or "undesirable" groups (Burleigh & Wipperman 1991; Hancock 1996; Milton 1990). Others insist, however, that the Jews were the only group targeted by the Nazis for total annihilation and that this fact makes what happened to them unique. This observation is not intended to create a hierarchy of pain or to minimize the suffering that so many endured. Rather, it is meant to point out that the Final Solution "happened to a particular people for particular reasons" and that "the Jews were, for the Nazis, the central enemy" (Bauer 2001:63, 67; see also Katz 1989; Lewy 1999).

Ironically, for over a decade after the war Jews did not have a preeminent place in public discourse about the Holocaust. During the postwar Nuremberg trials, for example, the particularity of Jewish victimization was acknowledged but subsumed under the broader categories of "war crimes" and "crimes against humanity" and soon half-forgotten. William Shirer's *The Rise and Fall of the Third Reich,* a 1960 bestseller, devoted just 2 to 3 percent of its some twelve hundred pages to the Jewish genocide. The word "Jew" was not even mentioned in Alain Resnais's otherwise brilliant 1955 documentary film, *Night and Fog.* Early works by Jewish victims and survivors, including Wiesel's *Night* and Anne Frank's diary, were first printed in limited editions and largely ignored. And survivors found that those outside the survivor community were not interested in hearing about their ordeal (Berger 1995; Davidson 1992; Hilberg 1991; Novick 1999).

All this, of course, eventually changed, for reasons we will explore later in this book. As historical scholarship on the Holocaust proliferated, Wiesel observed that perhaps "no other tragedy or . . . event has been as [thoroughly] documented" (quoted in Cargas 1986:5). At the same time, he still views the Holocaust as a phenomenon that defies comprehension. Although his own writings have achieved much acclaim, Wiesel says that he writes about the Holocaust to denounce writing, for words can never truly portray the nature of the evil and suffering that constituted this event (Freeman 1991; Sachar 1992).

Historians are respectful of this position but argue against mystifying the Holocaust as incomprehensible (Marrus 1987). "The Holocaust was a human event," argues Yehuda Bauer, "perpetrated for human reasons which can be historically explained" (1987:209). Historians have by now succeeded in integrating the Holocaust into the mainstream of their discipline. Sociologists, on the other hand, have paid far less attention to the Holocaust, although it affords opportunities to examine issues that are central to some "main themes of sociological inquiry" (Bauman 1989:xiii). This book, therefore, aims to advance sociological understanding of the Holocaust, not simply to describe its history but to examine its social construction, that is, to understand it as a consequence of concerted human activity. In doing so, I also hope to encourage the teaching of the Holocaust in the sociological curricula of higher education.[4]

HISTORIANS AND THE HOLOCAUST

Wiesel has said, "The more I read about [the Holocaust] the less I understand" (quoted in Cargas 1986:5). This retreat from clarity may stem, in part, from the ambiguities of evidence and interpretation that are typical of any scholarly enterprise. Researchers, at times, offer contrary evidence regarding the facticity of certain events and advance competing interpretations to explain the empirical record. Hence some are concerned that legitimate scholarly disputes will encourage Nazi apologists or open the door to Holocaust denial (Marrus 1987).

The contributions of historians to the study of the Holocaust are sophisticated and vast. Their perceptive analyses and empirical documentation constitute the primary corpus of knowledge that informs this book. Here I want to begin by briefly considering two levels or modes of analyses. The first entails what Saul Friedlander (1989) characterizes as "global interpretations" of Nazism, that is, efforts to understand Nazism broadly in terms of the evolution of German nationalism and the phenomenon of totalitarianism or fascism more generally. The second entails the more specific or concrete evolution of the Final Solution against the Jews.

Germany's Special Path

Historians have observed that Germany lagged behind other Western societies (e.g., Great Britain, France, United States) in building a consolidated nation-state and developing a tradition of political liberalism that valued democratic institutions and individual rights. This German *Sonderweg* (special or separate path) is viewed by some as key to understanding the eventual rise of Nazism in Germany (Fischer 1995; Herf 1984; Maier 1988).

Prior to unification as a nation, Germany consisted of several independent states. Among them Prussia was the only one that had an army comparable to those of any Western European power. In 1862 Prussian King Wilhelm I appointed Otto von Bismarck as prime minister of Prussia. Bismarck wielded a coalition of German states that fought four successful wars, established Germany as a military powerhouse, and culminated in unification of the previously separate German states in 1871. Wilhelm I became the *kaiser* (emperor) of Germany, and he appointed Bismarck as chancellor to head the government.

A parliament was established with jurisdiction over domestic matters, but the kaiser retained control of the army and foreign policy. The chancellor served at the pleasure of the kaiser and not of the parliament (Sheehan 1993).

In this way, Klaus Fischer argues, German nationhood was born not from a broad, democratic consensus arising from the grass roots, not from a yearning of a people wishing to be free. Rather, it was imposed by the "force of superior Prussian arms" and imbued with a militaristic spirit that valued authority over democracy and obedience over autonomy (1995:19). Thus as the country began to industrialize in the late eighteenth and early nineteenth centuries, its political system was especially vulnerable to the influence of totalitarianism and fascist social movements (Evans 1989; Herf 1984; Maier 1988).

Fischer believes that Nazism "represents the right-wing variant of modern totalitarianism, the ideological counterpart of Communism, or left-wing totalitarianism" (1995:4). He defines totalitarianism "as the monopolizing of human activities, private and public, by a modern technocratic state," a political system where the means of control and domination are centralized in an all-powerful government and where personal liberties are suppressed and social institutions (e.g., media, schools) are forced to serve the interests of the state. The totalitarianism account of Nazism focuses on "the will for total domination" rather than on particular ideological motivations such as anti-Semitism,[5] racism, or opposition to capitalism or communism (Friedlander 1989:10).

Some historians make a distinction between totalitarianism and fascism. According to Ernst Nolte (1965), fascism derives its peculiar character from its anticommunist stance. It is "a counter-revolutionary rival to communism, rather than its twin," and is hospitable toward private ownership of industry as long as economic production is consistent with state objectives (Jay 1993:38). Fascist policies favor limitations on imports to promote national economic independence, restrictions on labor unions and the right to strike, and the buildup of the military. Fascism not only idealizes militarism but celebrates a radical cultural nationalism, expressing a nostalgic longing for the restoration of a lost community that is rooted in a people's common heritage and that excludes alien elements. At the same time, it is forward-looking in its messianic vision of a glorious new day that will come about as a result of the fascist revolution (Herf 1984; Payne 1980; Turner 1975).

Because fascist movements are intensely nationalistic, they give rise to distinct orientations that reflect the particular circumstances and aspirations of each nation-state (Deák 1983; Payne 2001). What was characteristic of German fascism (Nazism) in the period between the two world wars—what distinguished it, for example, from Italian fascism—was the centrality of anti-Semitism to its political program and worldview. In Italy, anti-Semitism did not figure prominently in Benito Mussolini's (1883–1945) rise to power in 1922 (which preceded Adolf Hitler's by over a decade) and in the ideology of Italian fascism. While Mussolini had anti-Semitic and racist leanings, his government did not openly advocate discriminatory policies against the Jews until the latter part of the 1930s, when German fascism was exerting greater influence. Moreover, these policies never achieved the broad consensus of support that they did in Germany (Caracciolo 1995; Carpi 2001; De Felice 2001; Zuccotti 1987).

In Nazi Germany, on the other hand, anti-Jewish policies played a predominant role. Nazi ideology asserted that the "spiritual, moral, and physical redemption" of the German people, the German *Volk*, required the purging of the Jewish blight, for "the Jew" (*der Jude*) was the source—the very essence— of all that was vile, corrupt, and evil (Bauer 2001:115; see also Goldhagen 1996). This "redemptive antisemitism," as Friedlander (1997) calls it, envisioned a radical reordering of society premised on the elimination of Jews. It had its roots, as we shall see, in Christian anti-Semitism and in secular notions of a Jewish culture that was "culturally and spiritually inferior" (Hertzberg 1968:274). In the nineteenth century these views were given a modern foundation through pseudoscientific theories of race. In the twentieth century they were carried to messianic heights through Hitler's charismatic leadership (Bauer 2001; Rose 1990; Volkov 1989).

The Intentionalist-Functionalist Debate

Historians have also attempted to reconstruct the particular events that led to the Final Solution, and two schools of thought have emerged to explain this facet of the historical record. *Intentionalist* historians view Hitler as the primary if not sole strategist whose order to begin mass murdering the Jews in 1941 flowed directly from the plan he outlined nearly two decades earlier in his book *Mein Kampf* (My Struggle). The intentionalists emphasize the premeditation and planning of the Nazi leadership, which was following Hitler's explicit instructions, and the role of bureaucratic subordinates who carried out the orders of their superiors (Browning 2000; Friedlander 1989; Marrus 1987).

Functionalist historians, on the other hand, emphasize a broader range of responsibility. They portray Hitler as less directly involved in the development and implementation of anti-Jewish policies than is commonly assumed. They focus instead on the bureaucratic functionaries who often improvised and competed with each other to devise the most efficient means of removing Jews from Germany and its annexed territories. While Hitler may have set the goal of a Germany *Judenfrei* (free of Jews), he did not specify how this goal was to be accomplished.[6] In the functionalist view, the Final Solution emerged gradually through a process of incremental decision-making and "cumulative radicalization," as a bureaucratic system of interrelated but often disharmonious parts eventually coalesced into a coherent program of extermination (Marrus 1987:42; see also Browning 2000). According to the functionalist view, German expansionism and World War II created both the need and opportunity for more radical measures: The occupation of more territory made the previous policy of emigration and deportation less feasible as a solution to the "Jewish problem," and the war provided the cover and opportunity for mass murder. Thus Hitler's actions take on the appearance of a planned policy only from the vantage point of historical hindsight. As Karl Schleunes observes, "When the Nazis came to power, they had no specific plans for a solution of a [particular] sort. They were certain only that a solution was necessary" (1970:viii).

Hitler, World War I, and Its Aftermath   The value of the intentionalist view is its emphasis on Hitler's indisputable central role, for without Hitler arguably there would have been no Holocaust. Hitler (1889–1945) was born in Germany's neighboring country, Austria. At one time Austria had been part of the German empire and thus shared many German cultural traits. (Between 1867 and 1918, Austria was merged with Hungary as Austria-Hungary.) As a boy Hitler grew up on "stories of heroic Germanic battles and conquests . . . [and] was taught to admire nationalism, militarism, order, and discipline" (Poole 1997a:xix, xxi).[7]

The cultural environment of Vienna, where Hitler moved in 1908, was intensely anti-Semitic. But according to James Poole, Hitler was propelled down the road to radical anti-Semitism through his confrontation with Marxist socialism. While working as a laborer on a construction project, "he refused to join a socialist labor union" and was beaten up and "kicked off the job" (ibid.:xviii). In addition to this personal experience, Hitler acquired an intellectual distaste for socialism because this ideology (and its variants, e.g., communism) advocated international solidarity among workers and hence rejected nationalist beliefs. Hitler also noticed that many socialist leaders were Jewish. He started reading anti-Semitic pamphlets, some quite fanatical, and was exposed to the view that Jews were not simply a religious group but an inferior race as well.

In 1914 Archduke Francis Ferdinand of Austria-Hungary was assassinated while traveling through Sarajevo, then part of Serbia. With a promise of support from Germany, Austria-Hungary used this incident as an excuse to attack Serbia, its long-time enemy. Russia, Serbia's ally, began mobilizing troops on the Austria-Hungary border. Germany then declared war on Russia and also invaded Belgium and France. (France and Russia were allies.) Soon Great Britain and eventually the United States were drawn into World War I (Coffman 1993).

World War I was a formative experience for Hitler. Prior to the war Hitler had left Vienna for Munich, Germany. When the war broke out he volunteered for the German army and distinguished himself as a dispatch runner carrying messages from "regimental headquarters to men in the trenches" while dodging barrages of artillery (Poole 1997a:xxiv). He was wounded and hospitalized after a mustard gas attack, and was awarded the Iron Cross, a high military honor. The war undoubtedly hardened Hitler and reinforced his conviction that ruthlessness and violence were necessary to get what he wanted. Years later he would say, "If two million of Germany's best youth were slaughtered in the war, we have the right to exterminate subhumans who breed like vermin" (quoted in ibid.:xxvi).

When Germany was defeated in 1918, Hitler was furious over the armistice terms imposed by the Allies. He blamed weak German leaders and "Jewish interests from within" for stabbing Germany in the back and selling out the country (Rubenstein & Roth 1987:98). Under the terms of the Treaty of Versailles, Germany was forced to accept full responsibility for causing the war and was required to relinquish considerable territory, pay $33 billion in reparations, and dramatically limit the size of its armed forces (Fischer 1995).

In 1919 a democratic, constitutional government was established in Weimar (the Weimar Republic), but it never received the full support of the German population (Fischer 1995). Economic malaise and political rebellions undermined the government's legitimacy. Hitler's road to power was to culminate in the abolition of the republic. Along the way, after joining and becoming the leader of the National Socialist German Workers' party (*Nationalsozialistiche Deutsche Arbeiterpartei*), or Nazi party, Hitler wrote *Mein Kampf* ([1925] 1943), a book that reverberates with insidious epithets against the Jews. In that book he "claimed that the killing of twelve to fifteen thousand Jews in Germany during World War I by means of poison gas (!) might have saved the lives of hundreds of thousands of German soldiers" (Breitman 1991:21). Two years earlier, in an interview with journalist Josef Hell, Hitler had boasted:

> Once I . . . am in power, my first and foremost task will be the annihilation of the Jews. . . . I will have gallows built in rows—at the Marienplatz in Munich, for example—as many as traffic allows. Then the Jews will be hanged indiscriminately, and they will remain hanging until they stink. . . . As soon as they have been untied, the next batch will be strung up, and so on down the line, until the last Jew in Munich has been exterminated. Other cities will follow suit . . . until all Germany has been completely cleansed of Jews. (quoted in Poole 1997a:271–72)

According to Poole, however, by the time Hitler came to power in 1933, he had concluded that his goal of a Germany *Judenfrei* could be achieved through emigration and expulsion rather than through extermination. Richard Breitman (1998), on the other hand, suggests that Hitler may have simply become more circumspect in his public pronouncements and that he never lost

his murderous impulse. Still, Breitman acknowledges a point made by functionalist historians: "The scope and methods of killing" were not anticipated
early on and the details "evolved substantially over time" (ibid.:4).

Ordinary Germans and the Banality of Evil   While Hitler's central role is un-
deniable, so is the broader range of responsibility for the Holocaust. And this
responsibility goes beyond a small inner circle of dedicated Nazi ideologues.
Here the functionalist historians have made us aware of the widespread complicity and active participation of ordinary Germans who voted for Hitler and
the Nazi party, provided the state with voluntary denunciations of Jews and
anti-Nazi resisters, staffed the bureaucracy of destruction (the "desk murderers"), and directly killed innocent men, women, and children (Browning 1992;
Goldhagen 1996; Hamilton 1982; Johnson 1999).

One of the main goals of this book is to document this complicity and participation and to explore a thesis first advanced by Hannah Arendt (1963) in
her book *Eichmann in Jerusalem: A Report on the Banality of Evil*: the view that
evil was accomplished in large part by "ordinary persons [acting] in ordinary
contexts" (Schmitt 1989:288). Arendt arrived at this view as she watched
Adolph Eichmann (1906–1962) being tried by the Israeli government for
"war crimes" and "crimes against humanity." Eichmann, a former traveling
salesman, was the leading Nazi expert on Jewish affairs and a key engineer of
the Final Solution. Psychiatrists at his trial remarked that he seemed clini-
cally well adjusted and had positive relationships with family and friends.
Eichmann denied that he held any ill-feeling toward Jews and claimed that
he joined the Nazi party to further his career, not to pursue an ideological
objective. He represented himself as "an ordinary bureaucrat . . . carrying
out the duties of his office" (Popora 1990:16), a man who "would have done
the same job if he had been ordered to kill all men whose name began with
P or B, or all who had red hair" (Askenasy 1978:27). He was simply a man
who wanted "to follow—and be rewarded for following—orders" (Markle
1995:38).

As a criminal defense, the "I was only following orders" claim is self-serv-
ing and unconvincing, for Eichmann exhibited considerable initiative, zeal,
and persistence in helping to plan and carry out the Final Solution. He did not
simply follow orders but exceeded them in "his obsessive determination to
hunt down and destroy every last Jew he could lay his hands on, even when,
as the tide of war turned, both the time and power to do so were deserting
him" (Clendinnen 1999:103). Nonetheless, the banality-of-evil concept helps
us see that one did not have to be a madman or monster to perpetrate extraordinary evil. Rather, many individuals did their job (of killing) as if it were the
most ordinary thing to do. That they did so, however, should also lead us to
ask, Could they have acted otherwise? Why was following orders so commonplace that too few disobeyed? Were there punitive consequences for resistance?

Was anti-Semitism so taken for granted, so much a "natural attitude" (see Schutz 1962), that too few thought to question what they were doing?

Comments from members of the Order Police (*Ordnungspolizei*) who participated in the shooting of Jews shed light on these questions. The Order Police, who were deployed in Nazi-occupied Poland, were comprised largely of ordinary Germans who were not Nazi party members and who had received no special indoctrination or training in the killing of civilians. Were they forced to kill Jews? The answer is no. As one man recalled:

> In no case can I remember that anyone was forced to continue participating in the executions when he declared that he was no longer able to. . . . [T]here were always some comrades who found it easier to shoot Jews than did others, so that the respective commando leaders never had difficulty finding suitable shooters. (Browning 1992:128–29)

Another man agreed: "It was in no way the case that those who did not want to or could not carry out the shooting of human beings with their own hands could not keep themselves out of this task. No strict control was being carried out" (ibid.:65). Still another said, "Truthfully I must say that at the time we didn't reflect about it at all. . . . Only later did it first occur to me that [the killing of Jews] had not been right" (ibid.:72).

SOCIOLOGICAL FRAMEWORKS

Although the Holocaust begs for sociological insight, sociologists have lagged behind historians in grappling with this subject. In the remainder of this chapter I suggest several avenues of sociological analysis, indicating ways that historical research "might benefit from greater collaboration with sociology" and laying out the framework for the rest of the book (Rafter 1992a:29).

The View from the Classics

It seems appropriate to begin this sociological inquiry with insights drawn from some classical sociological theorists. According to Jeffrey Alexander:

> Classics are earlier works of human exploration which are given a privileged status vis-à-vis contemporary explorations in the same field. The concept of privileged status means that contemporary practitioners in the discipline in question believe that they can learn as much about their field through understanding this earlier work as they can from the work of their own contemporaries. (1989:9)

In one way or another, all classic formulations posit a theory of *social structure* and *social action*. Social structure refers to social relations that are external to individual actors, to forces that constrain behavior "by fixing in advance its material environment" (Alexander 1984:10). Social action refers to human activity that responds to these constraints, most often conforming to or reproducing predominant structural patterns, but sometimes challenging or modifying these patterns as well. Social action entails motivated behavior, whether it is rational (or instrumental) behavior based on calculation of self-interest or the means to achieve goals, or nonrational (or normative) behavior based on values, moral concerns, or emotional needs that are imbued with symbolic meaning. We will now turn to some themes associated with the work of three classical theorists—Karl Marx, Max Weber, and Émile Durkheim—and see how their ideas help illuminate Nazism and the Holocaust.

Karl Marx and Class Structure   Alexander considers the German social theorist Karl Marx (1818–1883) to be the "greatest theorist of social structure in the [rational] tradition" (1984:10), and some analysts believe that much social theory has developed as a debate with Marx (Zeitlan 1990).[8] For Marx the relationship between economic classes constitutes the basic element of social structure that constrains individual action. Members of different classes have different and often opposing economic interests, and they tend to act rationally in pursuit of these interests.

Capitalism—an economic system based on private rather than public ownership of the major means of production (i.e., factories, technology, raw materials)—often pits capitalists against workers over wages and working conditions. After World War I, rebellious mobs of German workers were calling "for the confiscation of private property" and workers' control over business (Poole 1997b:123). German economic elites feared that their country might "suffer the same fate as Russia," which had experienced a communist revolution in 1917. They were also concerned that the Versailles Treaty—which limited not only the German military but the merchant marine fleet as well—hurt their ability "to gain new export markets and . . . vital raw materials" (ibid.:129). And many capitalists did not like the fact that the Weimar constitution guaranteed "every German a living through productive work," and if no work was available "would provide the means necessary for a worker's livelihood" (Fischer 1995:184).

Thus Marxian interpretations of German fascism view it as the final outcome of a capitalist system in crisis, where owners of big business supported extreme measures to subvert their political opponents and secure conditions that would allow for the unfettered accumulation of profits (Brady 1937). According to R. Palme Dutt, the "open and avowed supporters of Fascism in every country are the representatives of big capital . . . [whose aim is] to defeat the working-class revolution and smash the working-class organisations" (1935:100, 102). During the Nazi period these capitalists went even further, hoping to exploit the Jews and others as slave laborers. This view, of course, leaves unanswered the question of why capitalists would favor a policy of extermination that destroyed this slave labor pool. Nor does it account for the virulent nature of Nazi anti-Semitism (Friedlander 1989).

Moreover, the Marxian thesis regarding capitalists' support of Nazism lacks empirical support. In his book *German Big Business and the Rise of Hitler,* Henry Ashby Turner notes that the leaders of the largest German corporations did not as a rule support Hitler's quest for power. Turner defines German "big business" as "large-scale private enterprises owned and operated by Germans in the fields of commerce, finance, industry, and insurance" (1985:xv).[9] The early growth of the Nazi party took place without significant support from these corporate enterprises, and throughout the 1920s the Nazis "languished in disrepute in the eyes of most men of big business" (ibid.:342). Only two industrialists—Ernst von Borsig and Fritz Thyssen—stand out as significant financial contributors to the party. And many capitalists were apprehensive about the Nazis' tax policies and support of price controls, trade restrictions, and job creation through deficit spending, which they thought were contrary to their interests (Fischer 1995; James 2001; Spielvogel 1996).

Richard Hamilton adds that big business is "not ordinarily . . . interested in radical transformation of existing institutional arrangements" but in the preservation of order. Before Hitler acquired power, most capitalists who were sympathetic to the Nazis viewed them primarily as "support troops in a broad conservative nationalist alliance" (1982:429). They did, on the other hand, eventually allow the Nazis into this alliance and granted them legitimacy by "inviting Hitler and other party spokesmen to address their gatherings" (Turner 1985:348).

Still another Marxian interpretation views the conflict within the German capitalist class and between the capitalist class and working class as creating a "class stalemate [that] allowed the state to escape domination by a ruling [economic] elite and to emerge with autonomous power as a dictatorial apparatus" (Maier 1988:88).[10] Marx ([1852] 1963) first advanced an interpretation like this in his study of Napoleon Bonaparte's rise to power in France in 1799. "The Bonapartist or fascist state imposed a dictatorship . . . precisely in the [economic elites'] own interests, which [they] could not guarantee under a [democratic political] regime" (Maier 1988:88; see also Abraham 1981). This view of Nazism, however, is contradicted by the fact that the Nazis had their own political and ideological agenda that was not subservient (and was often contrary) to capitalist interests (Turner 1985).

In a study of the IG Farben corporation, Peter Hayes observes that German capitalists tended to follow rather than lead Nazism. "To a mounting degree," especially after the war broke out, IG Farben "became a mere executor of government orders; and technical possibilities, not financial or commercial considerations, dominated the [managing board's] decisions" (1987:326). Nevertheless, German industry proved itself capable of pursuing its ordinary profit-making ambitions under rather extraordinary conditions (the banality of evil), as it exploited Jewish and other slave laborers and manufactured whatever was necessary for the war effort and the Final Solution (e.g., poisonous gas, crematory ovens) (Poole 1997a; Rubenstein & Roth 1987). Nazi economic policy was based on the recognition "that so long as a state displays its determination but permits businessmen to make money, they will let themselves be manipulated as to how" (Hayes 1987:379). The Nazis understood that business "interests are not immutable . . . but . . . capable of restatement according" to the political context (ibid.). And, indeed, many big businesses not only survived but thrived during the Nazi era (Fischer 1995; Hayes 1998; Simpson 1993; Spielvogel 1996).

In addition to its focus on big business, Marxian interpretations posit a class-based theory of fascism based on the thesis of a declining lower-middle class (see Marx & Engels[1848] 1948). According to this view, members of the lower-middle class (e.g., small shopkeepers, artisans, farmers) live at the margins of the middle class and are anxious about falling into the ranks of the working class or the unemployed (Lipset 1960). In Germany, members of this class blamed their precarious position on Jewish competition, even through it was competition from larger financial enterprises that most threatened their livelihood. The Nazis' anti-Semitic rhetoric and policies appealed to this lower-middle-class group, "for it legitimated hostility toward the hated Jewish competitor while providing an ideological basis for community with the owners of large-scale business and the managers of large-scale government" (Rubenstein & Roth 1987:105). Voting patterns in pre-Nazi Germany support this analysis insofar as a higher proportion of the lower-middle class (in comparison to the upper, upper-middle, and working classes), voted for the Nazi party. However, since the working class constituted the largest proportion of the voting public, it was "of equal importance in determining the result" (Hamilton 1982:46).[11]

Finally, a word should be said of two other class constituencies that supported the Nazis but that are left out of both the lower-middle-class and big-business interpretations of Nazism. One group includes businessmen who occupied a position between the lower-middle and big-business class, entrepreneurs who felt threatened by the "increasingly cutthroat competition for shrinking markets" (Turner 1985:344). The other group includes salaried white-collar workers in clerical, sales, and similar occupations who "jealously guarded" what they believed to be their superior status vis-à-vis blue-collar workers, and who were decidedly anti-Semitic, nationalist, and supportive of efforts to suppress labor unions (Speier 1986:2). Thus, as we have seen, there is no simple correspondence between class and Nazism. The Nazis both received and lacked support from all classes in German society, leaving no straightforward insight that can be drawn from analyses of class structure (Brustein 1998b; Deák 1984; Kater 1983).

Max Weber and Bureaucracy   The German theorist Max Weber (1864–1920) understood more than Marx that the actions of the state are not simply derivative of class relationships and that political power could be "sharply differentiated from economic power" (Alexander 1984:13).[12] For our purposes, however, Weber's most important contribution was his emphasis on the predominant role of bureaucracy in modern social life. Weber suggested that bureaucracy is not simply a mode of organization but an apparatus that can be used to exercise power. Bureaucracies constrain individual action by demanding efficiency and impersonality in the achievement of goals, by providing subordinates with authorization from superiors, by separating and diffusing responsibility, and by routinizing tasks (Bauman 1989; Gerth & Mills 1946; Kelman & Hamilton 1989; Markle 1995).

Raul Hilberg (1985) argues that it was the bureaucratic administration of death that made the Holocaust unprecedented and that distinguished it from a pogrom or mob action. Instrumental rationality supplanted rage. No one was spared; all were "murdered with equivalent proficiency" (Markle 1995:67). Personal feelings were set aside, and obligation to bureaucratic rules, to the task at hand, was "substituted for moral responsibility" (ibid.:72). The feelings, the very lives, of the targets of the action did not matter. "It [was] the technology of action, not its substance, which [was] subject to assessment as good or bad, proper or improper, right or wrong" (Bauman 1989:159–60). Authorization from superiors displaced the "authority of the private conscience" (Markle 1995:72). As Rudolf Hoess (1900–1947), the commandant of Auschwitz, explained, "It didn't even occur to me . . . that I could be held responsible. . . . [I]t was understood that if something went wrong, then the man who gave the orders was responsible. . . . I didn't think that I would have to answer" (quoted in Gilbert 1950:255). Similarly, a Gestapo interrogator recalled, "I was simply doing my duty—not more nor less! I had nothing to be ashamed of" (quoted in Engelmann 1986:280).

In the bureaucratic division of labor each individual was delegated a small portion of responsibility and the interconnections between the coordinated actions were often unclear (Bauman 1989). This made it easier for participants "to forget the nature of the product [i.e., death] that emerge[d] from the process" and to rationalize that what they were doing wasn't so bad (Kelman & Hamilton 1989:18). As Franz Grassler, the deputy commissioner of the Warsaw Jewish ghetto, asserted, "Our job was to maintain the ghetto and try to preserve the Jews as a work force. . . . [The] goal . . . was very different from the one that later led to extermination" (quoted in Lanzmann 1985:182). And Walter Stier, who booked Jews on the Reichsbahn (German State Railways) so they could be transported to Treblinka, claimed he did not know that Treblinka was in fact a death camp: "Good God, no! . . . I never went to Treblinka. I stayed in Krakow, in Warsaw, glued to my desk. . . . I was strictly a bureaucrat!" (quoted in ibid.:135–36).

To a large extent, it was the very routinization of tasks, the very mundane-ness of the work, that allowed some to convince themselves that what they were doing was "perfectly normal, correct, and legitimate" (Kelman & Hamilton 1989:18). Stier recalls that his "work was barely different from . . . [any other] work, . . . preparing time tables [and] coordinating the movement of . . . trains" (quoted in Lanzmann 1985:133). Writing of the so-called desk murderers, Hilberg observes:

> The questions with which these [bureaucrats] were concerned were almost always technical. . . . How were the borders of a ghetto to be drawn? What was to be the disposition of pension claims belonging to deported Jews? How should the bodies be disposed of? These were the problems [they] pondered in their memoranda, correspondence, meetings, and discussions. (1989:120–21)

Knowing all this, the banality-of-evil concept can be understood more fully. Ordinary bureaucratic processes were used to accomplish extraordinary deeds.

Nevertheless, bureaucratic constraints did not preclude innovation in devising solutions to problems (Blau 1955). Indeed, this is the essence of the functionalist historians' argument, for German bureaucrats "displayed a striking path-finding ability in the absence of directives, a congruity of activities without jurisdictional guidelines, a fundamental comprehension of the task even when there were no explicit communications" (Hilberg 1985:263). Practically speaking, the Final Solution could not have been accomplished "if everyone . . . had to wait for instructions" before they took action (Hilberg 1989:127).

Émile Durkheim and the Moral Order   In one way or another, both Marx and Weber were concerned with the ways in which external social structures affected the rational nature of social action (Alexander 1984). In doing so, they downplayed the ways in which actors' internal (psychological) states were constituted by nonrational considerations. It was the French sociologist Émile Durkheim (1858–1917) who understood that "social structure is located as much within the actor as without" and that a normative "collective conscience"—the "totality of beliefs and sentiments common to average citizens of the same society"—provides the moral glue that holds society together by "penetrating and socializing individual consciences" (Alexander 1984:9, 15; Durkheim [1893] 1964:79).[13] The collective conscience, according to Durkheim, consists of "collective representations"—culturally shared symbols, systems of meaning, or categorization systems—that divide the world "into contradictory patterns of sacred and profane," into that which is good and that which is evil (Alexander 1984:15; see also Douglas 1966; Durkheim [1912] 1965; Loseke 1999).

Earlier I noted that Nazi anti-Semitism characterized the Jew as the very essence of the profane, of all that was vile, corrupt, and evil. Nazism, however, did not create this representation out of "whole cloth." Rather, it drew upon a long-standing tradition of German anti-Semitism that characterized the Jew as the "malevolent and corrosive . . . opposite of the German" (Goldhagen 1996:55). German anti-Semitism provided the Nazis with a powerful symbolic code that expressed reverence for German culture by rejecting all that was not of it. Although a distinction should be made between the violent anti-Semitic impulses of the Nazis and the moderate anti-Semitism that was commonplace among Germans, all too many were indifferent to the Jews' plight and readily accepted their legal disenfranchisement (Browning 1998; Volkov 1989).[14]

Daniel Goldhagen argues that explanations of the Holocaust often fail to acknowledge the fundamental fact that the Nazis' primary victims were *Jews* and that Jews were not considered to be Germans. Many explanations, he observes, do not "emphasize the autonomous motivating force . . . of anti-semitism, . . . [as if] the perpetrators would have treated any other group of intended victims in exactly the same way" (1996:13). Thus Goldhagen, like Durkheim, wants us to understand "actors' beliefs and values . . . as crucial in explaining . . . [people's] willingness to act" (ibid.:13, 20).

If social action is understood as nonrational behavior imbued with symbolic meaning, then the perpetrators of the Holocaust can be viewed as not entirely coerced, as not simply following orders, but as acting out of conviction that what they were doing was right, or at least not thinking that what they were doing was wrong. As Goldhagen notes, many explanations treat the perpetrators as if they were "people lacking a moral sense, lacking the ability to make decisions and take stances" (ibid.:13). Although they "were working within institutions that prescribed roles for them and assigned them specific tasks, . . . they individually and collectively had latitude to make choices regarding their actions," and thus to some degree their participation may be considered voluntary (ibid.:15).

In the discipline of sociology, the tension between individual voluntarism and social-structural constraints has sometimes been addressed in terms of the question of "human agency." According to William Sewell, Jr., agency involves the capacity to exert control and to some extent even transform "the social relations in which one is enmeshed" (1992:20). It entails "an ability to coordinate one's actions with others and against others . . . and to monitor the simultaneous effects of one's own and others' activities" (ibid.:21). Individuals, however, "are born with only a highly generalized capacity for agency, analogous to their ability to use language" (ibid.:20). The form this capacity for agency takes varies with structural context. Perhaps some of the participants in the Holocaust lacked the moral socialization that would have motivated them to exercise agency to resist, for the Jews remained outside their society's universe of moral obligation, that is, outside "the circle of people with reciprocal obligations to protect each other" (Fein 1979:4). As one member of the Order Police involved in the killing of Jews remarked, "Under the influence of the times, my attitude to the Jews was marked by a certain aversion" (quoted in Browning 1992:182). And recall the comment of another member of the Order Police quoted earlier: "Truthfully I must say that at the time we didn't reflect about it at all. . . . Only later did it first occur to me that [the killing of Jews] had not been right" (ibid.:72).

Although Durkheim believed that "man is a moral being only because he lives in society," Zygmunt Bauman thinks that Durkheim was entirely too sanguine about the positive functions of morality in reinforcing social solidarity (quoted in Bauman 1989:172). To the contrary, Bauman suggests, morality may reside not in the observance of the normative moral order but in the subordination of it, "in action openly defying social solidarity and consensus" (ibid.:177).

Beyond the Classics: The Social Construction of a Social Problem

Even before the Nazi era, concern about the "Jewish problem" (*Judenfrage*), or "Jewish question" as it was often called, was a perennial theme in German public discourse (Goldhagen 1996; Rose 1990). After the war, sociologist Everett Hughes interviewed a German architect whose comments continued to reflect this concern:

> [T]he Jews . . . were a problem. They came from the east. You should see them in Poland; the lowest class of people, full of lice, dirty and poor, running about in their Ghettos in filthy caftans. They came here, and got rich by unbelievable methods after the first war. They occupied all the good places . . . in medicine and law and government posts! . . . [What the Nazis did] of course . . . was no way to settle the Jewish problem. But there was a problem and it had to be settled some way. (1962:5)

In contemporary parlance the term "social problem" is used to refer to a social condition that is perceived as troublesome or wrong and to the expectation or hope that something can be done to solve it (Loseke 1999). Typically we assume that social problems are constituted by some objective condition that exists in society. But social problems are also constituted by subjective definitions, that is, by the ways in which we interpret and assign meaning to the world. In sociology an influential theoretical perspective—social problems constructionism—has revolved around this latter theme.[15]

According to Joel Best (1995), an approach that focuses on objective conditions cannot provide a foundation for a general theory that is applicable to all social problems, since the particular conditions that cause disparate problems may have little in common. Social problems constructionism, on the other hand, offers an analytic vocabulary and theoretical framework capable of ordering disparate cases along a common schematic axis (see Berbrier 2000; Hall 1992). As first articulated by Malcolm Spector and John Kitsuse, social problems constructionism defines social problems as "the activities of individuals or groups making assertions of grievances and claims with respect to some putative condition. . . . The central [task] for a theory of social problems is to account for the emergence, nature, and maintenance of claims-making and responding activities" (1987:75–76). To put it another way, social problems constructionism treats social problems not as a *condition* but as an *activity*—what some call "social problems work"—that identifies and defines problems, persuades others that something must be done about them, and generates practical programs of remedial action (Loseke 1999; Miller & Holstein 1989).

Social problems constructionists observe that social problems have a "natural history," that is, they tend to evolve through a sequence of stages that entail "the development and unfolding of claims about problems and the formulation and implementation of solutions to problems" (Berger 1993:599; see also Fuller & Myers 1941; Peyrot 1984). However, social problems construction is an uncertain process, whereby prior stages provide a set of historical contingencies for subsequent stages with outcomes that cannot necessarily be anticipated. The process is by no means teleological. Events are moved forward by human beings making choices and responding to social-structural constraints. Thus what emerges in the later stages of social problems development "may be a far cry from how the problem was viewed" at an earlier point in time (Blumer 1971:303; see also Spector & Kitsuse 1987). In many respects, the process proceeds dialectically, as solutions to problems beget new problems that require solution, and so forth as time goes on (see Chambliss & Seidman 1982).

In an earlier work I offered the first application of constructionism to a genocidal event, showing how the processes that constructed the Holocaust paralleled those that constructed other social problems (Berger 1993). In so doing, I suggested a new way of understanding the banality-of-evil paradox: What made the construction of the "Jewish problem" and its Final Solution banal was the way in which its natural history was similar to those of other problems.

In this book I adopt what Best (1995) describes as a *contextual constructionist* rather than a *strict constructionist* approach. Strict constructionists ask sociologists to avoid theorizing outside claims-makers' perceptions or "symbolically demarcated . . . realities" and not to impute motives to social actors or concern themselves with broader sociohistorical circumstances (Ibarra & Kitsuse 1993:33; see also Troyer 1992). Contextual constructionists, on the other hand, are more inclined to evaluate claims-makers' assertions as warranted or unwarranted, to acknowledge objective conditions, and to situate social problems activity in its sociohistorical context (Neuman 1998; Rafter 1992b).

Strict constructionists are concerned about maintaining the theoretical purity of the "subjective definitions" approach to social problems but push the analyst too far into a contextual void "where claims-making may only be examined in the abstract" (Best 1993:143; see also Nichols 2000).[16] It is possible, Best argues, to consider objective conditions without abandoning a constructionist focus. As such, constructionism may be appropriated as a theoretical model that allows me to synthesize in logical progression a wide range of historical evidence and interpretation. The scheme is also flexible enough to absorb and capitalize upon insights from other theoretical traditions in sociology.[17]

The Aftermath of the Problem: The Construction of Collective Memory

Spector and Kitsuse criticized earlier natural-history models for assuming that "the official response or implementation of a policy as the final stage of the problem" (1987:142; see Fuller & Myers 1941). Thus a fully developed natural history of the Holocaust does not end with the implementation of the Final Solution or the defeat of the Nazi regime, for the postwar memory of the Holocaust constitutes a problem in its own right (Berger 1996; Marcuse 2001; Novick 1999). How do different collectivities, including nation-states, remember the Holocaust and to what ends? Is Holocaust denial or simply forgetting the past a problem? Has the memory of the Holocaust been trivialized or exploited in objectionable ways? Are some Jews obsessed with the legacy of their victimization? These are some of the questions that can be asked of the postwar legacy of this historical event.

To address this postwar context a constructionist approach needs to be infused with insights drawn from the literature on "collective memory." Maurice Halbachs (1950, 1992), a disciple of Durkheim, introduced the concept of collective memory to advance understanding of the collective conscience. Halbachs described collective memory as shared recollections of the "past that are retained by members of a group . . . that experienced it" (quoted in Schuman & Scott 1989:361–62). Barry Schwartz uses the term to denote a "society's retention and loss of information about its past" and observes that only part of this memory actually consists of shared individual experiences that construct members' autobiographical memories (1991:302; see also Coser 1992). Rather, individuals learn most of what they know about the past through social institutions that infuse disparate individual memories with common moral meaning (Young 1993).

Schwartz (1996) conceptualizes collective memory as a cultural system that connects publicly accessible representations of the past (e.g., museums, memorials, motion pictures, photographs, written narratives) to the experiences of the present in order to construct meaning in the present and connect "successive generations with one another" (Durkheim [1893] 1964:80). Present social structures, however, are not so much "causes by which memories are produced, but contexts in which memories are contested, selected, and cultivated" (Schwartz 1991:317). Groups with varying amounts of power compete with each other to construct the memory that suits their rational interests or symbolic needs. Nation-states, for instance, appropriate collective memory to legitimate their moral origin, their "natural right to exist," or even their "divine election," in order to "create a sense of shared values and ideals" that provide the foundation for a unified polity (Young 1993:2, 6). Thus the citizens of Germany tend to remember the Holocaust differently than the citizens of the United States or Israel, for example, for people do not generally wish to remember their nation's history in a predominantly negative light. Moreover, a nation is not always free to remember its history as it wishes, for the victors of war have the most power to construct the past. If Germany had won World War II, or even negotiated a peace settlement, the Holocaust would not be remembered in the same way(s) as it is today, if it were remembered at all.

Jeffrey Olick and Daniel Levy observe, however, that the "relationship between remembered pasts and constructed presents is one of . . . perpetual . . . renegotiation over time" (1997:934). There are those in Germany, for instance, who feel that their country should be allowed to forget its checkered past, that their national identity has been tarnished for too long (Berger 1996; Marcuse 2001). After all, they say, don't most nations have a "dark side," their own atrocities to atone for? Why should the Nazi era stand out among all others? Hence the problem of collective memory—in our case, the memory of the "Jewish problem" and its Final Solution—is never really solved. The construction of the past, and its meaning for the present, is never completed.

NOTES

1. Garber (1994) credits Wiesel with first bringing the term Holocaust into popular discourse when he began using it in print in the late 1950s. It has its etymological roots in Greek and the Greek translation of the Hebrew Bible, where the terms *holokaustos, holokaustuma,* and *holokaustosis* (based on the Hebrew *ólah*) were used to refer to a sacrificial burnt offering made to God. For this reason, some people object to it being used to describe the genocide of the Jews. It is now generally taken to mean total destruction by fire, thus alluding to the open-air pits and crematoria that the Nazis used to dispose of the dead bodies of Jews (Laqueur 1980; Rubenstein & Roth 1987). When used with a lowercase "h," holocaust is employed by some to refer to genocide more generally. Bauer (2000), however, prefers to reserve its use as an analytic category that designates genocides where an entire group is targeted for complete annihilation.

In Israel and among many religious Jews, the term *Shoah* is preferred, which in Hebrew means "catastrophic destruction." It also has a connotation that adds an element of doubt and even despair regarding the role of divine judgment and retribution (Rubenstein & Roth 1987). See Chapter 7 for an extended discussion of God's silence during the Holocaust.

2.   Following the Jews, the Gypsies are the group that the Nazis appear to have targeted for the most thorough elimination. Some people consider "Gypsy" a pejorative term and prefer to use Roma or Rom. The Roma are the largest Gypsy group, but the Sinti were also victimized by the Nazis (Hancock 1996). For this reason, as well as for consistency in the literature, Lewy (1999) recommends retaining the term Gypsy.

3.   Five million is the figure more often heard to refer to the number of noncombatant gentiles who were killed. This number is attributed to an assertion by Simon Wiesenthal, but it appears to substantially underestimate the non-Jewish dead (Novick 1999).

On the other hand, various demographic projections of Jewish birth and death rates suggest that, if not for the Holocaust, the number of *additional* Jews who would have been alive in the year 2000 would not have been just 6 million but 7.3 to 20 million (DellaPergola 1996).

4.   In a survey of Holocaust courses taught in U.S. colleges and universities, Haynes (1998) found that history departments accounted for over half of the offerings. Religion/philosophy and foreign language/English departments each accounted for about 10 percent. The rest of the courses were divided among other programs, including sociology.

Prior to Bauman's (1989) call for sociologists to examine the Holocaust, Fein (1979), Hamilton (1982), Horowitz (1976), Hughes (1962), and Tec (1986) were among the first to address this subject.

5.   The term anti-Semitism, based on the distinction between languages with Semitic and Aryan origins, is credited to the German ideologue William Marr and has been used to refer to different language-speaking groups as separate races (see Chapter 2).

6.   Nazi linguistic constructions such as *Judenfrei* will likely strike a contemporary German speaker as a perversion of the language.

7.   Hitler's ancestry remains somewhat of a mystery since his father, who was apparently a cruel man who beat his wife and children, was born out of wedlock and thus the religious background of Hitler's grandfather is unknown. This has led to some speculation that Hitler had doubts about the purity of his own racial makeup. For biographical accounts and psychological interpretations of Hitler, see Botwinick (1996), Kershaw (1998, 2000), and Rosenbaum (1998). For representations of Hitler in popular culture, see Rosenfeld (1985).

8.   Both of Marx's parents were from rabbinical families, but for business reasons his father converted to Lutheranism, and Marx was baptized as a Christian. In his writings, Marx disparaged religion and Judaism in particular. In his rather anti-Semitic essay, "On the Jewish Question," he characterized Jews as a parasitic group whose religiosity and class outlook needed to be transcended (Ritzer 1992; Rose 1990).

9.   This sector of the economy was marked by a high degree of capital concentration, with comparatively few corporations owning a disproportionately large percentage of

economic assets. These companies were also characterized by a high degree of vertical integration, as many produced their own sources of energy as well as the raw materials needed for their products.

10.   The capitalist class is not a unified group and is itself composed of different segments or factions that may have competing interests (Wright 1978). Poole argues that in Germany between the two world wars *light industry* (e.g., electrical, chemical, textiles) and *commercial establishments* (e.g., department stores, retail merchants), which produced or sold consumer goods, favored "a policy of collaboration with organized labor" that would improve economic "prosperity by restoring the purchasing power of the people" (1997b:135). *Heavy industry* (e.g., iron, steel, mining), on the other hand, "wanted lower labor costs that would give them an advantage in world markets" (ibid.:136). Heavy industry also favored an expansionist foreign policy that would allow them to profit from government munitions orders and help them obtain needed raw materials. However, as Turner (1985) points out, some of the major firms were conglomerates, owning companies in diverse areas of the economy, thus making the distinction between heavy and light industry somewhat obsolete.

11.   Some historians suggest that farmers and residents of agrarian towns and villages were among the Nazis' strongest supporters (Childers 1984; Spielvogel 1996). Indeed, votes for the Nazi party often varied inversely with community size. But Hamilton (1982) notes that this thesis holds only for Protestants and not Catholic rural communities.

12.   Weber's father was a bureaucrat and his mother an intensely religious women. While Weber was not religious himself, he was an astute observer of the history of the world's faiths (Gerth & Mills 1946; Ritzer 1992).

13.   Durkheim was descended from a long line of rabbis and studied to be a rabbi himself. However, by his teens he had become an agnostic, and his interest in religion turned from the theological to the academic (Ritzer 1992).

14.   The Holocaust, of course, can by no means be attributed to anti-Semitism alone. Moreover, Germany was arguably not the most anti-Semitic country in Europe, and collaboration of non-Germans with the Nazis was widespread (Browning 1998; Deák et al. 2000; Marrus 1987; Rubenstein & Roth 1987; see Chapter 3). For example, in July 1941 about half the gentile residents of the small Polish town of Jedwabne (some 1,600 people) rose up and killed the other half, who were Jews, with the approval but without the participation of the handful of Germans who occupied the area (Gross 2001).

15.   The term "social construction" first gained wide currency with Berger and Luckmann's (1966) *The Social Construction of Reality,* and social problems constructionism has been influenced by other subjectivist perspectives such as symbolic interaction, phenomenology, and ethnomethodology (Best 1995; Holstein & Miller 1993; Loseke 1999).

16.   The extreme relativism of those constructionists who deny any objective element of reality has led to mocking criticisms. Writing of the Holocaust, Bartov asks if there are not events of the past that exist independently of people's constructions: "[I]f a murder has taken place, we did not construct it in our imagination" (1993:113). Extreme relativism also encourages unwarranted criticism of legitimate constructionist insights. For instance, in his book *The Social Construction of What?*, Hacking (1999)

equates a constructionist approach to the Holocaust with Holocaust denial. This book will show that this characterization is simplistic and misleading.

17.   In particular, social problems constructionism has been enhanced by drawing upon the literature on social movements (e.g., Bash 1995; Mauss 1975; McCright & Dunlap 2001; Neuman 1998).

2

Constructing the "Jewish Problem" and Its Solution

Do not engage much in debate with Jews about the articles of our faith. . . . [T]here is no hope until they reach the point where their misery finally makes them pliable and they are forced to confess that the Messiah has come, and that he is our Jesus. . . . We are at fault in not slaying them. . . . They are real liars and bloodhounds. . . . [B]e on guard against the Jews, knowing that wherever they have their synagogues, nothing is found but a den of devils in which . . . blasphemy, and defaming of God and men are practiced most maliciously.

What shall we Christians do with this rejected and condemned people, the Jews? . . . First, . . . set fire to their synagogues or schools and . . . bury and cover with dirt whatever will not burn. . . . Second, I advise that their houses also be razed and destroyed. For they pursue in them the same aims as in their synagogues. . . . This is to be done in honor of our Lord and of Christendom, so that God might see that we are Christians, and do not condone or knowingly tolerate such public lying, cursing, and blaspheming of his Son and of his Christians. —Luther

It would be difficult for any hatemonger to match the viciousness of this condemnation of a group of people. Is this the ranting of Adolf Hitler or other fanatical Nazi? No. It is the writing of Martin Luther, founder of the Lutheran religion, one of the most important figures in the history of Christianity! In 1543 Luther wrote "On the Jews and Their Lies" in response to Jewish rabbis in Germany who challenged his interpretation of Scripture. According to Luther, the Jews were not only mistaken in their religious beliefs, they were "perverse and demonic" as well (Rubenstein & Roth 1987:55).

The "Jewish problem" in Nazi Germany had deep-seated roots. The Nazis built upon what came before, upon a long-standing collective representation of "the Jew." Recall, following Émile Durkheim, that collective representations refer to culturally shared symbols, systems of meaning, or categorization systems used by individuals to make sense of themselves and the society in which they live. When applied to a group of people, collective representations work somewhat like stereotypes by providing simplifying schemes of interpretation that enable individuals to view a heterogeneous group of people as constituting a homogeneous category whose members are "all alike." In this way, collective representations can be used to construct or typify particular kinds of individuals (e.g., Jews) as problems that warrant particular kinds of treatment.

TYPIFYING THE JEW

Studies of contemporary social problems often emphasize the ways in which particular types of persons have been constructed as victims who are morally deserving of public sympathy (e.g., abused children, battered women, rape victims) and whose suffering justifies remedial social action (Best 1995; Loseke 1999). In this book, however, I consider an obverse type of construction that was applied to an entire ethnic group: In Nazi Germany, Jews were typified as persons who victimized others, who were morally unworthy of sympathy, and whose continued presence constituted a problem that needed solution. The Jew as a social type was not merely an unsympathetic character but a despised and less-than-human being. As we shall see, a dehumanized group like the Jews can be constructed and then isolated and even exterminated through social processes that are in themselves quite ordinary or banal.

Christian Claims and European Discontents

Most constructionist studies examine social problems with relatively short histories and that are limited to individual countries, particularly the United States (Best 2001; Loseke 1999; Nichols 1995). Arguably the "Jewish problem" has one of the longest histories known to humankind and one that has been diffused across a wide range of geographical contexts. The Nazis drew upon a centuries-old tradition of anti-Semitism rooted in religious hostility and combined it with German nationalism and pseudoscientific racial theory to articulate a powerful collective representation of the Jew. This representation defined Jews and Germans in "complementary opposition," as groups whose motives, interests, and essential nature were diametrically opposed to each other (see Miller & Holstein 1989:8).

The general features of an oppositional collective representation of the Jew did not originate in Germany. Historical accounts suggest that since the dawn of Christianity, Jews and Christians were each others' "disconfirming other," for genuine belief in the veracity of one religion required belief in the falsity of the other (Rubenstein & Roth 1987:43). Although Jews were a powerless minority in Christian-dominated Europe, their continued presence constituted "a permanent challenge to the certainty of Christian belief," a constant reminder that Christianity was not universally accepted (Bauman 1989:37). This recalcitrance, observes Zymunt Bauman, was all the more disconcerting since it "could not be dismissed as . . . pagan ignorance," for Jews were in fact schooled in the Old Testament and refused to accept Christianity "in full consciousness" of its meaning (ibid.). Moreover, the Jews were forestalling the Second Coming of Christ, which, according to Christian prophecy, would occur only after they were converted to Christianity (Rose 1990). Thus, according to Bauman, "Christianity could not reproduce itself . . . without guarding and reinforcing Jewish estrangement," and the Jewish challenge "could be repelled, or at least rendered less dangerous, only by explaining Jewish obstinacy by a malice aforethought, ill intentions and moral corruption" (1989:37–38).

Social problems claimsmaking typically entails the assignment of responsibility or attribution of blame for problems (Gusfield 1981; Loseke 1999; Neuman 1998). In Christian culture the collective representation of the Jew was constituted through claims about Jewish responsibility for a host of horrific acts. In addition to holding the Jewish people almost exclusively responsible for Christ's death,[1] Jews were accused of engaging in "blood libel" (i.e., the murdering of Christian children for religious purposes), desecrating the body of Christ (i.e., despoiling the Christian sacraments of bread and wine), poisoning wells, and spreading plagues and famines (Rubenstein & Roth 1987). Christian theologians, like Luther, claimed that Jewish suffering was God's punishment for having rejected his Son and that God's hatred of Jews "was evident by their miserable state" (Botwinick 1996:16). In the *Book of John*, Jesus admonishes Jews who refuse to accept his authority:

> If God were your Father, you would love me, for I proceeded and came forth from God. . . . Why do you not understand what I say? It is because you cannot bear to hear my word. You are of your father the devil, and your will is to do your father's desires. . . . He who is of God hears the words of God; the reason why you do not hear them is that you are not of God. (John, 8:42–44, 47)

According to Richard Rubenstein and John Roth (1987), no greater defamation of one religious group by another can be found in the annals of religious history.

As a discriminated minority group, Jews were often forbidden from agricultural land ownership and hence excluded from a common source of livelihood (Hertzberg 1968). They thus sought their economic survival in areas that complemented the majority population. In a world where commerce was poorly developed, people lacked literacy skills, and usury was discouraged by Christian Scripture, Jews found a niche "as merchants, traders, artisans, physicians, and moneylenders" (Rubenstein & Roth 1987:38). However, their very success in these areas bred resentment. Importantly, Jews were perceived as unlike any other minority group, for the threat they posed did not emanate from local conditions of friction or conflict with the dominant population. Rather, the Jewish threat was ubiquitous, vague, and diffuse; and hostility toward Jews

could be found among people who had never "set eyes on [them] and in countries where Jews [had not lived] for centuries" (Cohn 1967:252). In this way,
the oppositional collective representation of the Jew was used to account for a
multitude of local problems even though it was "not causally related to any"
(Bauman 1989:41).

By the eighteenth century the Enlightenment, or Age of Reason, opened
up new possibilities for European Jews (Rubenstein & Roth 1987). Enlightenment philosophy promoted the belief that humanity could rely on rational
thought rather than on religious authority to govern its affairs. Historically
the monarchical states of Europe had used one brand of Christianity or another
to delineate the boundaries of national identity, even establishing "state religions" as the basis of their authority (Bell-Fialkoff 1999). But the Enlightenment, which promoted democratic ideals and the separation of religion from
politics, fostered Jewish emancipation. Jews achieved greater formal political
equality and moved forward on a path of assimilation. At the same time, tra-
ditionalists like church officials and royalists who favored religious-based
monarchies over secular, democratic governments blamed Jews for fostering
unwanted social change. Modernists, on the other hand, expected Jews to relinquish their religious "superstitions" in order to become full citizens of the
nation. They wanted to integrate Jews into the economy "so that no particular pursuit, not even moneylending, should be the Jew's own preserve"
(Hertzberg 1968:7). And they hoped to undermine the capacity of the "organized Jewish community" to advance any economic or political claims that
were considered distinct from the broader national community (ibid.:288).

Arthur Hertzberg argues that the architects of the Enlightenment were
themselves divided on the "Jewish question," and that "there was no straight
line from their corporate outlook to the granting of equality for Jews"
(ibid.:248). He suggests that modern anti-Semitism "was fashioned not as a
reaction to the Enlightenment" but as part of it (ibid.:7). Some of the most influential Enlightenment thinkers such as Voltaire were intensely anti-Semitic.
However, this prejudice was derived not from the Christian tradition but from
secular notions (which can be traced to Greco-Roman pagans) that viewed Jews
as "by the very nature of their own culture and even by their biological inheritance an unassimilable element," a people who were inherently deceitful,
greedy, intolerant, and arrogant (ibid.:11). It was a racist view that predated
nineteenth-century biological racism.

The more sympathetic Enlightenment thinkers thought that this inferior
Jewish character was due not to the nature of Jews but to their circumstances
or environment. According to this view, "the faults of the Jews were created
by the conditions under which they were made to live and earn a living. . . .
If the Jews were given opportunity and freedom, they would change and very
rapidly lose their bad habits" (ibid.:292). Others thought that the way to solve
"the Jewish problem was for the Jew himself to become 'enlightened' and de-

tach himself from his [religious] tradition" (ibid.:279). At the same time, many believed the Jews were "the most difficult of all peoples to enlighten and regenerate" (ibid.:286). Some considered them beyond regeneration altogether. At best the "new Jew" born of the Enlightenment was asked to "keep proving that he was worthy" of citizen status (ibid.:366). In practice, this often meant conversion to Christianity, for to remain un-Christian was to remain a perpetual and potentially disloyal outsider.

Thus Jews remained a "lightning rod" for the social strains and discontents of modern Europe (Volkov 1989). In France, for example, a French-Jewish army captain, Alfred Dreyfus, was arrested and tried for treason in 1894. Dreyfus was accused of passing military secrets to the German military attaché in Paris that allegedly contributed to France's defeat in the 1870–1871 Franco-Prussian War. The case became "a national obsession" as a trial that symbolized the trial of all French Jews (Rubenstein & Roth 1987:84). Church officials were among Dreyfus's most vehement critics.[2] For instance, the *Civiltà Cattolica,* the official journal of the Jesuit order in Rome, reported:

> The Jew was created by God to serve as a spy wherever treason is in preparation. . . . The Jews allege an error of justice. The true error was . . . the [French Constitution] which accorded them French nationality. That law has to be revoked. . . . Not only in France, but [throughout Europe] . . . the Jews are to be excluded from the nation. Then the old harmony will be re-established and the peoples will again find their lost happiness. (cited in ibid.)

Dreyfus, however, had been framed by army officials seeking a scapegoat for the military defeat. He was convicted on the basis of forged documents and sentenced to life imprisonment on Devil's Island. In 1899 he was pardoned by the president of France when the true story of the conspiracy against him finally came to light.

As a "curtain raiser" for the twentieth century, the Dreyfus affair illustrates the degree to which the Jew had remained a social type "construed as compromising and defying the order of things, . . . the prototype and arch-pattern of all nonconformity, heterodoxy, anomaly and aberration" (Bauman 1989:39). Jews were criticized for being both capitalists and communists, and they were disdained for both flaunting their wealth and social superiority and for being mired in poverty and being uncouth and diseased. In Mary Douglas's terms, the Jew was endowed with "pollution powers" and was the embodiment of all that was profane (1966:113).

German Nationalism and Nazi Claims

Joel Best (2001) notes that the cross-national diffusion of social problems requires the adopters of claims to define conditions in their own society as similar to those that are the source of those claims. Clearly, the geographical diffusion of Christianity established the basis for the diffusion of anti-Semitic constructions of the Jew. Still, each individual society puts its own stamp on this construction. In Germany the sixteenth-century theologian Martin Luther (1483–1546) is often credited with Germanizing the Christian critique of Judaism and establishing anti-Semitism as a key element of German culture and national identity (Rose 1990; Rubenstein & Roth 1987).

Luther denounced Jews as Germany's particular "misfortune," "plague," and "pestilence" (cited in Rose 1990:7). According to Paul Rose:

> The first great national prophet of Germany and the forger of the German language itself, Luther . . . shaped the overwhelmingly pejorative, indeed, demonic, significance of the word Jude. Through the influence of Luther's language and tracts, a hysterical and demonizing mentality entered the mainstream of German thought and discourse. . . . The Jews . . . were blocking the Germans' need to fulfill themselves in achieving both their "Christian freedom" and their political "freedom". . . . Having crucified Jesus, they were . . . intent on crucifying the German people. . . . Morally, the Jews were the worldly agents of the devil. . . . Materially, [they] were extorting money from . . . [the] German nation. . . . Germany's redemption [meant] her redemption from the Jews and Judaism. (ibid.4, 7–8)

Thus Luther was a path-breaking claimsmaker regarding the "Jewish problem," a key progenitor of the view, which prevailed among the German political right (including fascists), that Jews were a "'foreign nation' that lived symbiotically within German society" (ibid.:67). "Jewish character" was considered to be the polar opposite of "German character." As Uriel Tal observes, "Jewish character was not only corrupt and evil . . . [but] the essence of corruption and the principle of evil. . . . German character was not only deep, upright, diligent, and enterprising but the essence of profundity, probity, industry, and courage" (1975:276; see also Volkov 1989).

In the late nineteenth and early twentieth centuries, this religious-based collective representation of the Jew was given a new foundation through anti-Semitic interpretations of modern biological and anthropological research. This transformation of anti-Semitism from a religious ideology to a "scientific" theory of race elevated the social credibility (and eventual legal legitimacy) of Nazi claims about the "Jewish problem" (Rose 1990; Volkov 1989; Yahil 1990).

The British biologist Charles Darwin (1809–1882) postulated that life had evolved through a process of natural selection or survival of the fittest among diverse species, including humans. Social Darwinists in both Europe and the United States applied this theory to the social realm, assuming that some races had natural qualities that made them more fit, more adaptable members of society than others (Hofstader 1959). In addition, Sir Francis Galton (1822–1911), Darwin's cousin, had pioneered the eugenics movement. Eugenics,

which means "well born" or "good genes," was a philosophy that advocated social intervention to regulate the genetic composition of the population by encouraging the breeding of parents with good genes and discouraging the
breeding of parents with bad genes. The United States was in fact "the first
country to pass laws calling for compulsory sterilization in the name of racial
purification" (Rubenstein & Roth 1987:141). In 1923 a prominent German
medical director wrote to the Ministry of the Interior: "[W]hat we racial hy-
gienists promote is not all new or unheard of. In a cultured nation of the first
order, in the United States of America, that which we strive toward was introduced and tested long ago" (cited in Rubenstein & Roth 1987:141).

In Germany the belief that there were distinctive Jewish and German char-
acters or types led anti-Semites to conclude that Jews were an inferior race and
Germans were a superior race. William Marr (1819–1904), the German ideologue whose distinction between languages with Semitic (Middle Eastern)
and Aryan (Indo-European) roots popularized the term "anti-Semitism" in the
late 1870s, viewed the Jews as "a mixed people, of a strongly prevailing Caucasian character" (cited in Rose 1990:283).[3] In Aryan racial theory, Caucasians
were seen as superior, with the so-called Nordic race (Germanic people of
northern Europe, especially Scandinavians) characterized by tall stature, light
hair, and blue eyes viewed as the original Caucasian stock. German eugenicists
favored social policies that would promote the purity of this race.

Alfred Rosenberg (1893–1946), an early member of the Nazi party and its
chief anti-Semitic ideologue, impressed Hitler with his theory of a Jewish-
Communist conspiracy that undermined "the foundations of our existence"
(cited in Kochan 1990:1304). Rosenberg was one of the principal dissemina-
tors of the *Protocols of the Elders of Zion*, initially a Russian forgery that claimed
to be the minutes of a secret meeting in which Jewish leaders were plotting to
achieve world domination. In his major original work, *Der Mythus des 20
Jahrhunderts* (The Myth of the Twentieth Century), which had influence comparable to Hitler's *Mein Kampf*, Rosenberg claimed that "race was the decisive
factor determining art, science, culture, and the course of world history" and
that Aryans were the "master race" who were destined to dominate Europe
(cited in ibid.:1305).

Thus in Nazi doctrine race was viewed as the basic element of human
society:

> It was because of their race that [individuals] acted for good or bad and tended
> toward survival or extinction. When citizens were corrupted by the rule of an
> inferior race, government was corrupted. When they were governed by a posi-
> tive and lofty race . . . they enhanced humankind, its society, and its culture.
> (Yahil 1990:37)

While some historians doubt whether Hitler really believed the scientific basis of Nazi racial theory, he was nonetheless committed to translating these

ideas into action, to finally and once and for all doing something about the Jews (Volkov 1989; Yahil 1990). As Hitler is reported to have said:

> I know perfectly well . . . that in the scientific sense there is not such a thing as race. . . . [But] I as a politician need a conception which enables the order which has hitherto existed on historic bases to be abolished and an entirely new and antihistoric order enforced and given an intellectual basis. (quoted in Yahil 1990:37)

APPEALING TO AUDIENCES AND GARNERING SUPPORT

Social problems claimsmaking involves the construction of collective representations of types of persons who constitute problems. Successful claimsmaking, however, ultimately requires public endorsement if it is to achieve legitimacy and "move forward in its career. . . . [Otherwise] it flounders and languishes outside the arena of public action" (Blumer 1971:303).

Social movements are often the vehicles for advancing claims about social problems and translating these claims into publicly supported actions (Bash 1995; Mauss 1975; Neuman 1998). Social movements use an ideological "frame" or scheme of interpretation that provides members with a coherent explanation of a rather diverse and ambiguous set of facts and circumstances (Gamson 1992). This frame promotes solidarity among adherents and mobilizes them to work on the movement's behalf. It is also used to make appeals to new audiences that might support the movement in various ways—as rank-and-file activists, financial supporters, or voters, for example. A social movement has a greater chance of success when its frame is aligned with sentiments in the larger culture (Snow & Benford 1992). As we have seen, there was much sentiment in German culture that was congruent with Nazi claims about Jews. As Hitler observed in 1922:

> I scanned the revolutionary events of history and . . . [asked] myself: against which racial element in Germany can I unleash my propaganda of hate with the greatest prospects of success? . . . I came to the conclusion that a campaign against the Jews would be as popular as it would be successful. (quoted in Rose 1990:379)

It was not always (or even usually) anti-Semitism, however, that was the Nazis' most effective theme in garnering popular support. At various times and with different audiences the appeal to nationalism, complaints about the Versailles treaty, opposition to communism, and proposed solutions to economic problems were more attractive issues. Nevertheless, the Nazis' vehement anti-Semitism was well-known, and supporters were not bothered by this stance, at best (Allen 1984; Browning 1998; Kater 1984).

Attracting Rank-and-File Members

Richard Hamilton suggests that the Nazis' rise to power was not inevitable, not structurally determined, for "widely varying developments may occur within the same structural frameworks" (1982:443). Other political parties did not offer attractive alternatives to deal with Germany's problems, and the Nazis seized upon political opportunities that created an opening or historical contingency for change (see Neuman 1998). They were able to "generate a plausible program and . . . mobilize cadres to sell it" (Hamilton 1982:18).

The German Workers' party, later named the National Socialist Workers' party, or Nazi party, was founded in 1918. It was but one of many right-wing nationalist parties that existed in Germany in the post–World War I period (Spielvogel 1996). The party's initial financial sponsor was the Thule Society, a secret organization that took its name from an ancient legend of a "mythological land of the north, . . . Ultima Thule, believed to be the original home of the Germanic race" (Poole 1997b:7):

> Among the group's members were lawyers, judges, university professors, police officials, aristocrats, physicians, scientists . . . [and] rich businessmen. Only those who could prove their racial purity for at least three generations were admitted. . . . [Their] motto was: "Remember that you are a German! Keep your blood pure!" . . . [They] espoused German racial superiority, anti-Semitism, and violent anti-communism . . . [and their goal] was the establishment of a pan-German state of unsurpassed power and grandeur. (ibid.:7–8)

One of the Thule Society's primary strategies for accomplishing this end was "to bring the working man . . . into the nationalist camp."

Hitler was an early Nazi party member (board member #7) and provided the party with the leadership and inspiration that transformed it from a rather inchoate group of beer brawlers to a potent political force (Fischer 1995). He gained notoriety as an exceptional orator who could mesmerize audiences with his voice. He "spoke with certainty when others equivocated . . . [and] offered simple, bold solutions with an air of absolute assurance" (Botwinick 1996:55).

W. Lawrence Neuman (1998) observes that a social movement's success is in large part dependent on the development of a movement culture that links members' personal identity to broader political objectives. Indeed, Hitler had a keen appreciation for the role of symbols and a celebratory atmosphere in creating a sense of belonging among adherents. He adopted the swastika—an ancient occult symbol that invoked the power of the sun—as the party's official insignia, and this emblem was displayed on flags and members' uniforms during rallies and parades. Hitler also introduced the *heil* salute. The word *heil* in German had "a religious-medical connotation . . . meaning 'healed' or 'saved'" and was historically reserved for dignitaries like princes (Fischer 1995:130; see also Spielvogel 1996).

In 1920 Hitler changed the name of the German Workers' party to the Nationalist Socialist German Workers' party. This change was calculated to invoke positive feelings among seemingly incompatible constituencies—nationalists and socialists. According to Klaus Fischer, Hitler saw "national socialism" as a symbolic slogan that could unify diverse ideological orientations under one banner. Socialism, for Hitler, did not refer "to a specific economic system but to an instinct for national self-preservation," to the promotion of "a homogenous and prosperous whole" over private interests (1995:125–26).

> Germans must be taught that they work not just for their own selfish ends but for the good of the nation; and by working for the collective, Germans should be secure in the knowledge that the state, in turn, works on their behalf by guaranteeing them a good livelihood, conducive working conditions, unemployment benefits, old-age pensions, free education, and other social benefits. (ibid.:126)

German nationals living outside German territorial borders (e.g., Austria, Poland, Czechoslovakia) were to be included in this scheme, while non-Germans living within German borders (e.g., Jews, foreigners) were not. However, William Brustein (1996) argues that it was nationalism not anti-Semitism per se that was the issue that attracted most new members. Anti-Semitism was such a "taken-for-granted part of [German] political discourse" that party leaders viewed it as a weak recruiting device for distinguishing themselves from other groups (Bernston & Ault 1998:1201).

In the early 1920s Hitler thought that the Weimar Republic could be overthrown through armed resurrection rather than through the electoral process. Thus the Nazi Storm Troops (*Sturmabteilung*), or SA, became central to his strategy. First established under the auspices of a gymnastic and sport division of the party, the SA became the armed force of the movement. Hitler sensed that the SA could be used not only to intimidate opponents but to draw new members as well. According to Fischer, his "immediate aim was to attract recruits with military backgrounds" (1995:123). Indeed, the early Nazi rank-and-file was composed largely of "bands of World War I veterans who were unable to give up fighting and adjust to civilian life . . . [and] young people . . . attracted to a group that offered adventure in secret meetings, parades, the painting of slogans on buildings, and fighting with opponents" (Spielvogel 1996:14, 30–31).

Nonetheless, by 1923 the party (with a membership of about 55,000) attracted recruits from varying social strata. Thirty-six percent were working class, 52 percent were lower-middle class, and 12 percent were upper class (Kater 1983). In an analysis of Nazi party membership in Munich between 1925 and 1930, Helmut Anheier and Friedhelm Neidhardt (1998) argue that the party had more socioeconomic breadth than any other party of the extreme political right or left.

Raising Money from the Elite

Social movements, as previously suggested, play a key role in mobilizing resources to construct social problems and their solutions. The Nazi party, like other social movements, required financial resources to sustain its activities. Kurt Ludecke, an early member, describes the situation this way:

> The Nazi organization itself lived from day to day financially, with no treasury to draw on for lecture hall rentals, printing costs, or the other thousand-and-one expenses which threatened to swamp us. The only funds we could count on were membership dues, which were . . . merely a drop in the bucket. Collections at mass meetings were sometimes large, but not to be relied on. Once in [a] while, a Nazi sympathizer would make a special contribution, and in a few cases these gifts were quite substantial. But we never had enough money. . . . Instead of receiving salaries for the work we did, most of us had to give to the Party in order to carry on. Clerks and officers, except for a very few, got no pay, and the majority of members pursued their usual occupations during the day. . . . [O]nly two or three . . . who gave full time to Party work . . . had sufficient means to support themselves. The rest were chiefly recruited from the jobless men who would work for their meals. (cited in Poole 1997b:27)

The Thule Society and right-wing military organizations did contribute funds, but they gave to other nationalist groups "and there was only so much money to go around" (ibid.). With the creation of the SA in 1921, however, paramilitary funds originally targeted for other groups were increasingly funneled to the Nazis.

Harvard graduate Ernst Hanfstaengl, whose mother was American and whose "wealthy family owned an art publishing business in Munich," was the first upper-class contributor to invite Hitler into his home (ibid.:39). Hanfstaengl did not share Hitler's anti-Semitic views, though he did find his criticisms of Jews amusing and witty. He "donated some of his personal wealth to the party . . . [and] used his family connections" to introduce Hitler to other high-society donors, especially wealthy matrons (Fischer 1995:137).

A key Nazi party fund-raiser among businessmen and aristocrats was Max Erwin von Scheubner-Richter, who had been brought into the party by Rosenberg. Among Scheubner-Richter and Rosenberg's most important contacts were anticommunist Russian oil producers living in Germany in exile who hoped to overthrow the Soviets with German help. In many cases the contributions secured from the elite "did not take the form of cash" but of valuable art objects and jewelry that Hitler disposed of "as he saw fit" (Poole 1997b:49). Typically, Hitler would use these valuables as collateral to obtain loans. Between 1919 and 1923, however, Ernst von Borsig and Fritz Thyssen were the only German industrialists who gave the Nazis significant financial support. Borsig, who headed "an old Berlin firm that manufactured locomotives, boilers, and heavy industrial equipment," wielded considerable influence over the German business community as chairman of the Alliance of German Employers' Associations (Fischer 1995:139). Thyssen, who at the time was the "heir-in-waiting" to United Steel Works, a gigantic steel firm, was to eventually contribute over a million marks to the Nazi party (Wistrich 1995).

The party also solicited money from beyond German borders. Hitler himself went on several fund-raising tours in Switzerland, Austria, and Czechoslovakia. Italian dictator Benito Mussolini had his government provide support. Through Rosenberg the party received money from wealthy British oilman Sir Henri Deterding. And there is evidence that the U.S. automobile magnate Henry Ford contributed money as well. Ford shared Hitler's anti-Semitic and anticommunist views. In the United States he financed anti-Semitic propaganda, including the *Independent,* a newspaper with a circulation of half a million by the mid-1920s. In the early 1920s reprints of anti-Semitic articles that appeared in the *Independent* were published in a four-volume compilation called *The International Jew,* which was translated into sixteen languages and published throughout the world. In *Mein Kampf* Hitler specifically praised Ford for his views and appears to have taken passages from the *Independent* (Poole 1997b).

Another source of financial support came from Alfred Hugenberg, a German newspaper and film tycoon, who joined forces with Hitler in a 1929 campaign against the Young Plan (endorsed by the Allied powers), which would have required Germany to pay reparations for another fifty-nine years. According to James Poole's account, "Every speech made by Hitler and other Nazi leaders was carried by all the newspapers in Hugenberg's chain. Millions of Germans who had hardly ever heard of Hitler before now became interested in him, since he was given such good publicity in the 'respectable' press" (1997b:149). Although the anti–Young Plan forces lost, the campaign brought considerable revenues into the Nazi party, including contributions from the "well-to-do middle class" (ibid.:159).

Appealing to Voters and Acquiring Power

In November 1923 Hitler led a failed *putsch* (coup) against the Weimar government in the city of Munich. The idea of a coup at that time was not novel. The Communists in Russia and Mussolini's fascists in Italy had risen to power this way in November 1917 and October 1922, respectively. And in Germany there had been other attempted takeovers, albeit unsuccessful ones (Hilberg 1992).

Hitler was convicted of treason and sentenced to five years in prison, though he served little more than a year. Upon his release Hitler faced opposition for leadership of the Nazi party, especially from Gregor Strasser, who along with his younger brother Otto took "the socialist part of the Nazi program seriously" (Spielvogel 1996:43). Hitler, of course, triumphed, and in 1926 at the first party congress since the failed coup, he declared himself the undisputed leader of the party.

During this time Hitler became more interested in an electoral strategy for gaining power (Hamilton 1982). But while the party continued to grow, this progress did not translate into votes, and it remained a "membership organization without an electorate" (Anheier et al. 1998:1265). A key turning point was the Nazis' electoral failure of May 1928 in which the party received only 2.6 percent of the *Reichstag* (German parliament) vote. Hitler decided to reorganize the party into *Gaue* (regions) "that were nearly identical to national election precincts." He gave the *Gauleitern* (regional leaders) greater flexibility to plan their operations and shift strategies if necessary to respond to local conditions. In addition, the *Gaue* were "further divided into *Kreise* (districts), these into *Ortsgruppen* (local groups), which, in larger cities, were further subdivided into *Zellen* (cells) and *Blocks* (blocks)" (Fischer 1995:205):

> The entire operation . . . was held together through a steady stream of memorandums, suggestions, and guidelines coming down a chain of command, and activity reports passing up. . . . From the top came . . . [instructions] as to how issues should be handled in a given campaign, or a review of techniques that had proved useful in recent elections. . . . The activity reports let people at the top know which units were performing and which . . . were lagging. They also indicated which tactics had been used and with what success; such information in turn . . . [was] passed on to other units . . . for more general use. The higher echelons did, unquestionably, reserve an absolute right of intervention. But that was something to be used . . . [only] for a malfunctioning or insubordinate unit. The intended relationship of top to bottom was . . . one of close monitoring (as opposed to close control), of guiding, helping, encouraging. (Hamilton 1982:324)

The party also established the Reich Propaganda Office, under the direction of Joseph Goebbels (1897–1945), and a public speakers' program, the National Socialist Speakers School, to train members in rhetorical and propaganda techniques as well as the "official party responses to standard questions" (Brustein 1998a:1253; see also Hamilton 1982; Spielvogel 1996). More mass rallies were held, with speakers brought in from the outside. An emphasis was placed on making the rallies entertaining for audiences. In addition, a Christmas party might be held for children, a youth group taken on a hike or camping trip, or a soup kitchen set up for the unemployed. Loudspeaker vans, leaflets, and personal letters were used to communicate with voters. Hitler himself would travel throughout Germany "in whirlwind campaigns by car, train, and airplane" (Spielvogel 1996:57). In one tour he covered fifty cities in just fifteen days.

In the countryside, the party targeted farmers suffering from "high indebtedness and high interest rates combined with poor harvests and a general decline in land prices" who had been largely ignored by other political groups (Hamilton 1982:365). Appeals were made to restore traditional communal values shared by a common German *Volk*, and Jews were blamed for the farmers' problems, "especially when Jewish middlemen could be used as a convenient target" (ibid.:370). In the cities, anti-Semitism was used when it would work and "played down or abandoned" when it would not (ibid.:367). In an analysis of party speeches between 1925 and 1930, Helmut Anheier and colleagues (1998) found that anti-Semitic themes declined and were replaced by increasing references to anticommunism, economic problems, and the Young Plan. Rather than making negative references to certain groups (e.g., Jews, foreigners), the speeches were more likely to make positive references to the German people or nation and portray the party as the "savior" offering solutions.

At the same time, other political parties did little to effectively repel the Nazi challenge. On the left, for instance, the Communists tried to transform workers' discontents into more radical actions against the state. Workers, however, did not respond favorably when the Communists tried to turn wage strikes intended as short-term events with specific, immediate goals into protracted struggles that would keep workers off the job "for longer, indefinite periods and for goals that, at best, seemed a doubtful gamble" (Hamilton 1982:298). And workers were also turned off when the Communists attacked both fascism and democracy as if they were two forms of government that harbored "the same class content" (ibid.:304). Parties on the right, on the other hand, became more extreme in their attacks on the Weimar Republic, making the Nazis appear more mainstream. They attempted to engage the Nazis in "a competition of toughness" that they could not win (ibid.:264).

As a consequence of all this, the Nazis' public standing improved, and in September 1930 the party received 18.3 percent of the Reichstag vote, an eightfold increase from the 1928 election. Moreover, total party membership rose to 389,000. Only the Social Democrats now had more members than the Nazis in parliament. The Weimar Republic was in increasing disarray, and it became difficult to maintain stable political coalitions to run the government. Repeated elections were held, and in July 1932 the Nazis received 37.3 percent of the vote, and party membership rose to 450,000. Although the Nazi vote declined to 33.1 in November 1932, Hitler had emerged as one of the leading political leaders in Germany (Anheier et al. 1998; Hamilton 1982; Spielvogel 1996).

Perhaps the only politician of Hitler's public stature was the aging General Field Marshal Paul von Hindenburg (1847–1934).[4] Hindenburg had been president of Germany since 1925, and as president he was the chief dignitary of the country and the military commander-in-chief. He also retained the power to appoint the Reichstag chancellor to run the government. After the November 1932 election, Hindenburg selected General Kurt von Schleicher (1882–1934) to replace Franz von Papen (1879–1969) as chancellor. Previously, von Schleicher had supported von Papen, but now he wanted his job. In January 1933, however, von Papen persuaded Hindenburg to appoint Hitler as chancellor with von Papen as vice-chancellor. Von Papen managed to convince Hindenburg that Hitler could be co-opted and his radical impulses controlled. Von Papen, of course, was wrong (Fischer 1995; Spielvogel 1996).

On January 30, 1933 Hitler was sworn in as chancellor of Germany. He "had come to power legally and within the system" (Spielvogel 1996:67). Politicians who thought they could use Hitler for their own purposes were outmaneuvered. Hitler proved to be more formidable than they ever imagined. The Weimar constitution provided for the suspension of parliament and civil liberties in cases of national emergencies. Indeed, von Papen had invoked this power before, and Hitler got Hindenburg to agree to disband parliament for seven weeks and hold new elections in March 1933. In that period Hitler also convinced Hindenburg to issue an emergency decree directed at the Communists that curtailed freedom of the press and outlawed "public meetings that posed a threat to the vital interests of the state" (ibid.:69). The Nazis monopolized the state-directed public radio, enabling them to transmit Hitler's speeches throughout the country. In March 1933 the party received 43.9 percent of the Reichstag vote.

Hitler immediately pressed for the passage of the Enabling Act, officially called the Law for the Relief of the Distress of the Nation and State, which would gave him the power to issue laws without the Reichstag's approval for a period of four years "in order to solve Germany's economic and social problems, to create political stability, and to establish the new Germany" (ibid.:72). The Enabling Act was passed on March 24 with 83 percent of the Reichstag vote. Hitler then proceeded to suppress all other opposition—eliminating trade unions and other political parties—and turning Germany into a one-party state.[5] When Hindenburg died on August 2, 1934, Hitler merged the offices of the chancellor and president and became the "Führer of the German Reich and people" (ibid.:79). In a plebiscite held on August 19, 85 percent of the people gave Hitler their approval. The country was now run by the *Führerprinzip,* the leadership principle: "One man rules the whole . . . [and] that one man empowers his subordinates . . . to accomplish the goals set for them by their overlords and so on down the . . . chain of command" (Fischer 1995:297).

FORMULATING SOLUTIONS TO THE "JEWISH PROBLEM"

Having acquired political power, the Nazis were now in a position to translate their claims about the "Jewish problem" into specific policy proposals. However, as functionalist historians have pointed out, "When the Nazis came to power . . . [t]hey were certain only that a solution was necessary" (Schleunes 1970:viii). They had not yet worked out the details of what this solution would entail. As I will show, the solutions that were adopted evolved through progressively radical (though overlapping) stages. According to Raul Hilberg (1985), only with the Final Solution were the Nazis truly inventive, for at first they employed policies that were quite ordinary in their consistency with historical precedent—for instance, the laws prohibiting Jews from holding public office, from practicing law and medicine, from attending institutions of higher education, and from marrying or having sexual intercourse with Christians; and the laws requiring Jews to wear badges or specially marked clothing and to live in compulsory ghettos (Botwinick 1996). As Hilberg observes:

> [S]uch measures had been worked out over the course of more than a thousand years by authorities of the church and by secular governments that followed in their footsteps. And the experiences gathered over that time became a reservoir that could be used, and which indeed was used to an amazing extent . . . even in detail, as if there were a memory which automatically extended to the [Nazi] period. (quoted in Lanzmann 1985:71)

The Legal Solution

Social movements often perceive law reform as the primary means of achieving their goals, for the law confers legitimacy on new social norms (Handler 1978; Kidder 1983). To be sure, Hitler and other high-ranking Nazi officials countenanced and at times encouraged hooliganism and random violence against Jews. But they preferred more systematic, legal means to acquire and maintain public support for their anti-Jewish policies. All told, the Nazis issued over two thousand legal measures against the Jews (Adam 1990; Mommsen 1986).

In April 1933, for example, the Law for the Restoration of the Professional Civil Service and the Law Regarding Admission to the Bar were passed. These laws dismissed persons of non-Aryan descent from the civil service and denied them admission to the bar. The Law Against the Overcrowding of German Schools and Institutions of Higher Learning mandated that new admissions of non-Aryans not exceed the proportion of non-Aryans in the German population and that non-Aryans be prohibited from taking the final state exams for occupations requiring official certification. Such restrictions were "also introduced into the bylaws of professional organizations, societies, and clubs" (Adam 1990:53). In September 1933 additional legislation excluded non-Aryans from cultural enterprises having to do with literature, theater, music, art, broadcasting, and the press (Yahil 1990).

In September 1935 the Nazis' legal solution to the "Jewish problem" entered its second stage with the passage of the so-called Nuremberg Laws. The Reich Citizenship Law restricted German citizenship and all the rights contained thereof to persons of "German or kindred blood." The Law for the Protection of German Blood and German Honor prohibited marriages and sexual relations between Jews and persons of German or kindred blood, and forbade Jews from flying the German flag and from hiring German female domestic servants under the age of forty-five. It also prescribed penalties for violation, which included hard labor and imprisonment (Fraenkel 2001; Yahil 1990).

Hitler considered the Nuremberg Laws a milestone in the anti-Jewish campaign (Yahil 1990). The Nazis had succeeded in transforming the "Jewish problem" into a technical matter amenable to legitimate legal solutions. The question remained, however, as to how to define the target population. The Law for the Restoration of the Professional Civil Service, for instance, had defined "non-Aryan" as a person "descended from non-Aryan, particularly Jewish, parents or grandparents," even if only one parent or grandparent fit that category (cited in ibid.:65). But bureaucrats responsible for implementing the law encountered difficulty verifying non-Aryan status on the basis of just one grandparent's background. In the event of a dispute, an opinion had to be obtained from the expert on racial research in the Ministry of Interior. Moreover, at President Hindenburg's request, the law contained an exemption for non-Aryans who had held their positions since August 1, 1914 and who had either fought at the German front during World War I or were the son or father of a soldier who had been killed in that war.

With the Nuremberg Laws the term "Jew" replaced "non-Aryan." According to Leni Yahil (ibid.), a major reason for this change was the objections of non-Aryan countries (especially Japan) with whom Germany wished to curry favor. Still, at first "Jew" remained undefined, and it took a subsequent addendum issued in November 1935 to clarify the matter. The First Implementation Order to the Reich Citizenship Law defined a Jew as "anyone descended from at least three grandparents who were full Jews by race" (ibid.:72). The law also created the status of *Mischlinge,* which was composed of persons of mixed background. David Bankier describes the rather complicated Mischlinge status as follows:

> Mischlinge of the first degree, or half Jews, were those who had two Jewish grandparents, did not belong to the Jewish religion, and were not married to a Jewish person as of September 15, 1935. They had the rights of regular German citizens, although these were curtailed by a series of regulations: for example, they could marry only Mischlinge of the first degree. . . . Mischlinge of the second degree, or quarter Jews, were those with one Jewish grandparent. They were subject to certain limitations in [occupations] requiring full German origins, but were drafted into the army and allowed to marry Germans. . . . In all other matters they were treated like German "Aryans." (1990b:981)

For the most part it was Nazi policy to equate the Mischlinge of the first degree with Jews and "to absorb the Mischlinge of the second degree into the German nation" (ibid.:982). While many Nazis (including Hitler) remained concerned about the problem of all Mischlinge polluting German society, they did not reach consensus on this, and there was considerable variation in how officials responsible for implementing Jewish policy treated Mischlinge Jews. Similarly, while the Law for the Protection of German Blood and German Honor prohibited marriages between Germans and Jews, it did not cover already existing intermarriages, and Jews in mixed marriages were sometimes treated more benevolently than others (Ehmann 2001; Hilberg 1985; Johnson 1999).

Ian Hacking observes that particular types of individuals "come into being . . . with our invention of the categories labeling them" (1986:236). Thus in an important sense the Nuremberg Laws brought the "Jew" into being as a legally inferior entity. At the same time, these laws remained a far cry from the Final Solution. Although Hitler and the Nazi elite may have envisioned them as the first step toward a Germany *Judenfrei,* the German Information Agency reported that "the German people has no objection to the Jew as long as he wishes to be a member of the Jewish people and acts accordingly, but . . . [we decline] to look on the Jew as a national of the German Nation . . . and to accord him the same rights and duties as a German" (cited in Yahil 1990:72). Consequently, the new laws could be perceived as offering German Jews the opportunity to establish themselves as a "national minority" comparable to discriminated minorities in other countries (e.g., African Americans in the United States at that time). Some Jews even regarded the legal solution as somewhat acceptable, viewing them, as one survivor recalls, "as a sort of guarantee, . . . a definitive legal adjustment, which would make it possible for [us] to remain in . . . the homeland that meant so much to [us]" (quoted in Engelmann 1986:80).

The Nuremberg Laws, however, were just a prelude to countless other decrees that followed, including those that extended the list of occupations from which Jews were completely barred; closed schools and universities to Jewish students; prevented Jews from entering certain places (e.g., parks, theaters, hotels), from using public transportation, and from driving cars; required them to wear the "Star of David" insignia, to live in designated districts, and to relinquish their valuables (e.g., gold, jewelry, art objects); and restricted Jewish businesses to those that dealt only with other Jews, eventually requiring the complete transfer of Jewish-owned businesses to Aryan-German ownership (Botwinick 1996; Chesnoff 1999; Hilberg 1985).

The Emigration/Deportation Solution

As early as 1919, Hitler had written of the need to physically remove Jews from Germany (Browning 1990a). But it was not until the mid-1930s that Nazi leaders turned to a policy of expulsion to solve the "Jewish problem." This shift took place in the context of the Four-Year Plan, a directive issued by Hitler and carried out by Hermann Göring (1893–1946), who as *Reichs-*

marshall, was Hitler's designated successor, the second most powerful man in the country.[6] The Four-Year plan was designed to prepare the German economy and military for war aimed at the conquest of new living space (*Lebensraum*). Hitler wanted Germany to become economically self-sufficient, less dependent on foreign imports in the event of an economic blockade (Bankier 1990a).

At first the expulsion policy took the form of "voluntary" emigration. By creating conditions that were so bad for Jews, the Nazis hoped that they would simply choose to leave. However, disincentives for emigration were created by restrictions on "the amount of currency and property Jews could take with them" (Kaplan 1998:70). The Reich Flight Tax, first put in place before the Nazi era to prevent "capital flight," was raised to prohibitive heights. Many prospective emigrants "had to sell all their belongings simply to pay this . . . tax" (ibid.:71). And they were not allowed to directly transfer their after-tax money abroad but were required to deposit it in "blocked accounts . . . [from which] they could buy foreign currency—at very unfavorable exchange rates" (ibid.). In 1935 the exchange rate was only half the market value of the German mark, and it became progressively lower, falling to just 4 percent by 1939. Moreover, obtaining the necessary documents "took months of running a bureaucratic gauntlet," and German officials often demanded bribes and some demanded sexual favors from Jewish women (ibid.:130). Another significant barrier was the absence for most Jews of "relatives or friends abroad who could sponsor admission into a country of refuge" (ibid.:72). In addition, the Nazis issued "passports for emigration only," thus forbidding exploratory trips intended to assess opportunities elsewhere.

At times initiatives were developed to circumvent some of these restrictions to make emigration easier. The *Ha'avarah* (transfer) Agreement, for example, allowed the transfer of German-Jewish capital in the form of German goods into British-controlled Palestine, thus facilitating the emigration of those Jews whose capital was transferred. According to Yehuda Bauer:

> The details were rather complicated, but the general idea was that Jews with capital at their disposal would be permitted to buy German industrial goods, mainly tools of production—irrigation, pipes, cement mixers, machinery— that were in demand in Palestine. . . . The goods were shipped to Palestine, and when the German Jewish investors arrived there, they received their money back in pounds sterling. (1994:10)

With this policy the Nazis also hoped to expand Germany's export market in the Middle East and to undermine an anti-German economic and diplomatic boycott that had been initiated by several (mostly U.S.) Jewish organizations. This agreement was in effect until the outbreak of World War II.

In March 1938 German troops marched into neighboring Austria and took over the nation. The *Anschluss* (annexation) of Austria was followed by pogroms initiated against Austria's Jewish population and many were "arrested, humiliated, tortured, and sent to the Dachau concentration camp" (Yahil 1990:105). Adolf Eichmann—who was serving in the Jewish Section of the *Sicherheitsdienst* (Security Service), or SD, and who had emerged as a leading expert on Jewish affairs—was sent to Vienna "to organize the emigration of the Jews and introduce a new system" of *forcible* deportations. This system involved the confiscation of Jewish property, which left Jews with "only the sum required to enter their proposed countries" of destination, if such destinations could indeed be found. It was here that Eichmann introduced the methods that were later used to expel Jews from other areas: concentrate Jews in a central location, fix quotas, instruct designated Jewish leaders to fill these quotas, and force wealthier Jews to finance the costs of deporting Jews "who had no means of their own" (Cochavi 1990:1733).

The events in Austria diffused the "Jewish problem" into the international arena as U.S. President Franklin Roosevelt called for a conference on Jewish refugees that was held in Evian, France, in July 1938. At the Evian Conference delegates from thirty-two countries met, but no one (including the United States) was willing to modify its existing immigration policies to accommodate more Jews (Bauer 1994; Wyman 1990).

Hitler was quick to exploit this impasse, admonishing the Evian Conference nations that they had no right to tell Germany what to do with its Jews when they did not want to accept more Jews themselves. "The world has sufficient space for [Jewish] settlements," he warned, "or sooner or later . . . [the Jews] will succumb to a crisis of inconceivable magnitude" (quoted in Bauer 1994:36). Hitler argued that settlement of the "Jewish problem" was an international responsibility upon on which the peace of Europe depended, for as he said, "European questions cannot be settled until the Jewish question is cleared up" (ibid.). Failing an international agreement, Hitler told Göring that "The Jewish question is to be summed up and coordinated once and for all and solved one way or the other" (ibid.). Richard Breitman and Alan Kraut (1987) believe that Hitler was in fact contemplating extermination of those Jews who could not be emigrated.

In November 1938 the infamous *Kristallnacht* pogrom (Crystal Night or Night of the Broken Glass) showed just what the Nazis had in mind for the Jews. This pogrom was precipitated by an edict issued the previous month to deport all Polish-born Jews living in Germany back into Poland. When Herschel Grynzpan, a young Jewish man living in Paris, learned that his parents had been deported, he retaliated by shooting (and killing) an official at the German embassy in Paris. Goebbels, with Hitler's approval, instructed the Nazi cadre to attack Jewish businesses, homes, and synagogues. Amidst the looting and massive destruction that ensued, "thousands of windows were smashed and the broken shards glittered in the streets like crystal" (Botwinick 1996:122). About a hundred Jews were killed, countless others injured, and some twenty-six thousand arrested and herded into concentration camps (Bauer 1994; Fischer 1995).

While most of the Nazi leadership was pleased with *Kristallnacht,* Göring was concerned that too much property the Nazis could have otherwise seized was destroyed (Barkai 1989; Chesnoff 1999). To make the pogrom more profitable, Göring ordered an "atonement tax" to be paid by every Jew who owned assets of over 5,000 marks, an amount that yielded 1.25 billion marks. In addition, 250 million marks of insurance payments that were due to the Jews who lost their property during the pogrom were also confiscated. Göring also ordered the compulsory "Aryanization" of the economy, requiring the closure of all Jewish businesses and the "sale" of Jewish property and valuable possessions (through government-appointed fiduciaries) at a fraction of their market value. After the taxes levied by the Nazis, only "a small fraction of the . . . assets . . . [owned] by the Jews . . . ever left Germany with them" (Chesnoff 1999:21). Then, in January 1939, he instructed Reinhard Heydrich (1904–1942) to establish a Central Office for Jewish Emigration to further "the emigration of Jews from Germany by all possible means" (cited in Bauer 1994:38).[7] In essence this office was designed to expand and coordinate the methods of deportation previously used by Eichmann in Vienna. Still, the Nazis were concerned that it might take eight to ten years to accomplish full emigration of German Jews (Cochavi 1990; Yahil 1990).

The Final Solution

Earlier I noted that the construction of social problems is an uncertain process, and what emerges at the end may be quite different than what was initially envisioned (see Chapter 1). I also explained the functionalist historians' view that the Final Solution emerged only gradually through a process of incremental decision-making and "cumulative radicalization," as German territorial expansion made the emigration/deportation solution less viable.

World War II, which began with the German invasion of Poland in September 1939, was a crucial turning point in the formulation of a more radical solution to the "Jewish problem."[8] In the months before, Hitler had made it clear that the conquest of Poland would mark the beginning of a new set of expectations regarding the Jews, especially because Poland contained Europe's largest Jewish population. Following the invasion, "plans took shape in discussions . . . [between] Hitler and a [small] coterie of faithful followers" (Yahil 1990:128)—including Heydrich and Heinrich Himmler (1900–1945), head of the Nazi SS (*Schutzstaffel*) and the entire German policing system—for a "sweeping demographic reorganization of Poland" (Browning 2000:3).[9] Jews, Gypsies, and Poles were to be resettled into areas of German-occupied Poland further east, creating space in the western regions for the establishment of "pure German provinces" (ibid.:4). Heydrich was to coordinate the eastern resettlements, while Himmler was charged with the resettlement of ethnic Germans and the elimination of "harmful" indigenous elements in the west. To this latter end, a division of the SS, the *Einsatzgruppen* (Operational or Special Action Squads), were employed. The Einsatsgruppen, which were first introduced during the *Anschluss,* followed the German *Wehrmacht* (army) into occupied areas. The Wehrmacht secured the area militarily, and the Einsatsgruppen performed nonmilitary operations against the civilian population. During the Polish invasion the Einsatsgruppen murdered "thousands of prominent Poles and Jews" (Breitman 1991:146; see also Browning 1990c; Spector 1990a).[10]

Concentration of Jews into urban ghettos or reservations was the first step toward their eventual resettlement, and various proposals were circulated as to how this was to be done (Browning 2000). Plans were temporarily derailed, however, when the need to resettle Germans from Soviet-occupied Poland took precedence, trains for transportation were in limited supply, and Polish workers were needed for the war effort. Göring, whose first priority was the war, insisted that "all evacuation measures are to be directed in such a way that useful manpower does not disappear" (quoted in ibid.:12). Himmler was among those most disappointed with the curtailment of the deportation program.

As a result of the Polish invasion, Great Britain and France declared war on Germany. But by May 1940 prospects of a German victory in France emboldened Himmler to try to persuade Hitler to step up the deportations. He drafted a memorandum entitled "Some Thoughts on the Treatment of Alien Populations in the East," which he submitted to Hitler. Himmler proposed "completely to erase the concept of Jews through the possibility of a great emigration of all Jews to a colony in Africa or elsewhere" (cited in ibid.:14). The colony Himmler was referring to was Madagascar, an island off the coast of southeastern Africa that was controlled by the French. For decades anti-Semites had contemplated Madagascar as a place to send Jews, and it had been mentioned frequently in Nazi policy circles since 1938. Himmler's memo indicates that as of May 1940 the Nazis had not yet decided upon extermination as a solution to the "Jewish problem." Himmler wrote, "However cruel and tragic each individual case may be, this method is still the mildest and best, if one rejects the Bolshevik method of physical extermination of a people out of inner conviction as un-German and impossible" (ibid.). On the other hand, Breitman (1991) suggests that Himmler's mention of extermination in this memo indicates that this method had in fact crossed his mind and that his reservations about it may have been reserved for (non-Jewish) Poles. Breitman thinks that by this time the Nazis viewed forced emigration and murder of Jews as complementary rather than as alternative policies (Breitman & Kraut 1987).

Hitler read the memo and found the ideas, in Himmler's words, "very good and correct" (cited in Browning 2000:14). Himmler obtained Hitler's authorization to distribute the memo to other Nazi leaders, including Göring, along with the message that the führer had "recognized and confirmed" the plan. Franz Rademacher, the newly appointed Jewish expert in the German Foreign Office, proposed that Jews in German-occupied western Europe be sent to Madagascar as well, a suggestion that was quickly expanded by others to include all European Jews. In June, Heydrich referred to the Madagascar Plan as a "territorial final solution" (cited in Browning 1990b:491).

Nazi leaders anticipated that the Madagascar plan could be implemented at the end of the war, which they thought was eminent. They had quickly defeated France and expected to conquer Great Britain. The defeat of France and England "promised both the colonial territory and the merchant fleet necessary" for the realization of the plan (Browning 2000:17). By September, however, it was clear that a timely defeat of Great Britain was not possible, and the Madagascar plan was aborted. Nevertheless, the need to find a comprehensive solution to the "Jewish problem" was now on the table. "[T]he Nazi[s] were . . . committed to a way of thinking . . . that precluded any solution that was less than . . . 'final' and trans-European" (Browning 1990b:491).

Planning for Operation Barbarossa, an invasion of the Soviet Union that took place in June 1941, constituted the next major radicalization of the anti-Jewish policy.[11] According to a January 1941 memorandum written by Eichmann's close associate, Theodore Dannecker, Heydrich had "already received orders from the Führer . . . [to bring] about a final solution to the Jewish question within European territories ruled or controlled by Germany" (cited in Browning 2000:20). This solution would involve "the wholesale deportation of Jews as well as . . . the planning to the last detail of a settlement action in the territory yet to be determined" (ibid.). "Territory yet to be determined," it turns out, was a code phrase for the Soviet Union.

In the months before the invasion, Himmler and Heydrich reached agreements with the Wehrmacht to allow both the Einsatsgruppen and Order Police to engage in "pacification" measures to eliminate the "Bolshevist-Jewish intelligentsia" (Breitman 1991, 1998). Many army officers were receptive to this plan because they "equated Jews with Bolshevik agitators, guerrillas, and saboteurs" (Browning 2000:22). In addition to these killing operations, which in fact had no military objective, Nazi leaders made plans for the expropriation of local food supplies (to feed the German army and to export to Germany) and for the massive resettlement of Jews to the east, which they knew would result in starvation for millions of people.

Browning argues that Operation Barbarossa "*implied* nothing less than the genocide of Soviet Jewry. . . . Now mass executions, mass expulsions, and mass starvation were being planned . . . on a scale that would dwarf what had happened in Poland" (ibid.:25). However, Browning adds, the implied genocide was still a vague and unspecified policy that "commingled the fates of Jewish and non-Jewish victims." It did not yet entail an plan to exterminate all European Jews, or even all Soviet Jews, "down to the last man, woman, and child" (ibid.:30).

It was not until after the Soviet invasion that a second decision was made to target all European Jews for extermination. Most historians believe that this decision was made by Hitler in consultation with Himmler and Heydrich during the euphoria of the initial success of the Barbarossa campaign (Bauer 1991; Browning 2000). On July 31 Heydrich presented Göring with a written order that he had prepared for Göring's signature. This order, which brought Göring on board, authorized Heydrich to make "all necessary preparations with regard to organizational, practical and financial aspects for an overall solution of the Jewish question in the German sphere of influence in Europe" and to submit "to me promptly an overall plan of the preliminary . . . measures for the execution of the intended final solution" (cited in Bauer 1991:144).

By the fall the outlines of the plan began to emerge. Himmler ordered the end to all Jewish emigration, "experimental" gassing of Jews at Auschwitz was undertaken, and construction of death camps at Belzec and Chelmno was begun. In January 1942 Heydrich convened the Wannsee Conference, at which the decision to proceed with the Final Solution was officially transmitted to a group of high-ranking Nazi bureaucrats. Although most of those in attendance were aware of the killing operations, only at the conference were they informed of the full scope of the plan. By May 1942 the Final Solution to the "Jewish problem" was under way with full force (Browning 1990b, 2000).[12]

NOTES

1.   Jesus was a devout Jew but spoke out against the Jewish leadership for its corruption and abandonment of genuine faith. Biblical accounts implicate one of his disciples, Judas Iscariot, in turning him over to the Sanhedrin, the Jewish High Court. He was charged with blasphemy and false messianic claims and consigned to the Roman authorities. Under Roman law the Sanhedrin had no jurisdiction over capital offenses, and crucifixion was a method of "punishment that was exclusively the prerogative of Roman courts of law and reserved for political prisoners" (Rubenstein & Roth 1987:33). In a Biblical account that was written about a century later, the Roman procurator Pontius Pilate is said to have been reluctant to execute Jesus. He offered the Jewish crowd outside the courthouse a choice between sparing Jesus or Barabbas, a convicted murderer. The crowd chose Barabbas (Ausubel 1964; Botwinick 1996).

2.   Dreyfus was compared with Judas Iscariot (see note 1).

3.   Moses Hess was among the more moderate racial theorists in Germany who considered "race as a complex mixture of ethnic inheritance and cultural tradition solidified over thousands of years" (Rose 1990:322–23). He preached "racial harmony" rather than "racial domination."

4.   In March 1932 Hitler had run against Hindenburg for the presidency. Hitler received only 30 percent of the vote, but in a multicandidate field Hindenburg did not gain a majority. Hindenburg won in a run-off election, while Hitler got 37 percent of the vote (Shirer 1960; Spielvogel 1996).

5.   To appease the German military, which was concerned about the SA, Hitler decided to overthrow the SA leadership. In June 1934 a number of SA leaders, most notably Ernst Roehm, were arrested and killed in what has been called the "Night of the Long Knives." Subsequently the SA's function was increasingly confined to ceremonial duties. The SS (*Schutzstaffel*), originally established in 1925 as an elite core of the SA whose purpose was to protect Hitler and top Nazi leaders, became independent of the SA and took on expanded functions (Rubenstein & Roth 1987; Shirer 1960; Spielvogel 1996).

6.   Göring was also Commander-in-Chief of the *Luftwaffe,* the German air force.

7.   At that time, Heydrich commanded the SD, the surveillance and intelligence-gathering component of the SS, and the Gestapo (*Geheimes Staatspolizei*), the national secret police. Later that year these two organizations (and others) were combined into the RSHA (*Reichssicherheitshauptamt*), or Reich Security Main Office, which Heydrich also headed.

8.   Prior to that time, in 1936 the German army had moved into the Rhineland, the demilitarized zone that bordered France, and in 1938 it took control of Czechoslovakia, neither of which provoked serious opposition from Great Britain or France. In August 1939, in anticipation of the Polish invasion, Hitler signed a secret pact with Soviet leader Joseph Stalin in which the two powers agreed to divide and occupy Poland (Shirer 1960; Spielvogel 1996).

9.   Although Heydrich administered the SD and Gestapo, these organizations were under Himmler's command (see note 7). In 1943 Himmler also became minister of the interior (Wistrich 1995). Also see note 5 on the emergence of the SS.

10.   The Wehrmacht was complicit in the civilian killings (see Chapter 3).

11.   This was done in violation of the previous agreement with Stalin (see note 8).

12.   According to Weinberg (1998), by November Hitler had "made it clear that the project of killing Jews was by no means confined to Europe. As he explained to the Grand Mufti of Jerusalem," his hopes of military victory in Africa and the Middle East would bring about the destruction of Jews in the Arab world (ibid.:484).

3 Implementing Solutions to the "Jewish Problem"

Filip Müller was a Jewish concentration camp inmate who worked in the crematoria at Auschwitz-Birkenau. He describes the killing process this way:

> Zyklon gas crystals were poured in by a so-called SS disinfection squad through the ceiling . . . [or] side openings. With five or six canisters of gas they could kill around two thousand people. . . . The gas took about 10 to 15 minutes to kill. The most horrible thing was when the doors of the gas chambers were opened—the unbearable sight: people were packed together like basalt, like blocks of stone. How they tumbled out of the gas chamber! I saw that several times. That was the toughest thing to take. You could never get used to that. (quoted in Lanzmann 1985:124–25)

As we have seen, the ultimate decision that led to this systematic gassing of Jews in Nazi extermination camps was the gradual outcome of incremental (but increasingly radical) decision-making. I believe that intentionalist historians are correct in suggesting that Adolf Hitler was a driving force behind the policies that led to the Final Solution, although Nazi elites like Heinrich Himmler and Reinhard Heydrich shared his fanatical vision and were crucial in helping Hitler turn his dream into a reality (Breitman 1991, 1998). On the other hand, the functionalist historians are also right in pointing to a broader range of responsibility. Indeed, the Final Solution involved nothing less than the coordination of "German society as a whole" (Hilberg 1985:264). Countless individuals in various official and unofficial capacities engaged in the "social problems work" that was necessary to construct and implement the Final Solution to the "Jewish problem."

In general, successful implementation of solutions to social problems depends upon claimsmakers' ability to manipulate cultural symbols to legitimate their policies and to transform a potentially disputable claim into a neutral, technical issue that is amenable to rational action (Best 1990; Gusfield 1981; Loseke 1999; Neuman 1998). This is not to say that this stage of social problems development proceeds without resistance from those who organize to thwart or redirect the implementation process (Spector & Kitsuse 1987). During the Nazi period such challenges did in fact occur, and I will consider these in Chapter 4. In this chapter, however, I examine the organizational settings and processes that enabled the Nazis to implement the Final Solution.

CONSTRUCTING NAZI CULTURE

Social problems claimsmaking is in large part dependent on the effective use of mass media to garner public support for solutions to problems (Gusfield 1981; Hilgartner & Bosk 1988; Loseke 1999; Neuman 1998). Indeed, after acquiring state power the Nazis embarked on a systematic media campaign to build a new moral order or cultural fabric that, in Émile Durkheim's terms, would penetrate and socialize individual consciences and create a new "collective conscience" (see Chapter 1).

In March 1933 Hitler established the Reich Ministry for Public Enlightenment and Propaganda, which was headed by Joseph Goebbels. As Goebbels remarked, "It is not enough to reconcile people more or less to our regime, to move them towards a position of neutrality. . . . [W]e would rather work on people until they are addicted to us . . . [and] the ideal of the national revolution" (quoted in Welch 1993:24). Later that year Goebbels was put in charge of a new Reich Chamber of Culture, which consisted of seven divisions: radio broadcasting, the press, literature, film, theater, music, and the visual arts. In order to work in any of these areas, Germans had to become members of the division that represented their group. People could be denied membership if they lacked "reliability or suitability," that is, if they were Jews or insufficiently pro-Nazi (Spielvogel 1996:155). Numerous other organizations were also established to regulate cultural content in these fields, enabling the Nazis to control everything from the news to the entertainment that Germans were allowed to receive.[1]

The Nazis intervened in educational settings as well. The National Socialist Teachers Association "assumed responsibility for the ideological indoctrination of teachers," and the Reich Ministry of Education exercised control over the curriculum (ibid.:171). For example:

> Instruction in German . . . inculcate[d] racial ideology or "German awareness" and utilized literary works stressing the idea of folk, blood and soil, and national and military values. . . . History classes focused on the Nazi revolution and Hitler's role in it. The whole of history was reinterpreted in light of racial principles . . . [and] the significance . . . of the Aryan race. Biology . . . centered on the laws of heredity, racial breeding, and the need for racial purity. Children learned to measure skulls and to classify racial types accordingly. Biology classes

underscored the necessity of cultivating racial health by the correct choice of Aryan spouses and the bearing of large families. . . . [The teaching] of geography . . . justified [territorial] expansion and the need for *Lebensraum* (living space). (ibid.:172–73)

In addition, the Nazis created a number of elite schools for boys who were trained to become the future political and military leaders of Nazi Germany. The objective of these schools was to create a cadre of committed National Socialists who were ready to fight and die for their country.

The *Hitler Jugend,* or Hitler Youth, founded in 1926, was another means of indoctrinating boys into Nazi ideology. By 1936 the Hitler Youth attracted two-thirds of all ten- to eighteen-year-olds, and in 1939 membership was made mandatory. All Hitler Youth were required to swear allegiance to the führer: "I swear to devote all my energies and my strength to the savior of our country, Adolf Hitler. I am willing and ready to give up my life for him, so help me God" (quoted in ibid.:168). Although Hitler Youth participated in activities such as model-plane building, sports, hiking, and camping, the organization was modeled on military values and included constant drilling, the exaltation of German military heroes, the honoring of war dead, and weapons training. Boys were encouraged to cultivate a fighting spirit, to become hardnosed and ruthless in their pursuit of Nazi ideals (Koch 2000; Rempel 1989).

The female counterpart of the Hitler Youth was the *Bund Deutscher Mädel,* or League of German Girls (Spielvogel 1996). Girls were taught to serve the state by becoming dutiful wives and mothers and by bearing as many children as possible to propagate the Aryan race. Indeed, the Nazis envisioned a culture of gender roles based on presumed biological traits that was hypertraditional in delegating women to the private sphere of child rearing and housework, dependent upon men for support but also providing men with the nurturance that sustained them in their quest for economic, bureaucratic, and military power (Koonz 1987).[2]

Finally, the Nazis tried to exert control over the religious sphere of German culture. The vast majority of Germans were baptized Christians, with Lutherans comprising the largest denomination (Rubenstein & Roth 1987). German Lutheranism, as noted in the previous chapter, was characterized by its antipathy toward Jews and by its highly nationalist sentiments. Since early 1933, Lutheran and other Protestant denominations had been moving toward a unified Evangelical Church. In July, Ludwig Müller, Hitler's envoy to the Evangelical community, was elected as the first bishop of the Evangelical Reich Church. Müller was the leader of the pro-Nazi "German Christian movement," the radical right wing of German Lutheranism. Although relatively small in number (about 600,000), members of the German Christian movement came to occupy key positions "within theological faculties, in regional bishops' seats, and on local church councils" (Bergen 1998:567). They saw no contradiction between worshiping Hitler and worshiping Christ. They viewed

Hitler as "God's man for Germany, the savior himself," and his program of racial purity a "holy crusade" (Rubenstein & Roth 1987:203). Of the Jews, Müller wrote that once it was believed that "if a Jew was baptized, he was then a Christian. Today we know that you can baptize a Jew ten times, he still remains a Jew and a person whose nature is alien to us" (cited in Bergen 1998:568).

THE BUREAUCRACY OF DESTRUCTION

In the tradition of Max Weber, as noted in Chapter 1, many scholars consider the bureaucratic administration of the Final Solution to be central to the entire process (Browning 2000; Hilberg 1985). The German government under the Nazi regime consisted of a myriad of organizations that often had overlapping functions and jurisdictions that changed over time. Himmler and Heydrich in particular oversaw a complex terror apparatus that "struck fear into the hearts" of those who opposed it or were the targets of its actions (Spielvogel 1996:103).

In 1929 Himmler was selected to head the SS and given the title *Reichsführer-SS* (Breitman 1991; Wistrich 1995). At that time, the SS was a relatively small organization that had been formed from a select group of SA storm troopers for the purpose of protecting Hitler and other Nazi Party leaders.[3] Under Himmler's leadership the SS grew and became one of the most influential Nazi organizations, with Himmler eventually rivaling Hermann Göring as the second most powerful man in Germany. SS members wore black uniforms, which distinguished them from the brown-shirted SA, and were sometimes referred to as Blackshirts, the Black Corps, or the Black Order. As the SS expanded it took on multiple functions that were administered by various subunits. In 1931, for example, the SD became the surveillance and intelligence-gathering division of the SS. Himmler appointed Heydrich as its head. The Einsatzgruppen, first deployed during the Austrian *Anschluss,* was a division of the SD and hence came under Heydrich's control (Botwinick 1996; Koehl 1983).

In 1936, when the German policing system was reorganized to create a centralized national police force, Himmler was given the additional position of chief of the German Police. With this reorganization, the Gestapo was established as a national organization that handled political offenses, including Jewish matters. Again, Himmler placed Heydrich in charge. In 1939, when several SS institutions (including the SD and Gestapo) were combined into the Reich Security Main Office, Heydrich became its head (Aronson 1990; Taylor & Shaw 1987; see Chapter 2, note 7).

Donileen Loseke notes that "the practical process of transforming claims [about social problems] into actual policy" is facilitated by sponsorship from pre-existing organizations (1999:118). Although hard-core Nazi organizations were of course central to the Final Solution, many of the governmental bureaucracies that implemented the anti-Jewish campaign were not the creation of the Nazis (Hilberg 1992). To be sure, new offices were created and specialists in Jewish affairs placed in influential positions. But the Nazis "never had to restructure or permeate extensively" (Rubenstein & Roth 1987:237) the existing bureaucratic apparatus whose occupants tended to favor the "racial dissimilation" of Jews and who often acted as if they were engaged in the most ordinary of operations, following orders and performing routine tasks (Mommsen 1998a:220).

Many of the bureaucrats of the Nazi regime were bright, ambitious university (especially law) graduates who sought successful administrative careers and who "understood that power and influence were at stake in managing well the Jewish affairs that fell to them" (Rubenstein & Roth, 1987:237). They played an indispensable role in drafting legal decrees, maintaining files on Jews, investigating disputes about individuals' Jewish status, prosecuting and convicting Jews in stacked courts of law, expropriating Jewish property, segregating the Jewish population, deporting Jews to concentration (including extermination) camps, and even killing innocent people. They helped direct unsystematic Nazi violence into legal channels, hence sanitizing and legitimating anti-Jewish actions (Miller 1991; Spielvogel 1996).

These bureaucrats competed with each other to expand their organizational domains and sought their superiors' favor by pursuing and attempting to anticipate their wishes. Initially working without a blueprint for the Final Solution, they often improvised policies to operationalize rather vague Nazi goals (Browning 2000; Mommsen 1998a). Practically speaking, Raul Hilberg observes, the Final Solution could not have been accomplished "if everyone . . . had to wait for instructions" (1989:127). And it was this bureaucratic initiative that "eventually brought about the existence of experts accustomed to dealing with Jewish matters" (ibid.:128).

Finally, as Hilberg notes, the Final Solution was a European-wide operation and "a multiplicity of measures were taken by non-German authorities" in other countries to disenfranchise, segregate, and deport the Jews (1992:75). To be sure, officials throughout Nazi-occupied Europe differed in their degree of enthusiasm for the Nazis' anti-Jewish program, but sufficient numbers were willing to contribute to (and benefit from) this effort. They tried to carefully maneuver between drawing maximum benefit from an alliance with Germany and preserving "a modicum of independence as an assurance for the future" in the event that Germany would lose the war, which at first seemed unlikely (Deák 2000a:8; see also Deák et al. 2000; Marrus 1987; Vago 1989).[4]

The Role of the German Citizenry

In general, the implementation of solutions to social problems requires activity that assigns claimsmakers' typifications to specific individuals (Best 1995;

Holstein & Miller 1993; Loseke 1999). With the Nuremberg Laws and their amendments, a "Jew" had been officially defined, and the Nazis required those who met this definition to register with the authorities and otherwise identify themselves with special cards and insignias on their clothing (Hilberg 1985). Ordinary German citizens, however, also played a key role in identifying Jews who were allegedly in violation of anti-Jewish laws. By providing authorities with voluntary denunciations of others, they helped socially isolate the Jews and target them for official action (Gellately 1997; Johnson 1999). As Heydrich told Hermann Göring at a meeting in 1938, "The German population . . . [will] force the Jew to behave himself. The control of the Jew through the watchful eye of the whole population is better than having . . . a control of his daily life through uniformed agents" (quoted in Hilberg 1985:50).

The banality of the citizen denunciation process is suggested by the way in which anti-Jewish law enforcement operated much like contemporary, conventional law enforcement, where the majority of police interventions occur in response to citizen initiatives (Reiss 1971). During the Nazi period, the Gestapo was the policing agency empowered to "investigate and suppress all anti-State tendencies," especially violations of anti-Jewish laws (Gellately 1988:654). Although the Gestapo was undoubtedly a brutal, repressive organization, it lacked the personnel resources to exercise effective surveillance over the population. Eric Johnson (1999) estimates that in the cities there was on average only about one Gestapo officer for every 10,000 to 15,000 citizens; and in the countryside there were next to none. Thus "the perceived omnipresence of the Gestapo was not due to large numbers of Gestapo officials" but to the omnipresence eyes of the citizenry (Gellately 1997:187). As one Gestapo official remarked, the "officers let things come to them" (quoted in Johnson 1999:15).

Several studies of Gestapo case files indicate a high degree of unsolicited informing against Jews, especially for alleged violations of laws that restricted Aryan-Jewish contact (e.g., the Nuremberg prohibitions on sexual relationships between Germans and Jews). Robert Gellately (1997), for instance, reports that 57 percent of "racial mixing" or "race defilement" cases from the city of Wurzburg involved denunciations by citizens. If one adds the 11 percent of cases that indicate no source of the denunciation—but that include phrases like "This office has been informed" or "It has been discovered" and are thus likely to have come from ordinary citizens—the total is even higher (ibid.:189). Similarly, Johnson (1999) found that 41 percent of Gestapo case files from Krefeld were initiated by citizen denunciations. (Johnson's study includes a broader range of offenses, e.g., alleged business/property violations associated with Jews' attempts to secure their assets in preparation for emigration.) If one adds the 27 percent of cases in which the source was unknown, the proportion of citizen-initiated denunciations in Johnson's study rises to the level found by Gellately.[5]

Often the motivation for informing was quite banal. For example, a resident would denounce a neighbor with whom he or she had quarreled, a businessman would denounce an economic competitor or an employee he wanted to fire, a disgruntled employee would denounce an employer or coworker he or she didn't like, or a spouse would denounce a partner from whom he or she wanted a divorce. At times the Gestapo was so flooded with false accusations that government officials issued warnings not to misuse denunciations for personal gain. Ironically, even Hitler complained that "we are living at present in a sea of denunciations and human meanness" (quoted in Gellately 1988:679). In 1937 an article in the *Frankfurter Zeitung* offered "a reward of up to one hundred marks (the monthly wage of an unskilled worker) for anyone who could provide correct information about false informers" (Johnson 1999:153).

Johnson cautions against overstating the number of German citizens who provided denunciations to the Gestapo. He estimates that only 1 to 2 percent of the population were denouncers. At the same time, he notes that "considerable numbers of ordinary citizens used the repressive political means afforded by the Nazi dictatorship . . . to their own advantage" (ibid.:16). Gellately adds that the "Nazi system of party and state was certainly repressive and highly invasive, but it was almost immediately 'normalized' by many people as they began to accept it as part of the structure of everyday life" (1997:203).

To be sure, the Nazis, as we have seen, exercised considerable control over the social institutions that they used for propaganda and indoctrination purposes and that helped build broad popular support for their policies. And of course the regime dealt ruthlessly with those who opposed it in any meaningful way. Nevertheless, outside of Germany's defeat in the war, many Germans subjectively experienced the Nazi period as "liberating, ecstatic, and empowering" (Patterson 1991:404). As one citizen recalls, "To be honest . . . I wasn't really against the Nazis at that particular time. I often found their methods appalling . . . [but the] truth is, all that business about the 'unity of the German people' and the 'national rebirth,' really impressed me" (quoted in Engelmann 1986:15). Another person remembers the 1930s this way: "Of course later on we found out that mistakes had been made, that certain things happened that shouldn't have. But [Hitler] . . . really did accomplish the impossible! Millions of desperate people found new happiness, got decent jobs, and could face the future once more without fear" (ibid.:189).

Thus after the war many Germans interpreted the Final Solution not as an abomination for which they should be held responsible, but as a "mistake" made by a few bad Nazis (Marcuse 2001). They never expected things to go that far, but after all, "the Jews . . . were a problem . . . [that] had to be settled some way" (quoted in Hughes 1962:5).

Ghetto Management

The concentration of Jews into specially designated districts, or ghettos, was at first viewed by Nazi leaders as a transitional measure designed to facilitate

deportation elsewhere (Browning 2000; Hilberg 1985). Before the Final Solution was articulated, deportation meant emigration, primarily to the east.
After the Final Solution, it meant deportation to a concentration/extermina-
tion camp.

There is no record of a general order that was ever given for the creation of
Jewish ghetto communities. Rather, ghettoization appears to have evolved as
a decentralized process, with initiatives taken by local German officials at various times. In smaller Jewish communities an entire town might be ghettoized. In larger ones a Jewish district would be partitioned off (with barbed
wire, wooden fences, or brick walls) from the rest of the city. *Judenräte*, or Jewish Councils, were used to manage the Jewish population and administer Nazi
demands. The councils were generally headed by a group of 12 to 24 Jews who
were already respected as community leaders. They administered a ghetto bureaucracy that in some cases was quite elaborate, for they essentially performed
all the administrative functions of a city government. They dealt with the food,
housing, and medical needs of the population. They set up schools and a police force and supported cultural events. At the Nazis request, they arranged
for the confiscation of Jewish valuables and selected people for forced labor
and even transports to extermination camps (Gutman 1990a; Hilberg 1985;
Rubenstein & Roth 1987).

Although the councils relieved the Germans of the burden of administer-
ing the day-to-day operations of the ghettos, the Nazis of course remained in
charge. Recall Franz Grassler, the deputy commissioner of the Warsaw Jewish
ghetto, who said that his job "was to maintain the ghetto and try to preserve
the Jews as a work force. . . . [The] goal was very different from the one that
later led to extermination" (quoted in Lanzmann 1985:179; see Chapter 1).
But Grassler and others like him were not given the resources to do their jobs
without incurring mass starvation, disease, and death. There was inadequate
food, coal, soap, and medicine; and sewage and garbage littered the streets. To
be sure, there were some Nazis for whom the exploitation of Jewish labor was
more important than Jewish deaths; and there were periods, even after the Final Solution was announced, that proponents of the "productive use of Jewish
labor were permitted brief and precarious opportunities to pursue their goals"
(Browning 2000:59). After the Final Solution, however, the prevailing Nazi
policy was for Jewish workers to receive only a temporary reprieve from their
ultimate fate. They were to be literally "worked to death" or gassed in a camp.

Didn't Grassler realize he was in fact a manager of death? Perhaps, for he
admits that "people were dying in the streets. There were bodies everywhere. . . . [N]aturally with those inadequate rations and the overcrowding,
a high, even excessive death rate was inevitable" (quoted in Lanzmann
1985:183–84). But he does not want to accept responsibility for what happened: "I had no power. . . . [Don't] overestimate my role. . . . [Don't] overestimate the authority of . . . a lawyer who got his degree at [age] twenty-seven"

(ibid.:192–93). Nevertheless, overall, ghettoization and general privation overseen by ghetto bureaucrats like Grassler accounted for about 16 percent of Jewish deaths in the Holocaust (Hilberg 1985).

The Railways

Most of the Jews (59 percent) who died in the Holocaust perished in concentration camps (Hilberg 1985). And most of the Jews were delivered to these camps by rail. Thus the *Reichsbahn,* or German State Railways, was key to the annihilation process. The Reichsbahn was a large administrative unit housed in the Ministry of Transportation, which employed about 1.4 million personnel who serviced both civilian and military transportation needs. All told, the Reichsbahn used about two thousand trains to transport Jews to death camps and other locations where they were killed (Mierzejewski 2001; Spector 1990b).

Bureaucrats in the Reichsbahn performed important functions that facilitated the movement of trains (Hilberg 1989; Mierzejewski 2001). They constructed and published timetables, collected fares, and allocated cars and locomotives. In sending Jews to their death, they did not deviate much from the routine procedures they used to process ordinary train traffic. Recall Walter Stier, the bureaucrat who booked Jews on transports to the Treblinka extermination camp (see Chapter 1). "The work," he said, was "barely different from . . . [any other] work" (quoted in Lanzmann 1985:133). As Hilberg explains, the Reichsbahn was willing to ship Jews as if they were like any other cargo as long as it was paid for its services "by the track kilometer, . . . [w]ith children under ten going half-fare and children under four going free" (quoted in ibid.:142). While the guards on the train required a round-trip fare, the Jews only had to be paid for one way. The party responsible for payment was the Gestapo, which had no separate budget for its transportation needs. However, the proceeds from the Jews' confiscated property was usually enough to cover the costs if the Gestapo received group rates.

> The Jews were . . . shipped in much the same way . . . [as] any excursion group. . . . [The Gestapo was] granted a special fare if . . . enough people [were] traveling. The minimum was four hundred. . . . So even if there were fewer . . . it would pay to say there were . . . [more to] get the half-fare. . . . [I]f there [was] exceptional filth in the cars . . . [or] damage to the equipment, which might be the case because the transports took so long and . . . [so many] died in route, . . . there might be an additional bill. (ibid.:142–43)

Although Stier denies that he knew Treblinka was a death camp, he admits that "without me these trains couldn't reach their destination" (quoted in ibid.:135). For him, Treblinka was nothing but a destination, a place were people were "put up" (ibid.:136). "I never went to Treblinka. I stayed . . .

glued to my desk. . . . I was strictly a bureaucrat!" (ibid.:135). Indeed, Stier
and others like him did their job as "a matter of course," as if it was "the most
normal thing to do" (Hilberg in ibid.:143). But it was not really a " normal"
job, for Jews were in fact crammed into freight and cattle cars, without venti-
lation or protection from the cold in winter and heat in summer, filling every
inch until "there was no room to sit down" (Botwinick 1996:160). They were
given no food or water and just a single pail in the corner that "soon overflowed
with human waste." And upon arrival to their destination, most of them were
killed.

The Order Police

About 25 percent of the Jews killed in the Holocaust died in open-air shootings (Hilberg 1985). The Einsatzgruppen were the first troops deployed for
this purpose on a large scale (see Chapter 2). However, they were substantially
assisted by the Wehrmacht (Breitman 1991; Browning 2000). The Wehrmacht not only permitted the Einsatzgruppen to operate in the eastern territories under its control, but it also turned Jews over to the Einsatzgruppen and
even engaged in mass killings. In fact, Omer Bartov argues that Wehrmacht
troops were directly "involved in widespread crimes against enemy soldiers
and the civilian population, acting both on orders by their superiors and in
many instances also on their own initiative" (1997a:169). Thus, according to
Bartov, the military campaign on the eastern front was not simply a war of territorial expansion but "a war of annihilation."

The Order Police were also involved in the mass killing of Jews (see Chapter 1). This organization was established in 1936 when the entire policing system (including the Gestapo) was reorganized on a national basis under
Himmler's control as chief of the German Police. Under the command of Kurt
Daluege (1897–1946), who had risen through the ranks of the SS, the Order
Police consisted of both stationary and mobile formations that were initially
intended to carry out more-or-less ordinary civilian police functions. They
were organized into battalions and reserve units, much like the U.S. National
Guard, and those who enlisted in it were exempt from military conscription.
The Order Police grew from about 131,000 troops on the eve of World War
II to about 310,000 by 1943 (Browning 1992; Goldhagen 1996).

Whereas the Einsatzgruppen was a select group of Nazis who received special training for deployment in the killing of civilians, the Order Police consisted of men who "were not particularly Nazified in any significant sense save
that they were, loosely speaking, representative of the Nazified German society" (Goldhagen 1996:182; see also Spector 1990a). While Daluege was a dedicated SS man, only a fifth of the Order Police officers were SS, and a third were
not even Nazi party members. Among the rank-and-file, only a fourth were
Nazi party members and none were SS. The rank-and-file were older than the
average military recruit (especially the reserves, who constituted about 42 per-

cent of the troops), and many were thus socialized in the pre-Nazi era. They "were men who had known political standards and moral norms other than those of the Nazis . . . [and] would not seem to have been a very promising group from which to recruit mass murderers on behalf of the Nazi vision of a racial utopia free of Jews" (Browning 1992:48).

Some Order Police had participated in the civilian killings that began with the Polish invasion, but they were used to a greater extent during the Soviet campaign (Breitman 1998). Himmler in particular was aware that the execution of civilians would be difficult for these men. Thus at first the men were told they were eliminating anti-German resisters, saboteurs, and looters; and the victims were limited to male Jews between the ages of seventeen and forty-five. However, Himmler reasoned that "once they carried out mass murder in response to an alleged crime or provocation, it would be easier to get them to follow broader killing orders" and later kill men, women, and children of all ages (ibid.:48).

Himmler was right, for few men refused to participate. There is no evidence of significant dissent among the troops or of significant punishment for those few who were unwilling or unable to kill (Breitman 1998; Browning 1992; Goldhagen 1996). Nevertheless, as Himmler had expected, many of the men had difficulty coping with their task. They were instructed to position their rifles on the victim's backbone just above the shoulder blade in order to make a "clean" shot. But they did not always shoot their victims properly, and blood, bone, and tissue were splattered all over the ground and on the men's faces and clothes. Killing people one on one, face to face, can indeed be a messy business. Alcohol was passed out to dull the men's anxiety. Most of the men who quit shooting appear to have done so more because they were physically repulsed and less because they thought what they were doing was wrong. One participant described the range of reactions this way:

> When I am asked about the mood of [my] comrades, . . . I must say that I . . . observed nothing special, that is the mood was not especially bad. Many said that they never again wanted to experience something like that in their entire lives, while . . . others were content with saying an order is an order. With that the matter was settled for them. (quoted in Browning 2000:123)

Some police even developed astonishingly odd justifications. As one man admitted:

> I made the effort . . . to shoot only children. It so happened that the mothers led the children by the hand. My [comrade] then shot the mother and I shot the child that belonged to her, because I reasoned . . . that after all without its mother the child could not live any longer. It was . . . soothing to my conscience to release children unable to live without their mothers. (quoted in Browning 1992:73)

Other shooters were more enthusiastic about their work. One man observed that "with few exceptions, [they were] quite happy to take part in shootings of Jews. They had a ball!" (quoted in Goldhagen 1996:396). Some inflicted special humiliations, for instance, making the Jews run a gauntlet and beating them before they were killed, or making the Jews strip naked and crawl to the mass graves that awaited them. Some police took souvenir photos that they sent home to their wives and girlfriends. One officer, an SS man, even invited his new bride to watch a massacre (Browning 1992). At night the men would celebrate and make jokes about their actions or keep scores on the number of kill. When "Jew hunts," or *Judenjagd* as they were called, were organized to track down Jews who had fled into the forest, more men volunteered than was necessary for the job. Indeed, in German the term *Judenjagd* has a positive valence insofar as *jagd* suggests "a pleasurable pursuit, rich in adventure, involving no danger to the hunter, . . . its reward . . . a record of animals slain" (Goldhagen 1996:238).

To relieve the Order Police of its more gruesome duties, the Nazis increasingly relied on SS-trained, Ukrainian, Latvian, and Lithuanian prisoners of war to do the actual killing. These men were screened for "their anti-Communist (and hence almost invariably anti-Semitic) sentiments, offered an escape from probable starvation, and promised that they would not be used in combat against the Soviet army" (Browning 1992:52). This enabled the Order Police to be deployed mostly as "ghetto clearers" who rounded up Jews for deportation or delivered Jews to others who did the killing. After their earlier experiences, this type of work seem relatively innocuous to the men.

The Medical Establishment

It is important to situate the anti-Jewish campaign in the context of a broader Nazi policy aimed at purifying the Aryan race more generally (Burleigh & Wipperman 1991; Milton 1990). In particular, the medical establishment's acceptance of eugenics helped legitimize the claim that Jews were a distinct and biologically "unfit" racial group that threatened to contaminate the German *Volk*. Its endorsement facilitated the public's acceptance of the notion that Germany needed to be cleansed of Jews (Koonz 1991; Proctor 1988; see Chapter 2).

In July 1933 the Law for the Prevention of Progeny with Hereditary Diseases mandated that individuals be sterilized:

> If, in the opinion of a genetic health court, they suffered from certain specified . . . "illnesses" . . . [including] congenital feeblemindedness, schizophrenia, manic-depressive insanity, . . . epilepsy, Huntington's chorea, [hereditary] blindness, deafness, serious physical deformities, and . . . chronic alcoholism. (Fischer 1995:384)

Next, the Law for the Protection of the Genetic Health of the German People, established in October 1935, required that couples wishing to marry submit themselves to a medical examination to certify that they did not have a hereditary or contagious disease. Finally, a centralized system of regional State Health Offices with departments of Gene and Race Care were empowered to review marriage and sterilization proposals and to compile a national index of the "gene value" of all inhabitants of Germany (Bock 1983; Friedlander 2001).[6]

German medical professionals looked to their American counterparts for guidance and affirmation regarding the practice of involuntary sterilization (Muller-Hill 1998; see Chapter 2). As early as 1933 German doctors began conducting sterilization experiments using various techniques such as surgical castration and exposure to x-rays, and it is estimated that about 400,000 people were sterilized without their consent (Fisher 2001; Hilberg 1992; Rubenstein & Roth 1987).

Sterilization of the physically and mentally "unfit" was just a prelude to more radical actions. In a September 1939 order, Hitler authorized physicians "to be designated by name, to the end that patients considered incurable according to the best available human judgment of their state of health, can be granted a mercy death" (cited in Lipton 1986:63).[7] The euthanasia project that was hence established was called the General Foundation for Welfare and Institutional Care, or T-4, because it was headquartered at Tiergartenstrasse 4 in Berlin (Friedlander 2001). The T-4 program, which included some of the most prominent physicians in Germany (including psychiatrists), and which operated six main killing centers, began in January 1940 and was responsible for the death of over 100,000 men, women, and children. Staff decisions about which patients under their care were killed "were made without consulting either the victims or their families, who first learned of the fate of their loved ones by a duplicitous form letter . . . [notifying them] that the victim had died of heart attack, pneumonia, or some other fictitious ailment" (Rubenstein & Roth, 1987:143). These "mercy deaths" had nothing to do with euthanasia as the practice had previously been understood—as the release of "a terminally-ill patient from unbearable pain, usually with consent" (ibid.).

Initially the T-4 killers starved their patients to death, had them shot in the back of the neck, or injected them with drugs. Christian Wirth (1885–1944), a nonphysician SS officer who headed the euthanasia center at Brandenburg, was the first to experiment with gassing, which subsequently became the preferred method of inducing death. Gas chambers disguised as showers were constructed, and carbon monoxide (sometimes in the form of bottled gas) was piped in to kill the victims. The bodies were then disposed of in crematoria (Lipton 1986; Rubenstein & Roth 1987).

In early 1941 Himmler authorized the use of T-4 personnel and facilities to rid the concentration camps of physically and mentally ill prisoners. Under the code name *Aktion 14f13,* inmates were designated for "special treatment." According to Robert Lipton, the 14f13 program was a crucial step in the emergence of the Final Solution, for it was the first time that the camps "became connected with a principle of medical-eugenic killing," and it was broadly construed to encompass those who held aberrant beliefs—including political prisoners, draft evaders, and Jews (1986:138).

Nazi attempts at covering up the euthanasia operation were unsuccessful, and vocal protests from influential church leaders who decried the killing of German citizens led Hitler to "officially" terminate the program in August 1941 (see Chapter 4). Nevertheless, children continued to be killed in T-4 centers throughout the war, as were prisoners from concentration camps. All told, about 100,000 people died in the T-4 program (Friedlander 2001; Hilberg 1992; Rubenstein & Roth 1987).

As previously noted, Himmler was aware of the psychological strain imposed on Germans involved in the open-air shooting of Jews. In August 1941 he had attended the execution of some one hundred Jews by an Einsatsgruppen unit and was deeply disturbed himself, according to one eyewitness account, "Almost fainting, pale, limbs quivering" (cited in Adam 1989:139). Himmler was also concerned that his men remain internally "correct," that "despite the difficulty of the task," they not become brutes (quoted in ibid.).[8] Moreover, it took too long to kill large numbers of people this way, and too many dead bodies were left without efficient means of disposal. (Prior to the use of crematoria, the bodies were buried in mass graves or burned in open air fires.)

Chelmno was the first of six Polish camps that were specifically intended for extermination, and killing by gas began there in December 1941.[9] Fifty or more people were crowded into each of three vans, which looked like furniture delivery trucks. A hose was attached to the exhaust pipe of each van, filling the vehicles with carbon monoxide. The vans were driven around for about fifteen minutes, stopped near a pit, and emptied of their dead occupants. The executioners soon realized that this was an inefficient method of mass killing. The victims would bang on the doors, screaming and pleading with the drivers, who experienced much distress. It sometimes took longer than fifteen minutes to kill everyone, and gasoline to run the vans was in short supply. Clearly, another method for increasing "output" had to be found (Adam 1989; Botwinick 1996; Krakowski 1990a).[10]

Wirth, who regarded the Chelmno operation as amateurish, was soon brought in to revamp the killing process (Adam 1989; Rubenstein & Roth 1987). He was named commandant of the Belzec death camp and by February was supervising carbon monoxide executions in gas chambers modeled after those he used in the T-4 program. Wirth also oversaw the construction of gas chambers at the Sobibor and Treblinka extermination camps. Eventually about one hundred T-4 personnel were transferred to the Belzec, Sobibor, and Treblinka operations (Friedlander 1998).

Beginning with Aktion 14f13, Nazi physicians were also put in charge of the "selections," the process by which concentration camp inmates deemed capable of work were separated from those deemed incapable (Lipton 1986). Nazi leaders hoped that doctors' involvement in these decisions would lend a veneer of credibility to the killings by making it appear that the selections had been made for medical reasons, as one doctor explained, "with precise medical judgment" (quoted in ibid.:173).

In addition, during the war years Nazi physicians conducted horrendous medical-research experiments on an estimated seven thousand persons in hospitals and concentration camps. At least seventy projects of this kind were undertaken. Some experiments were designed to test human endurance under severe conditions. In conjunction with the German air force, for instance, high-altitude experiments tested the maximum height at which an individual could survive without oxygen equipment. Inmates were subjected to freezing cold temperatures to the point of unconsciousness to study methods of reviving them. Some were made to drink ocean seawater to examine its dehydration effects. Wounds were inflicted with the intent of causing severe infections in order to test remedies. Bones were intentionally fractured and even severed from inmates to develop transplantation techniques, and some people's limbs were amputated. Prisoners were injected with the typhus virus and other contagious diseases to experiment with immunization vaccines. Most of these inmates of course died (Cohen 1990; Fisher 2001).

Joseph Mengele (1911–1979?) was arguably the most notorious Nazi doctor. He ordered the deaths of prisoners with physical anomalies (e.g., dwarfs, hunchbacks) so he could dissect and study them. He is perhaps most well-known for the experiments he conducted on some 1,500 sets of twin children—subjecting them to x-rays and various chemicals, ultimately killing them so he could examine their internal organs—in the hopes of learning about the causes of twin births (Lipton 1986; Rubenstein & Roth 1987).

The Concentration Camp System

The Nazi concentration camp system consisted of hundreds of camps across Europe (Pingel 1990; Rubenstein & Roth 1987). "Concentration camp" is a term that designates a variety of camps with different (though sometimes overlapping) functions—for example, incarceration, forced labor, or extermination. Some camps, like Auschwitz, consisted of numerous subcamps. The camp system was run by the SS and guarded by a special unit known as the *Totenkopfverbande,* or Death's Head Units, named after the skull and crossbones insignia worn by members on their black caps. In 1942 the camps were incorporated into the SS *Wirtschafts-Verwaltunghauptamt* (WVHA), or Economic-Administrative Main Office, the division that ran a vast array of SS business enterprises that relied on inmate (slave) labor. These businesses included companies involved in armaments, building materials, furniture, textiles, leather, fishing, forestry, shale oil, printing, foodstuffs, soft drinks, and mineral water (Poole 1997a; Taylor & Shaw 1987).

Initially the Nazis used the concentration camps to incarcerate their political adversaries within Germany (e.g., Communists, leftists, trade unionists, oppositional church leaders). Next they sent so-called asocial elements (e.g., vagrants, beggars, criminals with prior convictions). After the *Kristallnacht* pogrom in November 1938, the camps were increasingly used to deal with the "Jewish problem." Dachau and Buchenwald, established in 1933 and 1937, respectively, are among the most well-known of the early camps operated within German borders (Marcuse 2001; Pingel 1990; Rubenstein & Roth 1987).

Elsewhere, in Nazi-occupied territories, concentration camps were opened at Mauthausen in Austria (1938) and Auschwitz in Poland (1940). The Auschwitz camp, which after expansion became known as Auschwitz I, was constructed on the site of an abandoned artillery barracks that originally had about twenty brick buildings (Adam 1989; Hilberg 2001; Rubenstein & Roth 1987).

Theresienstadt, established in Czechoslovakia in November 1941, was set up in a former military fortress as a ghetto-style camp, with a Jewish council that ran its internal affairs. Heydrich envisioned it as a "model" Jewish settlement, designed, in Eichmann's words, "to preserve appearances to the outside," to reassure foreign governments that conditions in the camps were not so bad after all (quoted in Browning 2000:55). In reality it was only a transit camp, a temporary holding place for Jews who were eventually sent to Auschwitz or Treblinka (Dov Kulka 1990; Bondy 2001).

Experimental gassings were first conducted on about nine hundred inmates (mostly Soviet prisoners of war) in Auschwitz I in September 1941. A gas chamber and crematorium were installed, and prussic acid (hydrogen cyanide)—which had been used in the camp as a disinfectant and pesticide—was used to gas the inmates. Crystalline pellets of the chemical, whose commercial name was Zyklon B, were dropped through small holes in the roof.[11] The pellets vaporized upon contact with the air and heat, killing the inmates. The corpses were then burned in the crematorium (Adam 1989; Friedrich 1994; Rubenstein & Roth 1987).

The use of Zyklon B to gas inmates was the brainchild of Auschwitz Deputy Commandant Karl Fritsch, who had been responsible for procuring the chemical for disinfectant/pesticide purposes. Rudolf Hoess, the Auschwitz commandant, was pleased with the results and discussed them with Eichmann (Breitman 1991; Friedrich 1994; Hilberg 2001).

When Himmler visited Auschwitz I in May 1941, he ordered the construction of an additional camp outside the main camp to be used for prisoners of war. Construction at Birkenau, a site about two kilometers away, began in October. However, its original mission changed, for by May 1942 the new

Auschwitz-Birkenau camp was receiving all types of prisoners, including Jews. Gas chambers with large holding capacities were added, and special crematoria ovens with two to three muffles (burning compartments) were built, enabling the killing and disposal of more bodies in less time (Public Broadcasting Corporation 1995). Birkenau became the largest killing center in the camp system. According to Hoess's estimate, when the gas chambers/crematoria were running at maximum capacity, it was possible to process as many as 9,000 bodies a day. It is estimated that 1.1 to 1.5 million people, most of whom were Jews, died at Birkenau (Adam 1989; Buszko 1990; Friedrich 1994; Greif 2001).

In addition, in November 1942 a third Auschwitz camp was constructed a few miles away at Monowitz, where the I.G. Farben corporation was contracted by the SS to operate a synthetic oil and rubber plant. Given the food rations and hard labor at that camp, most of the inmates at Auschwitz-Monowitz lasted no more than about three months before they were sent to Birkenau to be gassed (Hayes 1987; Rubenstein & Roth 1987).

Western-Occupied Europe

Over half of the Jews killed in the Holocaust were from Poland, and nearly a fifth were from the Soviet Union (Gutman & Rozett 1990). Indeed, Hitler and other Nazi elites had intended Eastern Europe as the "great field for the implementation" not only of the Final Solution but of the acquisition of living space for ethnic Germans (Marrus & Paxton 1989:177; see also Browning 2000). Gentile Poles and Slavs were considered racially inferior to Germans and subject to colonization and use as slave laborers. Although many were killed, they were not targeted for extermination. Moreover, Nazi actions toward Slavic-speaking people were rather inconsistent. For instance, Slovakia, Croatia, and Bulgaria were treated as "honorable allies," and many Slavs were even admitted into the Waffen SS, or SS army (Deák 2000a).

Regardless, about a fifth of the Jews killed in the Holocaust were from Western Europe, from countries where the Nazis did not view people (other than Jews) as inferior. Here, as elsewhere, the Nazis did not have the personnel resources to carry out their anti-Jewish policies (including deportations to concentration camps) without assistance from local officials. Such cooperation was most forthcoming when measures were directed against foreign Jews, for many western Europeans shared the Nazis disdain for refugees (Gutman & Rozett 1990; Marrus & Paxton 1989).

The Vichy government in France was among the most notable of the collaborating governments. After its military defeat, France was divided into an occupied zone that covered its western coast and northern region, and an unoccupied zone in the southeast, with Vichy as its capital. The Vichy government, which was permitted complete autonomy by the Nazis, initiated over one hundred anti-Jewish edicts between October 1940 and December 1941 and has the "distinction of being the only nation to have voluntarily turned over Jews to the Nazis from outside areas of German military occupation" (Chesnoff 1999:135; see also Marrus & Paxton 1981; Weinberg 2001).

BUSINESS AND MASS THEFT

Our earlier discussion of Karl Marx should remind us that economic self-interest is often a central ingredient of human action (see Chapter 1). Indeed, implementation of solutions to the "Jewish problem," though driven by racial ideology, was marked by myriad opportunities for self-enrichment in the name of broader national goals. Nazi officials and their collaborators profited financially in two ways: (1) through public and private businesses that served the Nazis' needs, and (2) through expropriation and mass theft of Jewish money and other valuable property (Barkai 1989; Chesnoff 1999; James 2001).

Government and Corporate Enterprise

The German economy under Nazism consisted of both government-owned and private corporate enterprises, with some involving both government and corporate ownership. Hitler was well aware that he needed the support of big business for reviving the economy and for building and maintaining his war machinery. Initially, corporate leaders were not enthusiastic about the Nazis' rise to power, and they were concerned about the state's interference with the market economy. Nevertheless, they understood that their profits depended upon their willingness to cooperate with the regime (Hayes 1987, 1998; James 2001; Spielvogel 1996; see Chapter 1).

With the advent of the Four-Year Plan aimed at German economic self-sufficiency (see Chapter 2), Göring was given virtual dictatorial control over the economy and "alternately cajoled and bullied big business into expanding factories . . . [that produced] synthetic rubber, textiles, fuel, and other scarce products" (Fischer 1995:377). He placed restrictions on imports and exports, initiated wage and price controls, and demanded that profits be limited and used for a firm's expansion and for buying government bonds to help finance the military buildup. In 1937, after industrialists found it unprofitable to invest in the conversion of low-grade iron ore to steel, Göring established the *Reichswerke Hermann Göring*, or Göring Reichs Works (GRW). GRW was primarily a state-owned enterprise, with the government financing 70 percent of its operations (with help from Dresdner Bank loans) and the private sector financing the rest. It soon became a huge industrial complex, employing some 700,000 workers, nearly 60 percent of whom were slave laborers. In the process Göring acquired a large personal fortune (Simpson 1993; Taylor & Shaw 1987; Wistrich 1995).

As noted earlier, the SS Economic-Administrative Main Office, or WVHA, ran another large economic operation. Relying on slave labor, valuables taken from extermination camp victims, and generous low interest loans from the Dresdner Bank and the *Reichsbank* (German state bank), the WVHA amassed huge profits. It was Himmler's intention to make the SS profitable enough to become a financially independent empire. Himmler and Oswald Pohl (1892–1951), head of the WVHA, were the principal shareholders of most of the SS-owned companies. Although they held these shares as representatives of the SS, they had extensive access to the funds and could use them as they saw fit (Breitman 1991; Poole 1997a; Taylor & Shaw 1987).

In addition, Himmler sought to profit from the leasing of inmate labor to private corporations. He had been trying to attract corporate interest in this idea since 1935, when a contingent of industrialists visited Dachau (Hayes 1987). Although corporate officials were at first reluctant to do this, the war depleted the available labor pool and thus made Himmler's offer more attractive. Auschwitz commandant Hoess recalls that

> prisoners were sent to enterprises only after [they] had made a request. . . . In their letters of request the enterprises had to state in detail which measures had been taken by them, even before the arrival of the prisoners, to guard them, to quarter them, etc. I visited officially many such establishments to verify such statements. . . . The enterprises did not have to submit reports on causes of death. . . . I was constantly told by executives . . . that they want more prisoners. (cited in Poole 1997a:326)

As more and more firms pursued this labor policy, the competition for inmates intensified. By mid-1942 the SS had become a major provider of slave labor for virtually every important sector of the economy. As time went on, the treatment of these workers became more ruthless, and many were either worked to death or sent to a concentration camp to be gassed.[12]

Arguably the most notable collaboration between the SS and private industry involved I.G. Farben, a huge chemical conglomerate whose subsidiaries included Bayer and Degesch. Farben, the largest corporation in Europe, and the biggest chemical firm in the world, produced products such as synthetic oil and gasoline, synthetic rubber, explosives, plasticizers, dyestuffs, and Zyklon B. Carl Krauch, a senior executive in the corporation, also served as Göring's plenipotentiary general for chemical production. In this latter capacity, Krauch was charged with filling Germany's chemical needs, a sphere that included fuel, explosives, and light metals. Eventually Farben became the government's main supplier of these materials, especially during the war years, and operated over 330 plants and mines across German and Nazi-occupied Europe. Nearly 40 percent of its workforce consisted of slave laborers (Hayes 1987; Rubenstein & Roth 1987; Simpson 1993; Taylor & Shaw 1987).

Farben's most infamous operation was the synthetic oil and rubber plant that the SS contracted the corporation to run at Auschwitz-Monowitz.[13] Farben officials had been attracted to this location because of its ample coal and water supply and convenient access to highway and rail facilities. There was, of course, a ready-made supply of concentration camp laborers. Peter Hayes argues that the company had decided on this location before the Final Solution and its interest in the site "contributed mightily to [Auschwitz's] expansion and . . . eventual evolution into a manufacturer of death" (1987:351). As SS demands for wartime production increased, Farben "partook more and more of the brutal madness that ruled its setting" (ibid.:356). In addition, the Degesch company, a Farben subsidiary, was a major supplier of the Zyklon B that was used for extermination at Auschwitz-Birkenau and Majdanek. Although the chemical was initially developed for use as a disinfectant and insecticide, Degesch officials were hardly unaware that their company was now manufacturing a product designed to induce death, for the "SS ordered that the special odor, required by German law as a warning, be removed. This odor was intended to alert humans to the lethal presence of the gas. Ordering its removal was a clear indication of the purpose it was to serve" (Gutman 1990d:1750; see also Hayes 1998: Rubenstein & Roth 1987).

But Degesch was not the only German corporation to provide Zyklon B or to aid in the extermination program in some other way. For example, J.A. Topf und Sohne, a manufacturer of ovens and incinerators, was contracted by the SS to help design and construct larger gas chambers and crematoria at Birkenau. Topf provided the special multiple-muffle ovens that could accommodate more bodies. And AEG, a major electrical equipment company, helped design and install the electrical system that was used in the new buildings (Hilberg 1992; Public Broadcasting Corporation 1995).

Finally, it is worth noting the Allianz insurance company, which the SS contracted to insure the buildings and contents of the concentration camps, including Auschwitz (Bower 1997). Allianz officials regularly visited the camps and regarded them as good risks. As one inspector remarked during a visit to Auschwitz, "Thanks to constant military supervision, impeccable order and cleanliness prevails" (cited in ibid:335).

Aryanization and Mass Theft

The Nazi solution to the "Jewish problem" entailed, among other things, an economic assault on the assets of the Jewish community in Germany and Nazi-occupied Europe. *Arisierung,* or Aryanization, was the term that was used to denote policies aimed at transferring Jewish-owned businesses to Aryan (i.e., German) ownership (Barkai 1989). In the early years, between 1933 and 1938, Aryanization took the form of unsystematic "voluntary" sales of Jewish property. The Nazis organized boycotts of Jewish businesses and harassed and intimidated merchants, sometimes violently. The Nazis tried to make conditions so bad for Jews that they would simply choose to sell their property and emigrate (see Chapter 2). For Jews who decided to leave, however, the prices they received were far below market value, and many Germans prospered from the bargains (Chesnoff 1999).

Although "few of the approximately 100,000 Jewish business in Germany were of sufficient size or importance to attract the avarice of the nation's major firms," in 1934 the *Frankfurter Zeitung* reported that there were twenty-one transfers of multimillion dollar Jewish companies (Hayes 1998:198; see also Simpson 1993). In his research, Hayes found that at first the larger German firms tended to offer Jews a better price than the smaller ones, but this was not always the case, and by 1938 many of the largest German companies "plunged into the scramble for the spoils" (1998:205). All told, corporate participation in Aryanization "was a crucial link in the cumulative radicalization" of a discriminatory process that excluded Jews from German society and ultimately led to the Final Solution (James 2001:4).

The banking industry was at the forefront of the feeding frenzy, with the Dresdner Bank setting "the standard for rapacity" (Hayes 1998:203). Some German bankers contended that failure to take advantage of Aryanization would make them uncompetitive and leave them open to charges of failing to protect their stockholders' and depositors' interests. In early 1938 Deutsche Bank headquarters urged its regional offices that "it is very important that the new business possibilities arising in connection with the changeover of non-Aryan firms be exploited" (cited in ibid.:206). To be sure, there were risks involved in taking over Jewish enterprises that were unprofitable or laden with debt. Nevertheless, the banking industry played "an active role in brokering deals, finding buyers and sellers, and [providing] the financing for purchases and acquisitions" (James 2001:43). By the end of 1938 it had assisted in the handling of about seventy-five major takeovers. According to Hayes, the Dresdner Bank "probably facilitated more" (1998:206). In addition, the banks began trading Aryanized securities "in New York, London, Zurich, and other financial centers" around the world (Simpson 1993:64).

As early as 1935, German Minister of Economics Hjalmar Schacht (1877–1970) realized that the government was losing out on the profits of Aryanization, so he initiated a variety of taxes and transfer charges to ensure that more of the capital gain would go directly to the state. And after *Kristallnacht*, Aryanization moved into its second stage, as Jews were required by law to sell their businesses and other valuable property in what amounted to a policy of legalized theft. Businesses, homes, securities, jewelry, gold and other precious metals, artworks, rare books, coin and stamp collections, antiques—anything of value—were virtually confiscated with little or no compensation (Chesnoff 1999; Simpson 1993).

As the Nazis conquered other countries the same pattern emerged, but what had taken years in Germany to accomplish was elsewhere carried out in months. Even before the Austrian *Anschluss,* for instance, Deutsche Bank director Hermann Abs was informed of the impending invasion. Abs "quickly assembled a team of the bank's foreign trade specialists to identify Austria's choicest Jewish-owned business and real estate for acquisition" (Simpson 1993:70). Although the corporate (and especially the banking) sector profited from the plunder, Hayes (1998) estimates that about 60 to 80 percent of the profits went into government coffers. In the year before the start of World War II, such proceeds constituted about 5 percent of the German national budget and were key to the financing of military rearmament. Nazi officials, of course, personally profited as well.

Moreover, gold from the teeth and jewelry (especially wedding rings) that were taken by the SS from concentration camp victims was shipped to the Reichsbank in Berlin. The Reichsbank credited the SS in marks and melted the stolen gold into ingots and mixed it with its other holdings. It was not just Jewish property, however, that was plundered, for the Nazis confiscated the gold reserves of the other nations it occupied (Bower 1997; Cooper 1996/ 1997).[14]

International Business Ties

One way in which the "Jewish problem" and its solution took on cross-national dimensions was through Germany's international business ties. It took more than the Reichsbank, for example, to help the Nazis convert the stolen property (gold and other items) into usable currency. Here, foreign art dealers, diamond traders, and bankers literally fenced or laundered stolen goods for the Nazis (Chesnoff 1999; Petropoulos 1997).

Among all the nations of the world, according to Tom Bower, Switzerland's banking industry had "the deepest and most crucial economic relationship with Nazi Germany" (1997:337). Although Switzerland was supposedly a "neutral" country, its business and political leaders "were convinced of Germany's ultimate victory and were untroubled by the Allied perception that [its banks were] acting as a partner to the Nazis" (ibid.:53). Swiss banks accepted over three-quarters of the gold transferred abroad by the Reichsbank and in exchange provided Germany with the foreign currency it needed to purchase materials on the international market for its war machinery. The Swiss National Bank in particular also laundered gold into other neutral nations (i.e., Portugal, Spain, Sweden, Turkey) that provided foreign currency to Germany. Thus between 1939 and 1943 Switzerland's national gold reserves increased from $503 to $1,040 million. The reserves in the other neutral countries increased dramatically as well.[15]

In addition, an international bank—the Bank for International Settlements (BIS)—located in Basel, Switzerland, played an important role during the Nazi period (Higham 1983; Simpson 1993). The BIS, founded in 1930, was the joint creation of the world's largest central banks, including the Federal Reserve Bank of New York, the Bank of England, and the Bank of France. Bankers throughout the world desired "an institution that would retain channels of communication and [collaboration] . . . even in the event of an international conflict" (Higham 1983:2). According to BIS by-laws, votes on the board of directors were allocated on the basis of financial contributions. During the war years the bank took in so much stolen Nazi gold that it was dominated by German representatives (e.g., Walter Funk of the Reichsbank and Hermann Schmitz of I.G. Farben), even though an American, Thomas Harrington McKittrick, became its president in 1940.

While Allied bankers are implicated in the activities of the BIS, this is only part of the story. In the 1930s, for instance, U.S. corporate investment in Nazi Germany "was expanding more rapidly . . . than in any other country in Europe . . . as U.S. companies sought to buy into European markets at bargain prices" (Simpson 1993:11, 47). Major U.S. corporations—such as Anaconda, Ford Motor Company, General Motors, Goodrich, International Business Machines,[16] International Harvester, International Telephone and Telegraph, Standard Oil of New Jersey, Texaco, and the United Fruit Company—were involved. Some of these companies invested heavily in German military vehicle and weapons production, operated German subsidiaries during the war years, and had joint investments with German corporations that exploited concentration camp labor and profited from the plunder of Jewish property (Billstein et al. 2001).

In 1937 the U.S. Ambassador to Germany, William Dodd, complained:

> A clique of U.S. industrialists is hell-bent to bring a fascist state to supplant our democratic government and is working closely with the fascist regime in Germany and Italy. I had had plenty of opportunity in my post in Berlin to witness how close some of our American ruling families are to the Nazi regime. On [the ship] a fellow passenger, who is a prominent executive of one of the largest financial corporations, told me point blank that he would be ready to take definite action to bring fascism into America if President Roosevelt continued his progressive policies. (quoted in Higham, 1983:167)

Indeed, some prominent figures in major U.S. corporations were known Nazi sympathizers. In 1933, for example, William Knudsen, president of General Motors called Hitler's Germany "the miracle of the twentieth century" (quoted in ibid.:163). By the mid-1930s his corporation "was committed to full-scale production of trucks, armored cars, and tanks in Nazi Germany" (ibid.:166). Walter Teagle, chairman of Standard Oil of New Jersey and director of a U.S. subsidiary of I.G. Farben, was a close friend of Henry Ford, whose anti-Semitic publications inspired Hitler (see Chapter 2). In the early war years, between 1939 and 1941, Standard Oil provided Hitler's regime with much needed synthetic rubber, and even after the United States entered the war, it shipped gasoline to Spain that was transferred to Germany, in spite of "desperate shortages in the United States" at the time (ibid.:59).

Six months before the outbreak of World War II, Chase National Bank (later named Chase Manhattan Bank) offered Nazi sympathizers in the United States an opportunity to buy German marks with dollars at discount rates. Pamphlets were sent out informing potential investors that "Germany could offer glorious opportunities to them and that marks would provide a hedge against inflation and would have much increased value after victory in the expected war" (ibid.:23). During the war, Chase kept its European branches open in "neutral" countries and in France. Its Paris branch "poured millions of francs into various French companies that were collaborating with the Nazis" (ibid.:26–27). Its Chateauneuf-sur-Cher Chase branch in the Vichy region enthusiastically enforced measures to expropriate Jewish property, "even going so far as to refuse to release funds belonging to Jews because they anticipated a Nazi decree with retroactive provisions prohibiting such release" (ibid.:25). Chase also acted as an intermediary for Nazis wishing to launder money into South America, and it handled "transactions for the Nazi Banco Aleman Transatlantico, which was, according to a [1943] Uruguayan Embassy report, . . . 'the actuality treasurer or comptroller of the Nazi Party in South America'" (ibid.:26).

All this demonstrates that for many corporations, in Germany and abroad, it was business as usual—the banality of evil—during the Nazi period. Ordinary capitalist profit-making continued as corporations accommodated themselves to the rather extraordinary nature of the times.

NOTES

1. See Kreimeier (1996) for an account of how the largest German film company, Universum-Film AG (Ufa), cooperated with the Nazi regime to produce movies consistent with Nazi propaganda.
2. In 1936 Himmler established the (Spring of Life) program, a home for unmarried and married mothers of "racially pure" stock who were impregnated by "racially pure" (especially SS) men. In 1939 he announced that it was the duty of women of "good blood" acting out of "profound moral seriousness" to bear the offspring of soldiers going off to battle (quoted in Spielvogel 1996:108).
3. See Chapter 2, note 5.
4. Gross (2000) suggests that we understand the motivation for collaboration not as something that was imposed by the Nazis but as endogenous to the social and political milieu of the collaborating localities.
5. In a study of Dusseldorf files in the Rhine-Ruhr area, which had a sizable Polish-immigrant population, Gellately (1997) found that 47 percent of the "forbidden contact" cases were initiated by citizens. Adding the cases listed as unknown brings the total to 60 percent. In another study of cases in three jurisdictions brought against

Germans for violating prohibitions against listening to foreign radio broadcasts, 73 percent were initiated by citizens.

6. While Nazi policy allowed for abortions performed on Jewish and other "unfit" women, it prohibited abortions for Aryan women. Doctors and midwives were obliged to inform State Health Offices of all miscarriages, and only after undergoing two cesarean operations did a woman have a right to an abortion, and then only after she agreed to be sterilized (Bock 1983).

7. This order appears to have been issued in October but was backdated to coincide with the Polish invasion (Lipton 1986).

8. In a speech to a group of SS leaders, Himmler said: "Most of you know what it means to see a hundred corpses lying together, five hundred, or a thousand. To have stuck it out and at the same time—apart from exceptions caused by human weakness—to have remained decent fellows, that is what has made us hard . . . [and] is a page of glory in our history which . . . shall never be written" (quoted in Wistrich 1995:114).

9. The other Polish extermination camps were at Auschwitz-Birkenau, Belzec, Sobibor, Treblinka, and Majdanek. There was also an extermination camp at Maly Trostinets in Minsk in German-occupied Belorussia. In addition, camps not initially intended for extermination, such as Mauthausen in Austria and Dachau and Ravensbruck (a women's camp) in Germany, were later used for this purpose (Adam 1989; Gilbert 2000).

10. Gas vans were first introduced by the Einsatsgruppen after the Soviet invasion (Rubenstein & Roth, 1987; Yahil 1990).

11. The name Zyklon B comes from the first letters of the German names for cyanide, chlorine, and nitrogen (Friedrich 1994).

12. The list of companies that used slave labor reads like a Who's Who of German business and includes corporations such as BMW, Daimler Benz, and Volkswagen (Simpson 1993).

13. This camp is sometimes called Buna-Monowitz, Buna referring to the synthetic rubber plant that was constructed but that never went into operation. Neither was much synthetic oil actually produced (Rubenstein & Roth 1987).

14. Bower (1997) estimates that Germany's gold reserves increased to about $120 million by 1939, while the Simon Wiesenthal Center puts the figure at $180 million in 1939 and $800 million by the end of the war (Cooper 1996/1997).

15. Supposedly neutral countries not only offered financial services, but also produced armaments or provided needed raw materials that aided Germany's war effort. Additionally, there was a general reluctance to accept Jewish refugees and in the case of Switzerland many were turned back at the border (Cooper 1998; Petropoulos 1997; see Chapter 4).

16. IBM had developed what at the time was an innovative computing technology, the Hollerith, a machine that processed data stored on punch-cards. These machines were used by the Nazis to help organize deportations of Jews and to process them at concentration camps, including Auschwitz (Black 2001).

4

Resisting the Final Solution

Michael Berger, a Polish-Jewish survivor of the Holocaust, arrived at Auschwitz-Birkenau in November 1943.[1] He had already been in two other concentration camps and was thus somewhat familiar with the camp experience:

> [W]e were surrounded by SS soldiers and ordered to line up in formation four deep. Then the . . . selection process began. Women and children were separated from the men. A couple of officers went through the lines and pointed a finger at each prisoner and ordered, "Step left, step right, left, right." . . . I quickly surmised that one group was probably going to be killed and that the other group might be saved to perform slave labor. I closely observed which group appeared to have a better chance of survival and assumed that the group with the stronger and taller people would be picked for work and that the group with the weaker people would be killed. I was standing next to a middle-age man who had an obviously crippled leg. When he was ordered to the left, I knew that this was not the group I wanted to be in. So when I was ordered left, I went right. The whole selection process . . . occurred with such speed that the guards did not notice that I had disobeyed the order and switched groups. (Berger 1995:67)

After toiling for a month at hard labor at Birkenau, Berger was fortunate enough to be transferred to the Auschwitz camp at Monowitz:

> On first impression . . . I could see that [Monowitz] . . . was an improvement over Birkenau. . . . While some inmates looked emaciated, others seemed well fed. I assumed that some prisoners were managing to get additional resources, and I knew that I would have to find out where these resources came from if I was to survive. . . . I learned that there were two classes of inmates—those who existed only on food rations allocated to them by the camp authorities and those who managed to supplement their rations with extra contraband food. These inmates were referred to as "organizers." An organizer was a person who was successful at finding ways of acquiring additional provisions. . . . Prisoners who

were unable to organize continued to deteriorate. Those who lost a lot of weight and became emaciated . . . either died of malnutrition or beatings [because they couldn't work] or were sent to the gas chambers after a selection. (ibid.:71, 75)

At Monowitz, Berger was able to become part of an organizing scheme by providing tailoring services for the Kapo (work-group leader) who was in charge of his work detail at the IG Farben plant:

> At great risk of getting caught and beaten . . . there were many ways an enterprising or opportunistic inmate could organize in the camps. . . . Some inmates were able to get extra rations by performing personal services, like tailoring, for prominent inmates like *Blockalteste* [barracks leaders], Kapos, or kitchen personnel. Some of the younger inmates performed sexual favors. . . . It was a known fact that many *Blockalteste* had their favorite boy, whom they sheltered, fed, and protected. . . . Some inmates, especially Kapos, were in a position to barter with the civilian employees who worked at the IG Farben plant. These civilians were interested in the various commodities that were being stored in the warehouses but that were not available on the open market. In return, civilians gave inmates food—a loaf of bread, a pound of salami or pork meat, or some butter. Since the inmate then had plenty to eat, he was no longer dependent on his camp rations and could give them to any inmate he favored. A Kapo in this position would share the food with his favorite underlings. In this way an inmate who was successful as an organizer, or who established a good relationship with a Kapo or other organizers, had enough food to sustain himself. (ibid.:75)

In his own small way, Berger's account belies the stereotype of the Jew who passively accepted his fate, for he was constantly appraising his circumstances to capitalize on even the smallest opportunity to maximize his chances of survival (Benner, Roskies, & Lazarus 1980). It is nonetheless common for Jewish victims and survivors to be characterized as having been overly compliant with the Nazi regime and for going "like sheep to the slaughter." Jews did in fact comply, but they resisted as well, sometimes on their own—as Michael did when he crossed over to the other line—or sometimes as part of organized resistance efforts (Bauer 1989, 2001).

In the previous chapter I suggested that social problems construction does not proceed without resistance from those who organize to thwart or redirect the implementation process. This resistance can take the form of "alternative, parallel, or counter-institutions" (Spector & Kitsuse 1987:142), or what some refer to as "countermovements," that is, social movements that emerge in response to an original movement (in this case, the Nazis) that "appears to be accomplishing its goals" (Zald & Useem 1987:254). Michael Marrus defines resistance during the Holocaust as "organized activity consciously intended to damage the persecutors of Jews or seriously impair their objectives" (1987:137). In this chapter I examine efforts by Jews and gentiles, including Allied governments, to subvert the Final Solution.

DILEMMAS OF JEWISH RESISTANCE

In the years between the Nazis' rise to power in 1933 and the start of World War II, many German Jews did try to leave Germany. I have already noted the disincentives to emigrate caused by restrictions on the economic assets Jews were allowed to take with them and the lack of places to go (see Chapter 2). Nevertheless, over 70 percent of German Jewry did manage to leave before the gates of immigration were closed (Rubenstein 1997). In addition, nearly 70 percent of Austrian Jews emigrated in the twenty-one months between the *Anschluss* and World War II, and over 20 percent of Czech Jews left in the five months between the annexation of Czechoslovakia and the war. To be sure, if the Allies' immigration policies had been more generous, more Jews might have found safe havens elsewhere (Breitman & Kraut 1987; Wyman 1984). I will discuss this issue later in this chapter. For now I consider the dilemmas facing Jews who were unable or unwilling to leave their homelands.

Hannah Arendt (1963) and Raul Hilberg (1985), among others, have criticized the ghetto Jewish Councils for being overly compliant with the Nazis and for collaborating, however unwittingly, in the destruction of their own people (see Chapter 3). But the councils were faced with a difficult and untenable task. Some council members genuinely believed that if they did not cooperate with the Nazis—even to the point of helping to register and round up Jews for deportation to the camps—the Jewish community would be even worse off. They tried to ameliorate conditions in the ghettos by negotiating (usual unsuccessfully) with the Germans for more resources and by helping to maintain the religious, educational, and cultural life of the community and provide social-welfare assistance (when available) for those who were in the most need. They pursued a strategy of "rescue through work," hoping that by making Jews economically useful to the Nazis, they might maximize the number of survivors who could hold on until the Allies won the war (Bauer 2001; Braham 1989; Marrus 1987; Rubenstein & Roth 1987).

In Chapter 2 I observed that social movements are typically the vehicles for advancing claims about social problems and that they provide a frame or scheme of interpretation to make sense of events. Movement frames allow certain lines of action to be defined as "morally imperative in spite of associated risks" (Snow, Rochford, Warden, & Benford 1986:466). In the case of the Jewish Councils, their task was to convince their Jewish audience that the circumstances called for compromise and accommodation to Nazi policies. Other Jewish groups, however, insisted upon engaging in armed resistance. Some councils tried to undermine these efforts, fearing they would provoke Nazi reprisal. They often withheld knowledge of the Final Solution from the rest of the population, denied rumors of atrocities, and maintained false hope that things were going to get better.

The impetus for a countermovement of Jewish armed resistance generally came from members of Zionist youth movements (Gutman 1990c). Zionism was a European-Jewish social movement that emerged in the last half of the nineteenth century to create a national Jewish state in Palestine (now Israel). Theodor Herzl (1860–1904) was arguably the most notable proponent of Zionism. Herzl was a Jewish journalist from Vienna who covered the trial of Alfred Dreyfus in Paris in 1894 (see Chapter 2). The conspiracy against Dreyfus, an assimilated French Jew, lead Herzl to conclude that emigration to Palestine was the only viable solution to the "Jewish problem." Subsequently, he published a book, *Der Judenstaat* (*The Jewish State*), and in 1897 became the first president of the World Zionist Organization. According to Herzl:

> The Jewish Question still exists. It would be foolish to deny it. It exists wherever Jews live in perceptible numbers. Where it does not yet exist, it will be brought by Jews in the course of their migrations. We naturally move to those places where we are not persecuted, and there our presence soon produces persecution. . . . We are one people—our enemies have made us one. . . . Distress binds us together, and thus united, we suddenly discover our strength. Yes, we are strong enough to form a state. . . . We possess all human and material resources necessary for the purpose. . . . Palestine is our ever-memorable historic home. . . . We shall live at last, as free men, on our own soil, and die peacefully in our own home. (cited in Mendes-Flohr & Reinharz 1995:534, 537)

The Zionist movement gave birth to a number of youth organizations of both the political left and right. In Poland, the country with the largest Jewish population in Europe, these youth movements were characterized by their rejection of traditional Jewish culture and what they perceived as the general passivity of adult Jewish society. During the German occupation they more quickly abandoned the "illusions still held by their elders" and clearly recognized "the threat to their existence" (Bauer 1989:239; see also Gutman 1990c).

Previously I noted that sponsorship of preexisting organizations facilitates social problems development (see Chapter 3). But preexisting organizations may also be used to counter this process (McCright & Dunlap 2000). During the war, Zionist youth groups built upon preexisting organizational ties to establish armed resistance groups in the ghettos and forests of Poland. However, a basic requirement of effective armed resistance was the acquisition of weapons, which Jews locked in the ghettos had difficulty obtaining. In addition, those outside the ghettos often encountered hostility from the local Polish population, including, anti-Nazi Polish partisan (armed resistance) units. Sol Berger, a Polish Jew who joined a non-Jewish partisan group in the forests of eastern Poland after escaping his small-town ghetto, reports that he had to conceal his Jewish identity from his comrades: "I never told them I was Jewish because I was fearful of what they would do to me. They often talked about the Jews—that the one good thing that Hitler was doing was killing the Jews" (Berger 1995:57).[2] Moreover, while the Allies parachuted arms to Polish partisan groups, they withheld similar assistance from Jews, "ostensibly because Jews were not a clearly defined national group" (Rubenstein & Roth, 1987: 175; see also Marrus 1987).

Arguably the most famous Jewish resistance effort took place in the Warsaw ghetto, the largest Jewish ghetto in Europe. By November 1940 the Jewish population of about five hundred thousand, which now included refugees from other communities, was sealed in a 3½ square mile area surrounded by an 11½ foot brick wall topped by barbed wire. Mass deportations to the Treblinka extermination camp began in July 1942, and the Warsaw Jewish Council complied with Nazi directives to deliver six thousand to seven thousand Jews a day. This predicament spawned the *Zydowska Organizacja Bojowa* (ZOB), or Jewish Combat Organization, a resistance group of less than a thousand members under the leadership of a young left-wing Zionist, Mordekhai Anielewicz (1919–1943). Anielewicz and his followers understood the implication of the deportations. Whereas the Jewish Council "acted as though the ghetto had a future," the ZOB realized that it did not (Rubenstein & Roth 1987:166; see also Botwinick 1996; Gutman 1990b).

In January 1943, with only about sixty-five thousand Jews left in the ghetto, Anielewicz led a small ZOB contingent "armed with a few pistols and hand grenades" against the Nazi troops who were trying to deport a large group of Jews (Lubetkin 1981:153). The revolt temporarily saved about 90 percent of the intended deportees and gave the Warsaw Jews an unaccustomed thrill of seeing the Germans retreat (Gutman 1990b).

For a while the Warsaw deportations were halted, but in April Heinrich Himmler ordered the total dissolution of the ghetto in three days. The Jewish resisters, vastly outnumbered by Nazi troops and local police who had far greater firepower (including armored vehicles and tanks), held out for four weeks. In the end, however, the ghetto lay in ruins and most of the Jews were killed (Botwinick 1996; Gutman 1990b).

The ghetto resisters were fully aware that they would eventually lose, and their slogan was "Let everyone be ready to die like a human being!" (cited in Mendes-Flohr & Reinharz 1995:674). Before the final defeat, Anielewicz took his own life rather than fall into Nazi hands. He left the following message:

> Only a few will be able to hold out. The remainder will die sooner or later. Their fate is decided. . . . [But] what we dared to do is of great, enormous importance. . . . [We will be] remembered beyond the Ghetto walls. . . . The dream of my life has risen to become fact. . . . Jewish armed resistance and revenge are facts. I have been a witness to the magnificent heroic fighting of Jewish men and women of battle. (cited in ibid.:675)

In the last analysis it is evident that neither the Jewish Councils nor Jewish resistance groups were able to thwart the Final Solution and save large numbers of Jews (Rubenstein & Roth 1987). To be sure, Jews fought valiantly both within Jewish and non-Jewish partisan units throughout Nazi-occupied Europe, defying the stereotype of Jewish passivity. One group of Jewish partisans, led by Tuvia Bielski (1906–1987), made protection of Jews a primary objective and provided shelter for over twelve hundred women, children, and elderly Jews in underground quarters (Tec 1993). There were even uprisings in the concentration camps, most notably at Auschwitz-Birkenau, Sobibor, and Treblinka. But it is simply a "failure of imagination to expect" a largely untrained and unarmed population (which included children and the elderly) to engage in meaningful acts of physical resistance against armed German soldiers who had been ordered to kill them and who engaged in the practice of collective reprisal, punishing innocent people for the actions of others (Clendinnen 1999:58). Richard Glazer, a survivor of the August 1943 revolt at Treblinka, observed that no one could have escaped that camp if it were not for inmates who had already "lost their wives and children" and who were willing to stay and fight it out with the guards in order "to give the others a chance" to escape (quoted in ibid.:59). Still, few of the inmates who made it out of Treblinka actually survived. Most were either killed in the minefield that had been planted around the camp, were caught in a dragnet and shot in the forest, or were discovered while in hiding and killed, mostly by hostile local Poles.[3]

Perhaps Michael Berger expresses the sentiments of the average inmate who understood resistance "realistically, not romantically" (Rubenstein & Roth, 1987:187):

> The opportunities to escape or in other ways resist were quite limited. Many of us were aware of the German's practice of collective punishment even before we got to the camp. If I, for example, would have decided to attack a German and thus risk my own death, I would have been a party to the execution of my family, friends, and neighbors. So even in the camps, we were not necessarily . . . inclined toward resistance. We did sympathize with the more skilled and experienced prisoners who were planning organized escapes or sabotage efforts that were more likely to be successful, but most of us were not privy to these schemes. . . . I don't think I would have joined them if I could have because I felt that my chances of survival . . . were greater if I didn't risk being executed for something I could choose to avoid. Others, however, may have felt that they would be killed anyway, which could have happened without notice at any time. (Berger 1995:82)

At the same time, Berger's survival, as noted at the beginning of this chapter, was dependent upon his ability to appraise his situation in order to take actions that would maximize his opportunities. "Any cessation of appraisal, as in the case of individuals who withdrew into . . . [a] state of apathy, was a signal of impending death" (Benner et al. 1980:235). Inga Clendinnen argues that perhaps "the most viable and effective 'resistance' occurred within the mind, with the determination not to yield to despair" (1999:60). But likelihood of survival was not altogether random. Research shows that prewar personality traits like assertiveness, tenacity, courage, willingness to take risks, optimism, and intelligence maximized one's chances. Jews who were relatively young (between their teens and thirties) and "in good health at the start of the ordeal" were better able to endure the physical hardship and withstand disease (Hilberg 1992:188). Those with particular occupational skills—such as tailors, carpenters, shoemakers, and physicians—also fared better, for they remained useful to others who might want to keep them alive (Berger 1995; Helmreich 1992).[4]

Regardless, Jews for the most part did not survive on their own. In the concentration camps, as we have seen, survival required an ability to "organize," and successful organizing was a collective effort. Similarly, Jews who survived outside the camps by hiding or passing as Christians were generally dependent on support from the non-Jewish population (Berger 1995; Berger, Green, & Krieser 1998; Oliner & Oliner 1988; Tec 1986).

GERMAN RESISTANCE TO THE FINAL SOLUTION

Although the Nazis dealt ruthlessly with their enemies, they remained concerned about maintaining their legitimacy in the eyes of the German public (Breitman 1998; Johnson 1999). To some degree they realized that knowledge of the Final Solution threatened to undermine this legitimacy. They understood that many Germans would not view extermination as acceptable, however much they were concerned about the "Jewish problem" and however much they favored or at least tolerated other solutions. Hence the Nazis tried to keep the Final Solution a secret, as much as this was possible. Heinrich Himmler even informed his SS troops that the course they had embarked upon was "a page of glory in our history which . . . shall never be written" (quoted in Wistrich 1995:114).

The Nazis used euphemisms such as "resettlement" or "special treatment" to obscure what they were doing to the Jews (Hilberg 1985). The Final Solution was itself an obvious euphemism. But the policy of secrecy was somewhat of a pretense, for it was an illusion to think that a crime of this magnitude could be kept secret for very long. Too many people were involved in the killings. Military troops, Order Police, and others wrote letters back home, or returned home themselves, telling people what they had witnessed. Photos were taken. A sizable portion of the population listened to foreign radio broadcasts, especially the BBC (British Broadcasting Corporation). The Allies dropped leaflets informing the German people about what was occurring. Some people, of course, lived in the vicinity of the concentration camps. Besides, everyone had heard Hitler's ominous pronouncements about what was in store for the Jews. They had witnessed the discrimination and segregation of Jews, the violence of *Kristallnacht,* and the deportations of their former neighbors. However, few chose to speak of this "terrible secret," few chose to openly break the silence (Breitman 1998; Johnson 1999; Marcuse 2001).

According to Eric Johnson, "The only open demonstration against the deportations of German Jews . . . was carried out by Aryan wives of Jewish husbands" (1999:423). As noted previously, Nazi policy regarding Mischlinge (Jews with mixed ancestry) and Jews in mixed marriages was somewhat ambiguous, and there was much variation in how local Nazi officials treated these people (see Chapter 2). On February 27, 1943, during the Nazis' final roundup of the remaining Jews in Germany, about two hundred German women "gathered outside of the administrative offices of Berlin's Jewish community . . . to inquire about the fate of their husbands, who had been arrested that same day." They began shouting, "Give us back our husbands! Give us back our husbands!" During the next week the protest grew in size and intensity, and the crowd of over one thousand refused to disperse in the face of repeated warnings from SS and Gestapo officers brandishing their weapons. On March 6, Joseph Goebbels, concerned with the adverse publicity that the protest was causing, called for the release of some seventeen hundred Jews. "The decision to deport intermarried spouses . . . [was] blamed on 'overzealous subordinates' . . . and Jewish spouses elsewhere in Germany were spared, since their deportation would have become too public, perhaps too unpopular," and might have caused more critical scrutiny of the killing program (Breitman 1998:162).

Johnson believes that "many more Jewish lives might have been saved" had similar protests been made earlier and more often by a broader segment of the German population (1999:423). He argues, however, that "there is no escaping the fact that Germans mounted next to no meaningful protest against" the mass murder of Jews (ibid.:379). To be sure, the German citizenry was not slavishly obedient to the Nazi regime. A majority listened to foreign radio broadcasts, which was against the law. People told political jokes that criticized Hitler and the Nazis. The young listened to swing music, which celebrated what the Nazis despised as "Jewish- and Negro-inspired American music" (ibid.:278). More significantly, trade unionists, Communists, and church officials were sent to concentration camps and even killed for their opposition to the regime.

One resistance group, which called itself the White Rose, involved a small cadre of students at the University of Munich, who passed out a series of six leaflets calling for nonviolent resistance and who used black tar paint to write anti-Nazi phrases like "Down with Hitler," "Freedom," and "Hitler mass murderer" on public buildings. But the protests were mounted late—between June 1942 and February 1943 and at a time when the tide of the war was already turning against Germany—and had little impact on the course of events (Johnson 1999; Moll 1994).

Of more potential significance was the attempted assassination of Hitler on July 20, 1944, by Claus Schenk Count von Stauffenberg. This "attempt was part of a broader conspiracy against Hitler organized by nationalist conservative leaders . . . [with] ties to some leading figures in the military, counterintelligence service, and aristocracy" as well as to some in the clergy and trade-union movement (Johnson 1999:305-306). This effort, however, was aimed primarily at minimizing Germany's loses and negotiating a favorable settlement with the Allies. Even Himmler seems to have had a general, though not detailed, knowledge of the plot and did nothing to stop it (Bauer 1994).

The German Churches

The role of the churches deserves special mention in understanding German resistance to the Final Solution. David Gushee, a professor of Christian ethics, writes:

> The Holocaust is an event in the history of the Christian faith and the Christian church. Both in its historical antecedents and in its wartime course, the annihilation of the European Jews was inextricably related to Christianity and the behavior of Christian people. . . . [E]very church official at every level who had the opportunity to help Jews faced a test of Christian moral leadership, while every Christian with similar opportunity faced a test of Christian moral character. (1994:13, 15)

Regrettably, during the Nazi period the vast majority of Germans who were in fact baptized Christians were not up to this test, and they instead did their best to stay clear of controversy (Rubenstein & Roth 1987).

In response to the establishment of the pro-Nazi Evangelical Reich Church in 1933 (see Chapter 3), an oppositional group of clergy formed the anti-Nazi "Confessing Church." The Confessing Church, which had the support of about one-third of the Protestant clergy, "rejected any belief that God's revelation" could be found through Hitler and the Nazi state (Gushee 1994:129). In the Barmen Declaration of 1934, leaders of the Confessing Church condemned "the false doctrine that the State, over and above its special commission, should and could become the single and totalitarian order of human life" (cited in Rubenstein & Roth 1987:204). They asserted that Christianity and Nazism were inherently irreconcilable and that Christian followers of Hitler had abandoned their true faith. But this declaration was not so much a repudiation of Hitler as a statement of the limits of secular authority. Even within the Confessing Church there was mixed opinion regarding the legitimacy of the regime, and not all of its leaders were thoroughly opposed to it.

Dietrich Bonhoeffer (1906–1945) was among the most notable leaders of the Confessing Church movement. Although he wrote in 1933 that "the church of Christ has never lost sight of the thought that the 'chosen people,' who nailed the redeemer of the world to the cross, must bear the curse for its

action through a long history of suffering," he nonetheless warned his followers that Nazi attacks against the Jews perverted the spirit of Christianity, and
he encouraged them to aid the victims of Nazi repression (cited in Rubenstein
& Roth 1987:208). Bonhoeffer himself plotted to assassinate Hitler and was
involved in efforts to help Jews escape from Germany. He believed that "those
who take upon themselves the mantle of Christian leadership must be prepared
to suffer and die in the service of Christian moral fidelity" (Gushee 1994:173–
74). In 1943 he was arrested and sent to a concentration camp, where he was
executed in 1945.

Unlike Protestants, Catholics (who comprised about a third of the German
population) had an organizational center with "ultimate ruling authority outside of Germany" in the Pope and the Vatican City in Rome (Spielvogel
1996:111). In 1933, however, the Vatican secretary of State Eugenio Cardinal
Paceli, a former papal diplomat to Berlin who later became Pope Pius XII,
signed a concordant with Hitler on behalf of Pope Pius XI that guaranteed religious freedom for Catholics. In return Pope Pius XI agreed to recognize the
legitimacy of the Nazi regime, to refrain from criticizing it, and to confine the
church's activity to purely religious matters (Botwinick 1996; Deák 2000b).

For the most part, German Catholic bishops admonished their followers to
be obedient to the Nazi regime (Braham 1999). They adopted an increasingly
nationalist stance and felt that Hitler's military expansion was justified. Some
even spoke out vehemently against the Jews, identifying them with communism and reminding the faithful that Jews were Christ killers who were
"harmful to the German people . . . [and who] in their boundless hatred of
Christianity were still . . . seeking to destroy the Church" (Zahn 1962:279).

Nevertheless, Hitler was not satisfied with Catholic cooperation and attempted to further erode the church's influence by closing Catholic schools,
prohibiting publication of Catholic literature, and dissolving Catholic associations such as the Catholic Youth League. Thus in 1937 Pope Pius XI issued
an encyclical entitled "With Burning Anxiety"—read in Catholic churches—
that condemned the Nazis' racial ideology and usurpation of religious authority. Still, for the most part both Pope Pius XI and Pope Pius XII (who served
as Pope from 1939 to 1951) "counseled prudence not boldness . . . [and] urged
that a lack of restraint would invite further evils" (Rubenstein & Roth
1987:215). They feared communism as much or more than Nazism and were
inheritors of a church tradition that viewed Jews as the carriers of modern ideas
that threatened established church doctrine (see Chapter 2). John Pawlikowski
notes that Pius XII had a "high regard for the German church" and to some
extent may have been relieved that "the Jewish community's 'subversive' influence on the traditional social order was being removed" (1998:564; see also
Braham 1999; Cornwell 1999; Deák 2000b).

While Pius XII's commitment to the "traditional social order" seems to
have waned as the war went on, the Vatican was concerned about losing the

allegiance of Catholics in Germany and elsewhere, and it used private diplomacy rather than public protest in its efforts to ameliorate the plight of Jews under Nazi control. Papal diplomats tried to persuade neutral countries (e.g., Spain, Portugal) to accept more Jewish emigrants, and when emigration was no longer an option, they tried to get Nazi-occupied governments (e.g., Hungary, Slovakia) to resist Nazi orders to deport Jews to the death camps. But the possibilities for influence differed from country to country, and we will consider these variations later (Deák 2000b; Pawlikowski 1998).

All told, many Catholic and Protestant clergy did speak out against the Nazi regime and some tried to help Jews escape (Johnson 1999; Phayer 2000; Zuccotti 1987). Few other gentile groups in Nazi Germany were put under as much surveillance by the Gestapo and had as many cases lodged against them. Most of the protests, however, took the form of critical sermons, and relatively few clergy were actually sentenced to lengthy prison terms or sent to concentration camps. Church leaders spoke most loudly when the Nazis invaded church prerogatives and persecuted Jewish converts to Christianity. Their protests were effective in curtailing the euthanasia program that was carried out against German citizens (see Chapter 3). But according to Richard Rubenstein and John Roth, rarely did they or speak out or act "on behalf of Jews as Jews" (1987:213). Never did they rally "their congregations to make a unified, principled protest against the Nazis' fundamental Jew-hatred" (ibid.:207).

In Germany only the Jehovah's Witnesses, a small Christian minority, refused to make any compromises with the regime, and they continued to "meet, organize, and proselytize" even after they were banned in 1933 (Johnson 1999:238; see also Reynaud & Graffard 2001). They refused to join any Nazi organizations, attend political rallies, give the Hitler salute, or serve in the armed forces. They even passed out "literature that pointed out specific instances of Nazi atrocities, cited Gestapo, police, and Nazi Party torturers by name, and called on the German people to turn away from the false prophet Hitler and to place their faith in the true savior, Jesus Christ" (Johnson 1999:239). Although estimates vary, about a third of their twenty-five thousand to thirty thousand members were imprisoned or sent to concentration camps, and some twelve hundred were killed.

THIRD-PARTY RESISTANCE

Samuel and Pearl Oliner (1988) estimate that less than 0.5 percent of the gentile population under Nazi occupation tried to defy the Final Solution by lending assistance to Jews. These individuals are often called "righteous gentiles" or "righteous Christians."[5] Paul Levine refers to them as "third-party protagonists who attempted, at least on some occasions, to stop the Germans from killing" Jews (1998:520). According to the Oliners' (1988) research, the majority of these individuals lent assistance to more than five people and were involved in some form of helping or rescue activity for at least two years. Helpers/rescuers (H/Rs) stored personal possessions for Jews and provided food, shelter, medical assistance, and critical information (e.g., about Nazi activity, useful contacts, escape routes). They helped Jews find sources of livelihood and, in some cases, ran businesses for them, diverting profits to their former Jewish owners. They smuggled arms, bribed officials, and provided false documents (e.g., food ration cards, identification papers). They hid Jews (for the short and long term) and helped them escape to safe havens (Fogelman 1994; Paldiel 1996; Tec 1986).

The Question of Altruism

The subject of Holocaust helping/rescue activity or third-party resistance has often been framed as a question of "altruism," which may be defined as voluntary behavior directed toward increasing another's welfare without the expectation of external reward (Berger et al. 1998; Oliner et al. 1992).[6] Postwar interviews with Holocaust H/Rs and with non-H/Rs suggest that some individuals were more predisposed than others to engage in such conduct. They had acquired a commitment to helping the needy before the war and continued this commitment in the postwar years (Oliner & Oliner 1988; Tec 1986).

Altruism research has found that certain socialization experiences are associated with the development of both cognitive altruism based on cultural values regarding what is "right" and "wrong" as well as affective altruism based on sympathy, empathy, or an emotional concern for another's well-being (Oliner et al. 1992; Piliavin & Charng 1990). Interviews with Holocaust H/Rs indicate that they were more likely than non-H/Rs to come from homes where parental-child interaction was close, nurturant, and affectionate. Their parents were less likely to rely on physical punishment and authoritarian disciplinary styles and more likely to rely on reasoning or cognitive discipline that socialized children to consider questions of right and wrong and the consequences of their actions on others. Parents also modeled altruism, as H/Rs reported seeing their parents behaving kindly toward others. Tolerance as a general moral value and toward Jews in particular was stressed in their homes, as was an orientation that emphasized treating individuals as equals regardless of social status and that promoted a feeling of obligation, hospitality, and generosity toward people in need. Before the war, H/Rs were more likely to have had Jewish friends as well as friends from different class backgrounds. In addition, parents taught H/Rs to be independent, self-reliant, and self-confident, which enabled them to act even in the face of disapproval from others and grave risks to their own safety (Berger et al. 1998; Oliner & Oliner 1988; Tec 1986).

Nechama Tec (1986) observes that altruism may be *autonomous,* that is, without social support, or *normative,* that is, reinforced or supported by one's group or society. During the war, normative altruism was more likely in countries that had a national culture or general cultural environment that was more hospitable toward Jews. Historical data indicate that, all other things being equal, the degree of prewar anti-Semitism had an impact on the number of Jewish deaths during the Holocaust.[7] Countries with a tradition of religious tolerance and civil equality were more likely to "engender sympathy for Jews that sometimes found expression in efforts to save them" (Baron 1988:17). Belgium, Bulgaria, Denmark, Holland, and Italy are often cited on this score. In these countries "Jewish acculturation and socioeconomic integration often created strong business or personal relationships with non-Jews" (ibid.). While the mere absence of anti-Semitism was insufficient to instigate third-party resistance, it created a broad consensus that made accommodation or collaboration with the Nazis less likely. Moreover, during the war these sentiments facilitated the emergence of collective networks that considered aid to Jews a part of their opposition to Nazism (Baron 1992; Berger et al. 1998; Fein 1979).

Collective Networks and Resource Mobilization

In their research, Eva Fogelman (1994) found that about one-fifth of H/Rs participated in collective rescue networks, and Tec (1986) reported that about one-third were involved in both individual and collective forms of assistance. The Oliners (1988) found that 44 percent of their sample participated in formal resistance or rescue groups, and nearly all cooperated at least informally with other H/Rs, including family, friends, and neighbors. One Polish H/R estimated that it took the support of at least ten people to save one Jew. Michael Gross, whose study uncovered few instances of solo rescue, argues that third-party resistance was not "simply the cumulative effect of . . . high-minded individuals collaborating to oppose an unjust regime" but of collective efforts at coordinated action that could not be undertaken by individuals on their own (1994:464, 468).

Research on social problems, as previously noted, highlights the role of social movements in mobilizing resources to construct social problems and their solutions (see Chapter 2). Following Gross's (1994) suggestion, the question of altruism can be recast in terms of a countermovement movement theory of resource mobilization, that is, an account of how rescue groups mobilized resources to resist the Final Solution. More specifically, I consider how these movements utilized leadership, ideological, and organizational resources to mobilize third-party resistance on behalf of Jews (Berger et al. 1998).

Leadership Resources   Direct invocations from civic and religious leaders who had established legitimate authority before the war were often important in mobilizing potential H/Rs to action (Baron 1992; Gross 1994). In Nieuw-

lande, Holland, for example, a number of H/Rs cited the persuasive appeals of
Johannes Post, a highly regarded councilman, as the main reason for their involvement. In Bulgaria, vigorous condemnation of "anti-Semitic laws by the
Bulgarian Orthodox clergy, various professional organizations, and prominent
politicians contributed to the government's lax enforcement of these laws and
eventual refusal to deport native Jews" (Baron 1988:18–19; see also Gilbert
2000; Todorov 2001a). In France, Catholic congregants were at times ordered
by church authorities to assist in rescue activity; and in Poland, Catholic nuns
engaged in third-party resistance at the behest of their convent superiors
(Gushee 1994; Kurek-Lesik 1992). In October 1943 Pope Pius XII finally ordered the Vatican clergy in Rome to provide sanctuary for "non-Aryans" who
faced German deportations to the death camps, thus saving the lives of over
5,600 Jews (Gilbert 2000).[8]

The village of Le Chambon-sur-Lignon in southern France, where over three
thousand Jewish adults and children were given sanctuary, helped to find hiding places, or smuggled to safety in Switzerland, is often cited as the classic
example of collective rescue (Baron 1988; Gilbert 2000; Gross 1994). In that
village Pastor André Trocmé drew upon a tradition of Protestant leadership
that had evolved through the community's historical experience of religious
persecution. The collective memory of the state-sponsored persecution of their
Huguenot ancestors predisposed the community to favor its local religious
leadership over other governmental authority.[9] This historical legacy was
"foundational for the community's persistent practice of hospitality to the
needy" (Gushee 1994:127). For centuries Le Chambon had been a safe haven
for Protestant refugees. In the 1930s, for instance, the village sheltered
refugees from the Spanish civil war, and during World War II it was only natural to identify with the plight of the Jews and unite around their pastors in
defiance of anti-Jewish policies.

Ideological Resources   As we have seen, social movements provide frames or
schemes of interpretation to help members interpret events. As was the case
in Le Chambon, religious or political sentiments could be used as ideological
resources that mobilized third-party resistance.

While Holocaust H/Rs were more likely than non-H/Rs to describe themselves as very religious, only a minority attributed their actions to their religious beliefs or sense of religious duty per se (Oliner & Oliner 1988; Tec 1986).
This apparent anomaly is perhaps explained by the fact that some even helped
Jews when this was opposed by church officials. According to Kristen Monroe, religious altruists shared "something that may bear superficial resem-
blance to but differs critically from what we would commonly think of as
organized religion or even religious belief" (1996:129). They were following
their own feelings of concern and compassion for human suffering, or their own
interpretations of what God wanted them to do, rather than specific instruc-

tions or teachings of the church (Caracciolo 1995; Fogelman 1994; Gushee 1994).

Gushee (1994) observes that religious-based H/Rs came disproportionately from reformed Protestant denominations rooted in Calvinist teachings that expressed a special religious kinship with the Jewish people. John Calvin, a sixteenth-century French Protestant who settled in Switzerland, advanced a Christian ideology that differed from both Catholicism and Lutheranism in its respect for "Old Testament moral law and its continuing validity for Christians" (ibid.:122). Calvin encouraged his fellow Christians "to appreciate rather than to deride continuing Jewish fidelity" to the Old Testament, while other Christian faiths "juxtaposed Old Testament 'law' with New Testament 'grace,' denigrating and deemphasizing the former" (ibid.:123). In countries like Denmark and Holland, prewar Calvinist ideology proffered pro-Jewish sentiments that made citizens less inclined to support Nazi policies against Jews.

Often, however, Jewish rescue activities simply went hand-in-hand with a more general anti-Nazi orientation. As Gushee suggests:

> Some gentiles rescued Jews because they hated the Nazis and simply wanted to thwart them at every opportunity. . . . Those acting on this basis were more likely to have been involved in general underground resistance activities [sabotage, gun-running, armed actions, etc.] . . . and rescued Jews as one part of their underground work. . . . [Others] saw the rescue of Jews . . . as a defense of their fellow citizens and national values. . . . This response was more likely to occur where Jews had won full and unequivocal citizenship rights before the war and where there existed little or no political sentiment in favor of [Jewish] disenfranchisement. (ibid.:110)

Similarly, socialists and communists often cited general antifascist sentiments as their motivation for helping Jews (Oliner & Oliner 1988; Tec 1986). Although most H/Rs described themselves as apolitical, individuals committed to leftist politics or a belief in democratic pluralism were more likely those with other political orientations to engage in rescue efforts. At the same time, not all anti-Nazi resistance groups included protection of Jews as part of their activities. In Poland, for example, aid to Jews was an issue that divided the underground, and many Polish partisans agreed with Hitler's anti-Jewish campaign and even killed Jews who escaped into the forests.[10] In France, on the other hand, Jews comprised about 20 percent of some resistance groups. Thousands of Jews were also active in the Soviet partisan movement led by escaped Soviet prisoners of war (Baron 1988; Berger et al. 1998; Fogelman 1994; Gilbert 2000).

Organizational Resources   It is axiomatic that organizations are a resource for collective action that individuals cannot engage in on their own. During the war, organizational resources were necessary for the acquisition of valuable information and the procurement of food ration cards, false IDs, places of hiding, and so forth. Officials often had to be bribed and persons who transported and sheltered Jews paid for their expenses. Even in as pro-Jewish setting as Denmark, fishermen smuggling Jews to safety in neutral Sweden demanded substantial fees, which they reduced only after the Danish underground insisted that they do so (Fogelman 1994; Yahil 1990).

Although several studies have found that the diffusion of responsibility in larger groups may increase the passivity of bystanders, other research shows that willingness to help in risky situations increases with group size (Crader & Wentworth 1984). In larger groups the capacity to overcome initial fear is augmented by a sense of social support, the risk of being exposed is reduced, and altruistic impulses are reinforced rather than discouraged.

At times prewar organizations could be adapted for rescue activities. The Le Chambon H/Rs, for example, were able to draw upon a national network of like-minded Protestant educators to aid in the hiding of Jewish children. In Poland over 60 percent of the nunneries were engaged in Jewish rescue. When Pope Pius XII ordered the sheltering of Jews, over a hundred monasteries, convents, and other church organizations were available to provide sanctuary (Gilbert 2000; Gross 1994; Kurek-Lesik 1992; see note 8).

In other cases, wartime organizations not initially intended for Jews could be transmuted for such efforts. In Holland, for instance, a network established to aid gentiles fleeing Nazi conscription for forced labor was later used for Jews. In Denmark several anti-Nazi resistance groups were eventually coordinated into one larger group, the Freedom Council, that organized a "fishing armada," which transported about 7,900 Jews, half-Jews, and Christians married to Jews to safety in Sweden (Fogelman 1994; Gilbert 2000; Gross 1994).

Situational Contingencies

The ability of individuals or groups to engage in third-party resistance on behalf of Jews was contingent on various situational factors, the most important of which was the degree of Nazi control, that is, the extent of Nazi military occupation, their use of terror, and their direct involvement in the administration of anti-Jewish policies (Berger et al. 1998; Marrus 1987). In Eastern Europe this control was greatest in Poland, and in Western Europe it was greatest in Holland and Norway. This helps explains the high percentage of deaths among Dutch Jews (over 70 percent) in spite of "Holland's long tradition of religious tolerance and civic equality" (Baron 1992:307; see also Yahil 1990).

In Italy most of the population and "even some Italian Fascists openly voiced support for and solidarity with Jews" (Carpi 2001:334). Government officials, including policemen and soldiers, often tried to delay compliance with German requests for Jews while maintaining plausible "pretexts or reasons to justify the lack of action" (quoted in Caracciolo 1995:61). According to Florette and Richard Koffler, the situation that prevailed was one of "willed inefficiency in the face of an inhumane order" (1995:xxviii). In the latter part of 1943, however, the Italians surrendered to the Allies, who occupied the southern part of the country. Germany, in turn, took control over the central and northern regions, the home of most of Italy's Jews. At this point the fate of Italian Jews took a dramatic turn for the worse.

In France the Germans left significant elements of control in the hands of the Vichy government (see Chapter 3). Although the Vichy regime is known for its cooperation with the Nazis, it was reluctant to deport native French Jews. According to Leni Yahil, the Vichy government's "attitude toward the Jews vacillated between xenophobic antisemitism and a democratic tradition that stood for offering refuge to the persecuted" (1990:590). French authorities maintained a sense of loyalty to French citizens but were also greedy for Jewish property. They capitulated to the Nazis but desired a degree of independence. These fluctuating tendencies led to both the persecution of Jews and to occasional opportunities for escape. Moreover, in the latter years of the war "French cooperation with the Nazis and indifference toward Jewish persecution decreased as the strains of German occupation and prospects of Germany's ultimate defeat became greater" (Baron 1988:39).

Indeed, the changing tide of the war provided a new context in which resistance to the Final Solution became more feasible. By early 1943 the Nazis had suffered a series of military defeats against Allied forces in North Africa and on the eastern front. Under these circumstances foreign leaders and church authorities in German-aligned and neutral countries became more willing either to resist Nazi edicts to deport Jews or to help Jews find refuge in safe havens. In some cases, as in Italy and Hungary, the Nazis had to exert more control over the deportations to the death camps when local cooperation was not forthcoming (Caracciolo 1995; Weinberg 1998; Yahil 1990).

Geographical location was also an important contingency that affected third-party resistance. In Eastern Europe hiding places for Jews were quite primitive, "with people hiding in holes underground, beneath rooms, or in fields or forests" (Paldiel 1996:14). In Western Europe, however, a small, secluded side room, a section of a room, or a corner of an attic were more likely to be available. In cities it was easier for Jews to blend in with their surroundings and "to flee and mingle with the crowd at a moment's notice" (ibid.:24). But in the countryside there was less anonymity and greater precaution was required to guard against betrayal by informers. In addition, certain types of terrain made concealment of fugitives, escape across borders, or guerrilla maneuvers more feasible. As Lawrence Baron observes:

> The sparsely populated and rugged wilderness of eastern Norway, the extensive and thick forest of Belorussia, and the mountainous regions of southern France, Greece, and Yugoslavia served as natural arenas for these kinds of activities. . . . Denmark's proximity to neutral Sweden . . . allowed the Danes to relocate most

of their Jews. . . . Access to [neutral] Spain [and] Switzerland, territories under
Italian control, and Mediterranean sea routes to Palestine favored Jewish escape
from Vichy France and the countries of the Balkan Peninsula.(1988:21)

Conditions confronting Holland, on the other hand, were more difficult to
support, as it was bordered by waters heavily patrolled by the Nazis and surrounded by other occupied countries and Germany itself (Baron 1992).

THE UNITED STATES, THE ALLIES, AND NEUTRAL COUNTRIES

The Statue of Liberty, standing tall in New York Harbor since 1886, was at
the time of the Holocaust an international symbol of freedom and hospitality
for immigrants seeking a better life in the United States (Bell 1993). A poem
by Emma Lazarus inscribed on a bronze plaque in the interior wall of the monument reads:

> Give me your tired, your poor,
> Your huddled masses yearning to breathe free,
> The wretched refuse of your teeming shore.
> Send these, the homeless, tempest-tost to me.
> I lift my lamp beside the golden door!

The sentiment expressed in this poem, however, was not generally consistent with U.S. immigration policy. As Richard Breitman and Alan Kraut note,
"Before 1933 the United States was far more the aloof isolationist seeking to
insulate itself from the world's troubles than it was the defender of universal
'human rights,'" (1987:248). Thus even if Jews could have managed to escape
Nazi-occupied Europe, where were they to go? Ultimately, third-party resistance to the Final Solution not only required the mobilization of countermovements under optimal situational contingencies but also the mobilization
of resources available only to governmental nation-states.

Donileen Loseke observes that successful social problems claimsmaking requires formulation of the problem in a way that makes it "a proper matter of
government . . . concern" (1999:113). Governments have limited "carrying
capacities," that is, there are countless issues that might benefit from their actions but only a limited number that can be effectively addressed. Thus third-
party resisters had a formidable task trying to convince U.S. policymakers that
the "Jewish problem" warranted their attention.

Practically speaking, no nation can be expected to take in all those who wish
to enter. And in the 1920s U.S. immigration law had established specific limits on the number of people who would be allowed to immigrate in any given
year from any given country. The quotas for different countries were "set at a
small percentage of those resident in America, but born in that foreign coun-

try, in 1890" (Rubenstein 1997:33). The year 1890 was chosen because it occurred prior to the large influx of eastern and southern Europeans (mainly Italians, Poles, and Russian Jews) and was designed to favor those of Anglo-Saxon
descent. Although Great Britain received 43 percent of the 153,774 annual
quota slots, Germany received 17 percent, the second highest allotment of any
country in the world (Breitman & Kraut 1987).

In 1930, in the midst of a devastating economic depression, President Herbert Hoover issued an executive order to further restrict immigration by more
narrowly interpreting existing immigration law that already denied visas to
all persons who were "likely to become a public charge" (LPC), that is, who
were unable to financially support themselves. Although the LPC stipulation
"was originally aimed at persons who lacked physical or mental skills required
for constructive employment," it was now construed to include "anyone unlikely to obtain a job under current market conditions" (Breitman & Kraut
1987:7–8).[11] Throughout the 1930s and the war years the annual immigration quota was never filled beyond 54 percent, and this was not due to a lack
of demand, especially from Jews.

Even before the Final Solution emerged, Nazi emigration policy had diffused the "Jewish problem" cross-nationally and created a dilemma for other
countries that did not wish to modify their immigration policies to accommodate more Jews (see Chapter 2). When Franklin Roosevelt assumed the
presidency in 1933, government officials and citizen advocates debated the
country's immigration policy, which was framed in terms of *humanitarian* versus *nationalist* claims about what the United States should do.

According to Loseke, a humanitarian frame consists of the view that appropriate moral action requires efforts to eliminate pain and suffering, while
a nationalist frame insists that the greater moral good lies in advancing the interests of the nation. U.S. protagonists in the debate about the refugee problem engaged in what Loseke describes as a "reality-definition contest" about
which morality should receive priority as they used these two frames to mobilize political support for various solutions (1999:57).

Frances Perkins, Roosevelt's secretary of labor and the first female cabinet
member in U.S. history, favored reversal of the Hoover order and a liberaliza-
tion of immigration quotas to accommodate "visa applicants seeking to avoid
racial or religious persecution" in Germany (Breitman & Kraut 1987:13).
While the Immigration and Naturalization Service (INS) was under the auspices of the Labor Department, the State Department had jurisdiction over the
issuance of visas by U.S. consuls abroad. Perkins had learned that since 1930
State Department officials had been instructing their "consuls in Germany to
reduce the number of visas issued to 10 percent of the quota levels," which in
her view ran contrary to the American humanitarian tradition of offering
refuge to those fleeing persecution (ibid.:15).

On the other hand, career bureaucrats and Roosevelt appointees in the State

Department, who were typically upper-class elites who were insensitive if not hostile to non-Anglo-Saxon immigrants, were among the staunchest opponents of reversal. They took the position that the State Department's primary responsibility was to protect the national interest and that this interest was best served by neutrality on the question of Germany's treatment of its own citizens. State Department officials also believed that the economy simply could not absorb more people and that liberalizing immigration policy would provoke an anti-immigration backlash among the U.S. population that might induce Congress to pass legislation that would reduce quotas even further (Breitman & Kraut 1987; Wyman 1984).

For the most part, prominent Jews in the United States weighed in on the side of immigration reform. Roosevelt had never hesitated to include Jews among his advisors or to appoint them to public positions. Among them were Secretary of Treasury Henry Morgenthau, Jr., and U.S. Supreme Court Judge Felix Frankfurter, who tried to persuade the president to modify his restrictionist stance.[12] Representatives of influential Jewish organizations, such as Rabbi Stephen Wise of the American Jewish Congress, had access to Roosevelt as well. Although the president tactfully listened to these men, his openness to Jewish appeals was largely symbolic, aimed at mollifying them "without making any promises," and he generally sided with the restrictionists (Breitman & Kraut 1987:226).

Roosevelt had little to gain politically, and much to lose, by a policy that favored increased immigration of Jews. Public opinion polls conducted in the late 1930s and early 1940s revealed less than hospitable attitudes toward immigrants in general and Jews in particular. For example, polls showed that about 70 to 85 percent of U.S. respondents opposed increasing immigration quotas to help refugees, and about two-thirds wanted to kept refugees out altogether, even objecting to a one-time exception to allow ten thousand children to enter outside the quota limits. While a poll taken after *Kristallnacht* found that 94 percent disapproved of Nazi treatment of German Jews, another poll showed that nearly half thought the persecution of Jews was partly their own fault. In addition, various polls found that about 35 to 40 percent said they would actively support or sympathize with policies that were unfavorable to Jews, about 15 to 25 percent thought that Jews were a menace to the United States, over half considered Jews greedy and dishonest, and about a third to a half believed that Jews had too much power in business, politics, and government, a figure that rose to 56 percent during the war years (Breitman & Kraut 1987; Wyman 1984).

Nevertheless, there were times when the contingent events of the Nazi period created a political opportunity for advocates of change (see Neuman 1998). As long as the INS remained in the Labor Department, Perkins had some leverage over immigration policy, and the State Department was willing to make some modest accommodations if Roosevelt approved of them.[13] The

Nazis' program of legalized discrimination against Jews that culminated in the 1935 Nuremberg Laws did not go unnoticed, and at least one U.S. consul in Germany reported that his office had been "inundated with visa inquiries and applications" (Breitman & Kraut 1987:48).

Up to this time advocates of immigration reform had been proposing various remedies. Perhaps children, spouses, and parents of current U.S. residents could be treated more leniently. Or U.S. relatives or friends could be allowed to post a bond to "guarantee that a potential immigrant would not become a public charge" (ibid.:18). Also, some of the red tape required of applicants who had to submit copies of documents (e.g., birth certificates, military records, police dossiers) that the German government made difficult to obtain could be waived.

The Nuremberg Laws provided a new political context that gave reform advocates some additional moral leverage. Roosevelt felt compelled to make some symbolic gesture of concern, for instance, by making public statements that condemned what the Nazis were doing. He "spoke out on the need to rebuild Palestine, the Jews' ancient homeland," and urged the British who controlled Palestine to keep this area open for Jewish immigration (ibid.:227). He also made it known that he would appreciate some leniency from the State Department on immigration policy. The State Department agreed to instruct consuls abroad that they were to use their discretion to deny visa requests only if they thought applicants would "probably" become a public charge but not if they thought applicants would "possibly" become a public charge. As a result, refugees began "experiencing an unusual easing of consular requirements, especially on matters of documentation and proof of support" (ibid.). After the German invasion of Austria in March 1938, Roosevelt also ordered that the German and Austrian quotas be combined, enabling the unused portion of the German quota (which was considerably larger than Austria's) to be used for Austrian refugees. And following *Kristallnacht* he instructed "the Labor Department to extend the visitors' visas of over 12,000 German Jewish refugees in the United States for another six months" (ibid.:230).

William Rubenstein (1997) believes that the U.S. response to the Jewish refugee problem in the latter half of the 1930s was better than many critics of U.S. immigration policy suggest (see Wyman 1984). For example, the annual number of Jews allowed into the United States increased from 6,252 in fiscal year 1935 to 43,450 in fiscal year 1938, and Jews were the largest single group of immigrants allowed into the country in that period. Still, by June 1939 there was a backlog of over three hundred thousand Jews from Germany, Austria, and Czechoslovakia who had applied for immigration visas but who were not allowed in (Breitman & Kraut 1987).

Critics argue that the United States could have done more before the Nazis stopped all emigration and began implementing the Final Solution in the latter part of 1941. Secretary of Labor Perkins, for instance, favored legislation that would have allowed children to enter the country outside the quota limits. But the Wagner-Rogers Bill that was introduced in February 1939 by Senator Robert Wagner of New York and Representative Edith Nourse Rogers of Massachusetts—which would have allowed twenty thousand German children to come into the United States over a two-year period—died in Congress for lack of support. Similarly, a 1940 bill that would have relaxed quota limits and allowed refugees to go to Alaska foundered as well (ibid.).

The plight of the passenger ship the *St. Louis* is often used to illustrate the critics' point (Rubenstein & Roth 1987). In May 1939 the *St. Louis* left Hamburg, Germany, for Havana, Cuba, with 933 passengers who were mostly Jewish refugees. Over seven hundred of the passengers had applied for U.S. visas and had secured affidavits of support. They expected to qualify for entry into the United States in a matter of months and hoped to wait their turn in Cuba rather than in Germany. Before their arrival, however, the Cuban government changed the policy that had previously allowed immigrants to seek temporary refuge in Cuba, and only twenty-two of the *St. Louis* passengers were given approval to land. The captain of the ship then headed for Florida but was denied permission to dock. A U.S. Coast Guard cutter was dispatched "to prevent anyone from trying to swim ashore" as a telegram from the ships' passengers to the president went unanswered (Breitman & Kraut 1987:71). The *St. Louis* cruised for a month on its way back to Hamburg before Great Britain, France, Holland, and Belgium finally agreed to accept the passengers. Seventy percent of them were killed in the ensuing Holocaust (Gilbert 2000).

Internationalizing the Refugee Problem

Roosevelt sought to relieve the burden that the refugee problem posed to the United States by diffusing it into the international arena. Recall that in 1938 he promoted the Evian Conference, which was attended by delegates from thirty-two countries (see Chapter 2). By demonstrating leadership on this issue, Roosevelt hoped to symbolically cast himself and the United States as upholding humanitarian principles. But neither he nor the other nations in attendance wanted to commit themselves to a serious solution. According to Breitman and Kraut, it was clear that the other countries were gauging their own response to that of a "reluctant United States" (1987:97).

In the Balfour Declaration of 1917 the British had promised to establish a Jewish national homeland in Palestine (Rubenstein & Roth 1987). However, in May 1939 they issued the so-called White Paper, which reversed this position. The White Paper outlined "plans for a Palestinian state with a permanent Arab majority" that would put an end to Jewish immigration in 1944 after seventy-five thousand Jews (fifteen thousand per year) were admitted, unless the Arabs agreed otherwise, which was most unlikely (ibid.:124). As a consequence of this policy, critics contend, European Jews lost a place of refuge at precisely the time they needed it the most.

The new British policy was a response to increased Arab resistance to Jewish immigration, which was encouraged by Germany, and to Britain's concern about its ability to contain an Arab uprising and hence to maintain itself as a colonial power in the region (Breitman 1998). Moreover, once World War II was under way, the British planned to rely substantially on troops from India, two-thirds of whom were Muslim, to defend "the southern approach to Palestine through Egypt" (Weinberg 1998:485). Gerhard Weinberg observes that these troops were unlikely to fight if they thought they were being asked to defend Jews. In addition, at the time it was not a foregone conclusion that the Allies would stop the Germans from taking over the Middle East. Indeed, in November 1941 Hitler informed the Grand Mufti Haj Amin El Husseini of Jerusalem at a meeting in Berlin that he intended to kill every Jew living in the Arab world, including those in Palestine as well as "Syria, Iraq, Iran, the Arabian peninsula, Egypt, and French Northwest Africa" (ibid.:484). Thus more Jewish immigration to Palestine, Weinberg argues, could have jeopardized the survival of the Jews.

As for Britain's policy regarding immigration into its own country, Rubenstein (1997) sees the response in a more favorable light than most critics (see Wyman 1984). He argues that after *Kristallnacht* (until the outbreak of the war) emigration visas to Great Britain were granted "virtually without limit" (Rubenstein 1997:27–28). Weinberg points out, however, that Britain's relaxed immigration policy "was at the time intended for, and restricted to, those who had prospects of leaving Great Britain for the United States or another country after what was expected to be a short time" (1998:481).

Given the British position on Palestine, Roosevelt began to consider alternative plans for a Jewish homeland and the possibility of raising private funds to purchase land, in Asia or Africa, for example (Breitman & Kraut 1987). But the outbreak of World War II dramatically changed Roosevelt's priorities and those of the nation. Now, fear of foreign subversives, especially from Germany and the Soviet Union, who "might be planted among the refugees by the warring powers . . . nourished the restrictionism that long predated it" (ibid.:112, 232).[14] Roosevelt signaled the State Department that he favored tighter immigration regulations, and the subsequent decline in the issuance of visas was dramatic. For instance, the number of Germans and Austrians (or former citizens of these nations) who were given immigration visas fell from 27,370 in fiscal year 1939 to 4,883 by 1942.

Breitman and Kraut argue that there is little evidence that refugees were a source of internal subversion in the United States. In fact, after the United States entered the war in December 1941, "hundreds of thousands of these refugees served in the armed forces and in defense-related industries" (ibid.: 124–25). Nonetheless, "State Department officials stiffened their resolve not to allow a misplaced humanitarianism to interfere with their duty" to defend the country's interests. Military victory was now the nation's top priority, and "Americans might recoil at the sacrifices" they were being asked to make if they thought the United States was at war to protect Jews (ibid.:138). And like the British, the State Department was concerned that alienating the Arabs might endanger U.S. troops that were being deployed in North Africa. Roosevelt hastened to reassure Saudi Arabia that no action would be taken that altered the status quo in Palestine without consulting them fully.

Responding to the Final Solution

Neither the humanitarian nor nationalist framings of the refugee problem were sufficient to characterize what was occurring in Europe as a "genocide" or "Holocaust." These latter frames, which might have established a greater moral imperative to act, were for the most part postwar constructions of the events.[15] But how much did the Allies really know about what the Nazis were doing to the Jews?

As early as spring of 1940, British intelligence operatives were receiving and decoding German radio messages on a regular basis (Breitman 1998). Consequently, they were aware of the atrocities the Nazis committed during the summer 1941 invasion of the Soviet Union. They had reports of staggering numbers of Jews who were killed, although they had not yet understood the full implications of what had occurred, nor had the Nazis quite yet arrived at the Final Solution, which emerged in the ensuing months. Knowledge of the killings, however, did not provoke official reaction, other than efforts to prevent such information from being made public. Any public confirmation of Jewish causalities, the British believed, would be contrary to the national interest, for it would narrow the anti-Nazi cause and reinforce Nazi claims that "the Allies were fighting a war on behalf of Jews" (ibid.:105). There is no evidence that the British shared this information with the United States, but in the fall of 1941 a U.S. official in Berlin reported that he had learned that "SS units were killing Jews in many occupied localities in Russia" (ibid.:124). The U.S. response was the same as the British—suppress public exposure to the information.

By the summer of 1942 reports from the Polish underground were beginning to confirm what was happening. In November the Poles informed the British government that tens of thousands, mostly Jews and Soviet prisoners of war, had arrived at Auschwitz-Birkenau "for the sole purpose of their immediate extermination in gas chambers" (cited in Breitman 1998:116). This information reinforced evidence the British had obtained from decoded messages from Himmler's minions. Later, in the spring of 1944, four escaped prisoners from Auschwitz, most notably Rudolf Vrba and Alfred Wetzler, provided more detailed (and more widely disseminated) information on the operation of the gas chambers and crematoria.

It is understandable that people would be skeptical of such reports. The Final Solution was unprecedented and unimaginable. Furthermore, reports from

Jewish sources were especially held in suspicion, since Jews, some thought, had reason to exaggerate their plight. In August 1942, Dr. Gerhart Riegner, the Swiss representative of the World Jewish Congress (WJC), went to the U.S. and British consulates in Geneva hoping to pass a cable to Rabbi Wise and to Sidney Silverman, a British parliament member who was the WJC representative in London. The cable included the following message:

> Received alarming report that in Fuehrer's headquarters a plan has been discussed and [is] under consideration according to which [the] total of Jews in countries occupied [or] controlled by Germany numbering three and one-half to four million should after deportation and concentration in east be at one blow exterminated. . . . Informer is reported to have close connections with highest German authorities and his reports to be generally reliable. (cited in Hilberg 1992:238–39)

The informant was German industrialist Eduard Schulte. While traveling in Switzerland, Schulte had contacted a Jewish journalist who conveyed the information to Riegner (Bauer 2001; Browning 1996).

The Riegner cable was first forwarded to the U.S. State Department and the British Foreign Office. The State Department, which did not want to make the report public, did not pass it on to Wise. The British Foreign Office, on the other hand, felt compelled to inform Silverman because he was a government official. Silverman, at Riegner's request, sent the cable to Wise. Wise contacted the State Department, which asked him not to make the cable public until the information could be verified.[16] Wise did not inform the press, but he did contact a number of high-ranking governmental officials outside the State Department, including Treasury Secretary Morgenthau, the only Jew in the Roosevelt cabinet and one of the staunchest advocates of intervention. Finally, in November the State Department confirmed the report and gave Wise the go-ahead to make the information public. Wise held a press conference that was carried by the national media and that generated more publicity about the Final Solution than anything previously (Breitman 1998; Breitman & Kraut 1987).

Social problems claimsmaking, as suggested earlier, is largely dependent on the effective use of mass media to garner public support for solutions to problems (see Chapter 3). Thus the Riegner cable and the publicity around it dramatically altered the context in which claims about the "Jewish problem" and its solution were addressed. Although the news had not been welcome "for those who wanted the [Allies] to focus solely on military goals," it gave those lobbying for action more credibility (Breitman 1998:141). Moreover, as the Allies' prospects for a military victory improved the next year, proponents of rescue gained momentum, receiving more backing from the media and some public officials, including Eleanor Roosevelt, the president's wife (Wyman

1984). One of the most frequent proposals that was advanced called "for the Allies to facilitate the escape of Jews into neutral countries and to . . . resettl[e] refugees already in neutral lands" (Breitman 1998:168). The record of neutral countries like Switzerland and Spain had up to that time been rather mixed, for while thousands of refugees had been let in, thousands of others who had reached neutral borders were denied entry and were turned back to face their deaths. The Swiss government even requested that a "J" be put on German passports to make it easier to identify Jews and bar them from entering the country (Cooper 1998; Yahil 1990).

In April 1943 the United States and Great Britain held a conference in Bermuda to discuss what could be done. Both sides were reluctant to ac-knowledge the specifically Jewish character of the problem, preferring to frame it as a more general refugee issue affecting a number of different groups. The conference delegates seemed more bent on creating the illusion of action than on doing anything concretely. They agreed to take steps to encourage neu-tral countries to accept more refugees temporarily, to find other temporary havens for them (e.g., in North Africa), and to provide financial assistance for these efforts. The British agreed "in principle to admit 29,000 Jews to Pales-tine, the number remaining under the White Paper limit" (Breitman & Kraut 1987:179). Only children, however, with some accompanying adults, would be allowed to immigrate. Otherwise, neither Britain nor the United States were willing to assume ultimate responsibility for the refugees after the war (Breitman 1998; Wyman 1984).[17]

Nevertheless, several events in the next few months compelled Roosevelt to take further action. In July 1943 the president met with Jan Karski, a lieu-tenant in the Polish underground army who had firsthand knowledge of what was occurring in Poland. Karski tried to persuade Roosevelt that the Nazis' treatment of Jews was fundamentally different from their treatment of other groups, and that if the Allies did not intervene, Polish Jewry would be anni-hilated (Breitman 1998; Breitman & Kraut 1987).

In the meantime, U.S. Jewish activists staged public protests, and organi-zations such as the WJC proposed that they be allowed to deposit funds in blocked bank accounts to help finance relief and evacuation efforts.[18] WJC representative Riegner, for example, submitted a request that would have per-mitted the WJC to finance efforts to relocate Jews from Rumania and south-ern France. The proposal was approved by the Treasury Department but opposed by the State Department (as well as by the British Foreign Office). In January 1944, after months of delay, Treasury Secretary Morgenthau met with Roosevelt and advised him of the need to take action in order to avoid a pub-lic scandal over the State Department's obstructionist stance. He asked the president to sign an executive order that would create an independent agency to handle rescue operations (Breitman 1998; Breitman & Kraut 1987; Wyman 1984).

Roosevelt finally felt compelled to act. On January 22, 1944, he signed the order that established the War Refugee Board (WRB), charging it with the responsibility "to take all measures within its power to rescue the victims of enemy oppression who are in imminent danger of death and otherwise afford such victims all possible relief and assistance consistent with the successful prosecution of the war" (cited in Yahil 1990:609). The departments of Treasury, State, and War were instructed to provide the WRB, which operated with a small staff of about thirty people in Washington, D.C., with information and assistance and to execute the measures the WRB deemed necessary. The WRB was also permitted to accept contributions, financial and otherwise, from private individuals and groups. Ultimately, 85 percent of its money came from Jewish sources (Breitman & Kraut 1987; Wyman 1984).

Under the leadership of its executive director John Pehle, an official in the Treasury Department, the WRB abandoned the Allies' policy of downplaying the Nazis' targeting of Jews. For the first time the doomed Jews of Europe had a special agency of an Allied government committed to thwarting the Final Solution. WRB activities focused on three areas: (1) threats to prosecute Nazis and collaborating officials for war crimes, (2) aid to people trying to escape Nazi-controlled Europe and find refuge in safe havens, and (3) provision of relief supplies to those who could not be evacuated but were lingering in ghettos and concentration camps (Breitman & Kraut 1987; Wyman 1984).

David Wyman (1984) credits the WRB with helping to save about two hundred thousand Jewish lives. The WRB was created at a time when European governments were already reconsidering their policies in light of the turnabout in the war. Definitive U.S. expressions of concern and threats to punish Nazi collaborators helped persuade German-aligned governments in Rumania, Bulgaria, and Hungary to think twice about complying with Nazi requests to deport Jews to extermination camps. Neutral nations became more willing to offer temporary havens and to provide transit visas to Jews who managed to escape from German-controlled territories. The International Red Cross modified its previous neutral stance, which had prevented it from providing relief to the ghettos and camps. And Jewish organizations such as the WJC and the American Jewish Joint Distribution Committee (AJJDC) were given more support to pursue various rescue schemes of their own (Breitman & Kraut 1987; Yahil 1990).

Negotiating for Jewish Lives

One of the biggest problems facing the WRB and others engaged in rescue efforts was the Nazis' unwillingness to release Jews. Rubenstein (1997) observes that with the emergence of the Final Solution the Jews under German control were no longer refugees—they were prisoners. Hitler, Himmler, and others were fanatical in their resolve to continue with the extermination program even as Germany's prospects of winning the war were turning bleak. As we shall see, however, there is evidence that some Nazi officials were willing to consider the release of some Jews in exchange for substantial concessions and that this willingness increased with the certainty that they would lose the war (Bauer 1994; Hindley 1996).

According to Levine (1998), German-aligned and neutral countries that maintained diplomatic ties with Germany had the best chance of negotiating for Jewish lives. He offers neutral Sweden as a case in point. Insofar as the Nazis relied on Sweden for iron ore, ball bearings, and ball-bearing parts, they had an interest in placating Swedish demands. When the Nazis began implementing the Final Solution in neighboring Norway, the Swedish government asked that Swedish Jews residing in Norway be allowed to return to their homeland. Germany acceded to this request, as it did to a subsequent Swedish demand to allow all Jews in Norway to emigrate to Sweden.

It was at this point that Sweden developed the tactic of offering to naturalize and issue "protective passports" to Jews who under normal conditions would have had no claims to Swedish citizenship. As long as these Jews possessed the appropriate documents that verified their right to Swedish protection, German Foreign Service bureaucrats were at times willing to respect normal diplomatic protocols and release Jews to their home country or at least temporarily exempt them from deportation to extermination camps. The leverage that Swedish diplomats had to pursue this strategy increased with the changing tide of the war as German bureaucrats "began to seek alibis for future eventualities" (ibid.:528). Levine argues that Sweden's response to the Final Solution (which included its acceptance of some 7,900 Danish Jews) illustrates how "determined intervention by an officially recognized third party [could] be decisive" (ibid.:531).

Levine adds that the highly regarded rescue efforts of Swedish diplomat Raoul Wallenberg in Budapest, Hungary, in 1944 must be understood in this context. Prior to his arrival in Budapest, Wallenberg had been introduced to Iver Olsen, the WRB representative in Sweden. The Swedish Foreign Office agreed to dispatch Wallenberg to Budapest to negotiate with the German-aligned Hungarian government to try to exempt Jews from deportation to death camps. Wallenberg essentially became the WRB representative in Hungary and was given WRB financial backing with money that came mostly from the AJJDC (Rubenstein 1987; Wyman 1984).

Even before Wallenberg's arrival, the Swedish foreign minister in Budapest had issued protective passports to several hundred Hungarian Jews who had family or business ties with Sweden, delaying the deportations that Adolf Eichmann began organizing in March 1944 after the initial German occupation of Hungary (Yahil 1990). Before that time "Hungarian killing and deportation of Jews [had] occurred only sporadically," and the eight hundred thousand Jews in Hungary represented the largest concentration of Jews remaining alive in Europe (Breitman & Kraut 1987:210). Within two months over half the Hungarian Jews were deported, and most of them were killed at Birkenau (Bauer 1994; Breitman 1998).

In response to the Hungarian deportations, King Gustav V of Sweden, Pope Pius XII, and Max Huber, the president of the International Red Cross, had appealed to Hungarian regent Admiral Miklos Horthy to stop any further deportations of Jews. In addition, Roosevelt had warned that "Hungary's fate will not be like that of any other civilized nation . . . unless the deportations are stopped" (cited in Breitman & Kraut 1987:213). In July the United States had also bombed Budapest (for military not humanitarian reasons), and the Soviet army was advancing toward the Hungarian border. All these factors combined to persuade Horthy to try to cooperate with the Allies and temporarily halt the deportation of the 250,000 Jews who remained in Budapest. He submitted the so-called Horthy Offer to high-ranking German officials, requesting that particular categories of Jews be allowed to emigrate. Historical accounts differ on the specifics of the proposal, but they place the number at about 400 to 450 Jews who held Swedish passports and about 7,000 who held immigration certificates to Palestine (Bauer 1994; Breitman 1998; Yahil 1990). Some accounts also indicate that the proposal included a request to send an additional 10,000 to 20,000 children to Palestine. The offer was apparently relayed to Hitler through the German ambassador in Hungary and the German minister of foreign affairs. Hitler is reported to have approved the release of some Jews provided that Horthy agreed to immediately resume the deportations of the remaining Hungarian Jews. According to Yehuda Bauer (1994), the Nazis were willing to consider the release of about 7,000 Jews to Palestine, 87 to Sweden, and a handful to other neutral countries.

It is not at all clear that the Nazis ever intended to abide by the agreement. They may simply have been trying to get Horthy to resume the deportations or to embarrass the Allies, whom they doubted really wanted to accept the Jews. Indeed, it took the Allies about a month to assure Horthy that they would in fact be willing to arrange for the transportation and temporary resettlement of the released Jews, and they made no commitment to allowing Jews permanent residence in Palestine. There is evidence that Himmler opposed sending the Jews to Palestine and that Eichmann intended to get German emigration officials "to procrastinate in granting transit permits," assuming that that once the deportations began, "all the Jews would be included . . . [and] would disappear . . . before anyone realized it" (Bauer 1994:213; see also Yahil 1990).

Nevertheless, the negotiations helped extend the moratorium on deportations and gave Wallenberg and other neutral diplomats (from Switzerland, Spain, Portugal, San Salvador, and the Vatican) more time to issue additional protective passports to Jews. By the end of August over seventeen thousand Jews had received such papers. The actions of these diplomats also provided

cover for Jewish activists in the Budapest Zionist youth movement who distributed thousands of additional forged documents as well—not just protective passports but food coupons, work passes, military papers, and the like
(Bauer 1994; Rubenstein 1997).

In October a Nazi-backed Hungarian military coup by the more staunchly
fascist and anti-Semitic Arrow Cross party forced Horthy's ouster, and the deportations to Auschwitz were resumed. Although the passports that had been
issued by the neutral governments were not always honored, the Jews holding
them were often released before or even during the deportations. Wallenberg
in particular is credited with heroically pursuing transports that had already
left Budapest and with managing to secure Jews' release before they crossed
the Hungarian border. He also tried to use his diplomatic leverage and the
sheer force of his personality to save Jews who had not yet received protective
documents (Bauer 1994; Wyman 1984).

In November, as the deportations continued, a coalition of neutral diplomats issued a formal communication to the Arrow Cross government protest-
ing the deportations and the government's failure to honor the protective
documents. The Arrow Cross agreed to establish an "international ghetto"—
a safe haven apart from Budapest's main ghetto—that held over thirty thousand people who were crammed into rented quarters without adequate resources to meet food, heating, health, and sanitation needs (Yahil 1990).

When the Soviet army liberated Budapest in January 1945, over one hundred thousand Hungarian Jews were still alive. Nonetheless, Bauer (1994)
notes that Wallenberg's singular role in saving these Jews has often been exaggerated, for Swiss diplomat Charles Lutz actually arranged for more protective passports than Wallenberg. Rubenstein (1987) adds that the WRB's role
in saving Hungarian Jews has been overestimated as well, since both Wallenberg and Lutz's influence derived not from their association with the WRB
but, as Levine (1998) suggests, from their status as neutral diplomats.[19]

At its inception the WRB was limited in the official mandate that required
its actions to be "consistent with the successful prosecution of the war." This
mandate was thus constrained by a previous agreement reached by the United
States, Great Britain, and the Soviet Union at the Tripartite Conference in November 1943, where the Allies committed themselves to demanding unconditional surrender from Germany. The three nations also agreed not to enter
into any separate negotiations with Germany, and if Germany solicited such
negotiations they were obligated to inform each other immediately. Thus the
Tripartite agreement imposed severe limits on the negotiations that could take
place between the WRB and the Nazis with respect to the release of Jews
(Hindley 1996; Weinberg 1998).

Bauer (1994) notes that as early as December 1942 Himmler had approached Hitler with the idea of ransoming a limited number of Jews for
appreciable quantities of foreign currency and that Hitler appears to have ap-

proved the idea so long as the money was substantial and the Final Solution would continue unabated. At the same time, both men doubted that the Allies would in fact be willing to accept more refugees and that their refusal to do so could be used as propaganda to counter Allied criticism about Nazi treatment of Jews. Moreover, if the Allies did agree to pay ransom money for Jews, this might stimulate anti-Semitic reaction abroad and thus help Germany's cause. Later, in April 1944, Eichmann contacted Joel Brand, a Zionist member of the Budapest Relief and Rescue Committee (RRC), to broker a deal with the western Allies. Eichmann offered to exchange 1 million Jews for 10,000 trucks, 800 tons of coffee, 200 tons of cocoa, 200 tons of sugar, and 2 million bars of soap. The Jews would be allowed to emigrate to any Allied-aligned country with the exception of Palestine. The proposal appears to have originated with Himmler for the purpose of sowing dissension among the Allies and opening up negotiations with the West for a separate peace agreement that would isolate the Soviet Union. Eichmann agreed that the trucks would be used only for civilian purposes or on the eastern front (Bauer 1994; Teveth 1996; Yahil 1990).

In May, Brand was sent to neutral Turkey to bring the offer to the western Allies. Although it was extremely unlikely that the United States and Great Britain would violate the Tripartite agreement, Allied proponents of rescue—including WRB director Pehle, Treasury Secretary Morgenthau, and leaders of influential Jewish organizations—hoped to string out negotiations to delay the deportations. Once the Russians were informed, however, the scheme was quickly abandoned. Nevertheless, while Brand was on his mission to Turkey, Budapest RRC member Rezso Kasztner took over negotiations with Eichmann and succeeded in securing the release of about twenty thousand Hungarian Jews in exchange for ransom money provided by the AJJDC (under the auspices of the formally neutral Swiss Funds for Aid to Refugees) and the Hungarian Jews themselves.[20] Although these Jews managed to avoid deportation to Auschwitz, they were not released outright but were sent to work and transit camps in Germany, Austria, and Czechoslovakia. Ultimately about 13,700 of them survived the war (Bauer 1994; Teveth 1996; Yahil 1990).

Bauer (1994) and Levine (1998) remind us that the Final Solution evolved gradually through a process of cumulative radicalization. They suggest that this radicalization could have been reversed as the wartime context that facilitated its emergence changed. Nazi concessions on Jewish policy that allowed for the emigration of Jews may have been a retreat from the Final Solution but were nonetheless consistent with the more modest goal of achieving a greater Germany *Judenfrei*. Some Jewish lives could be spared if it was in Germany's interests. Moreover, Himmler's anti-Semitism led him to hold an exaggerated view of the power of international Jewry to influence Allied policy. The reality was that Jews were never in a position to deliver what Himmler ultimately wanted—a separate peace with the Allies that would preserve the Nazi regime at the expense of the Soviet Union (Hindley 1996; Teveth 1996; Yahil 1990).

Nevertheless, Wyman (1984) believes that the WRB could have played a greater role in rescue efforts if it had been established earlier and given more support. These efforts, however, were constrained not only by the Tripartite agreement but by the Allies' firm belief that the military defeat of Germany was their primary—if not only—concern. Only "victory would end the killing, and anything that might delay victory would only hurt, not help, those whom the Germans had marked out as victims" (Weinberg 1998:489). Williamson Murray (2000) adds that from the hindsight of history Allied victory sometimes seems inevitable. At the time, however, victory was very much in doubt.

Walter Laqueur (2000) is among those who think that it would have been possible for the Allies to save more Jews if that had been a priority when, in fact, it was not. Weinberg agrees, noting that "every single life counts . . . and each person saved could have lived out a decent life" (1998:490).[21] He doubts, on the other hand, that the "general picture in terms of overall statistics" could have been altered very much, and he cautions against shifting the blame for the Holocaust from the killers to the bystanders. While the question of whether enough was done to help the Jews will likely remain and tarnish the Allies' record with regards to the Holocaust, "[o]fficial indifference to suffering in faraway lands and unwillingness to take responsibility for persons . . . [in need are] still with us" today (Breitman & Kraut, 1987:10).

NOTES

1.   Michael Berger (1921–1994) was my father.
2.   Sol Berger (1919–) is my uncle. Unlike Berger's experience with the Poles, Western-European resistance groups more readily accepted Jews as members. There was also a Polish group, the *Zegota* (code name for Council for Aid to Jews), that was explicitly involved in the rescue of Jews (Bauer 1989; Botwinick 1996; Prekerowa 1990).
3.   Only about a dozen of the 150 to 200 Treblinka escapees survived. Later, in October 1943, a Jewish-Soviet prisoner of war, Lt. Aleksandr Pechersky, led an escape from Sobibor. Eleven SS and several hundred Ukrainian guards were killed, but only 40 to 50 of the some 300 to 400 escapees survived. That same month, *Sonderkommando* inmates who worked in the crematoria at Auschwitz-Birkenau got word that some of them were to be liquidated. They attacked the guards and set one of the buildings on fire. Three SS guards and about 250 inmates were killed during the uprising (Arad 1987; Botwinick 1996; Hilberg 2001).
4.   Several accounts of concentration camps characterize inmates' behavior in primarily negative terms—as fatalistic, self-destructive, divisive, corrupt, and predatory (Bettleheim 1960; Dimsdale 1980; Levi 1986; Marrus 1987). However, others suggest that Jews who survived the camps often emerged from an initial period of shock,

despair, and disbelief able to take strategic courses of action through calculated risk-taking and disobedience; and many were able to do so without complete abandonment of prewar norms of human reciprocity and systems of morality. Des Pres, for example, notes that survivor accounts emphasize the "all against all" atmosphere, but they also regularly include reports of people holding onto their humanity and offering each other "help and mutual care" (1976:99). Pawełczynska argues that individuals "who made no revisions" in pre-existing humanitarian values perished if they "applied them in an absolute way," but there were always those who united "together in the practice of the basic norm, 'Do not harm your neighbor and, if possible save him'" (1979:144). Langer (1991) makes a distinction between acts that were "selfish" and acts that were "self-ish." "The selfish act ignores the needs of others through choice when the agent is in a position to help without injuring one's self in any appreciable way. Selfishness is motivated by greed, indifference, [or] malice. . . . [In the] self-ish act, however, . . . [one] is vividly aware of the needs of others but because of the nature of the situation is unable to choose freely the generous impulse that a more compassionate nature yearns to express" (ibid.:124).

5.   In 1953 Israel established Yad Vashem, "The Memorial Authority for the Martyrs and Heroes of the Holocaust," which has as one of its missions the recognition and remembrance of "the Righteous among the Nations" who risked their lives to save Jews (Spector 1990c; see Chapter 5). This category excludes those who saved Jews primarily for monetary gain, a group that includes anti-Semitic individuals (Fogelman 1994; Tec 1986).

6.   Study of altruism is an interdisciplinary field that focuses on a wide range of areas, including blood and organ donation, bystander intervention, disaster research, philanthropy, and volunteerism. Some analysts believe that self-interest or egoism ultimately underlies altruistic conduct. Batson (1991) describes three variations of this point of view. According to the "empathy-specific reward" hypothesis, individuals learn through socialization that rewards follow the helping of others. The "empathy-specific" hypothesis postulates that individuals expect that punishment in the form of guilt, shame, or censure will follow failure to help. The "aversive-arousal reduction" hypothesis suggests that concern for others evokes internal distress that is relieved by helping others. However, other analysts believe that genuinely altruistic behavior does in fact exist (Berger et al. 1998; Piliavin & Charng 1990; Simmons 1991).

7.   But "all other things," as we shall see, were not necessarily equal.

8.   Some researchers suggest that there is no evidence that the Pope ever gave a direct order to the Italian clergy to help Jews, although "local archbishops, bishops, priests, and nuns . . . [often] worked out their own methods" for lending assistance (Deák 2000a:48; see also Zuccotti 1987).

9.   The Huguenots were French followers of Calvinism.

10.   See note 2.

11.   The State Department had already been using this interpretation to limit immigration from Mexico.

12.   Frankfurter was appointed to the Court in 1939 and served until 1962.

13.   When the INS was transferred from the Labor Department to the Department of Justice in 1940, the State Department tightened its regulations again.

14.   The United States, as is well-known, interned Japanese Americans in camps, although it never did this to German Americans and Italian Americans.

15.   In August 1941 British Prime Minister Winston Churchill observed that "in the face of Nazi atrocities in Eastern Europe . . . the world was faced with 'a crime without a name'" (Ignatieff 2001:26). It was Raphael Lemkin, an American-Jewish refugee from Poland, who first advanced the term "genocide" to refer to the Nazi assault on the Jews in his book *Axis Rule in Occupied Europe*, published in 1944. After the war, Lemkin drafted and lobbied for the passage of the United Nations Convention on the Prevention and Punishment of Genocide. For further discussion of this issue, see Chapter 7.

16.   Although Riegner's cable contained some errors of detail, Browning considers it "an astonishingly accurate piece of wartime intelligence" (1996:3).

17.   Roosevelt did agree to allow one thousand refugees from Italy to receive temporary asylum in a camp at Oswego in northern New York.

18.   One of the most vocal activists was Peter Bergson, a Zionist who led the Bergson Group. Bergson was critical of Jewish-American leaders' inaction and of what he considered to be their obsequious behavior (Wyman 1984).

19.   Fenyvesi (2001) notes that Wallenberg not only worked for the WRB but for the Office of Strategic Services, the wartime precursor to the Central Intelligence Agency, and that his influence was due in part to this association. In January 1945 he met with Soviet military officials who controlled the area at the time and was subsequently imprisoned. The Soviets claim that he died in 1947, but others believe he was alive as late as 1989.

20.   See Bauer (1994) for the details of the rather complex rescue schemes Kasztner was involved in, and Chapter 5 for a discussion of the postwar accounts of his efforts.

21.   Novick (1999) estimates that a more aggressive Allied rescue policy could have saved about 1 to 2 percent of the Jewish deaths.

   In Chapter 6 I will discuss the controversy over proposals for the Allies to bomb the gas chambers at Auschwitz-Birkenau and the railways leading to them. Although the bombing issue often figures predominantly in postwar accounts, Lipstadt suggests it is more a symbolic issue that pertains to "a relatively late stage of the destruction process" that is often "substituted for anger about the whole [of] the United States' apathetic response to Jewish suffering" (2000:229).

5

The Politics of Holocaust Memory in Israel and the Federal Republic of Germany

Holocaust survivor Simon Wiesenthal recounts an incident in which he was called to the hospital death bed of a twenty-one-year-old SS soldier. At the time Wiesenthal was interned in a concentration camp in eastern Poland. A group of Jews had been marched outside the camp for a work assignment on the grounds of a school that had been converted into a hospital. A Red Cross nurse approached him asking, "Are you a Jew?," and took him to see an SS soldier named Karl, who had asked to speak with a Jew (Wiesenthal 1998).

Karl, whose head was "completely bandaged with openings only for mouth, nose, and ears," proceeded to tell a reluctant Wiesenthal of his participation in the murder of innocent Jewish men, women, and children (ibid.:25). Raised as a devout Catholic, Karl had joined the Hitler Youth and later volunteered for the SS. The images of the dying innocents haunted Karl, and he pleaded with Wiesenthal for absolution: "I cannot die . . . without coming clean. This must be my confession. . . . I have longed to talk about it to a Jew and beg for forgiveness from him. . . . I know that what I am asking is almost too much for you, but without your answer I cannot die in peace" (ibid.:53–54). Wiesenthal was torn, for the soldier sounded genuinely repentant. He did not think it was his place, however, to offer forgiveness for crimes committed against others. He stood up and left the room without saying a word.

For years to come Wiesenthal remained conflicted by his decision, and his dilemma has provoked soul-searching discussions "on the possibilities and limits of forgiveness."[1] According to Jean Améry, another Holocaust survivor, "forgiving or not-forgiving in this specific case" is a psychological question, one of "temperament or feeling" (1998:107). But *politically*, Amery adds, "I do not want to hear anything of forgiveness! . . . I refuse any reconciliation with the criminals, and with . . . all those who helped prepare the unspeakable acts with their words" (ibid.:108). Politically neither did Wiesenthal offer forgiveness, for he devoted the rest of his life to pursuing the capture and prosecution of Nazi war criminals. Through the Jewish Historical Documentation

Center in Austria, which Wiesenthal established in 1947, over eleven hundred Nazis have been brought to justice.

The question of forgiveness dovetails with the question of forgetting, for some believe that to forgive is also to forget. Indeed, forgetting about the Holocaust is arguably one of the greatest concerns of survivors. Elie Wiesel's greatest nightmare is that "when we die, no one will be left to persuade people that the Holocaust occurred," no one will be left to remind people that what happened to the Jews must never happen—to anyone—again (quoted in Miller 1990:220). But such issues—of forgiveness, of forgetting—are part of a broader and more complex problem of "collective memory," which in the first chapter of this book I defined as shared recollections of the past that link "successive generations with one another" and that infuse disparate individual memories with common moral meaning (Durkheim [1893] 1964:80). The question of Holocaust memory, however, may not be one of *whether* the genocide will be remembered but of *how* it will be remembered.

Earlier I noted that the development and unfolding of claims and solutions to social problems is an ongoing process and that the natural history of the "Jewish problem" did not end with the Final Solution or the defeat of the Nazi regime. Thus the *postwar* context of the Holocaust presents itself as a social problem in its own right, and a constructionist approach to this period needs to be infused with insights drawn from the collective memory literature.

All nation-states construct collective memories to legitimate their moral origins and provide a foundation for social solidarity and a unified polity, creating an imagined community, or what Pierre Nora (1986) calls the "memory-nation." National state-sponsored memory, however, is a disputed terrain where the dominant view is continuously confronted with challenges, alternatives, or countermemories. Thus collective memories have a contingent, negotiated character, and countermemories emerge as groups with competing material interests and symbolic needs attempt to revise or deconstruct the dominant memory (Berger 1996; Foucault 1977; Funkenstein 1992; Marcuse 2001).

In this chapter I focus on the construction of collective memories in Israel and the Federal Republic of Germany (FRG). Among existing nation-states, these countries best serve as "emotional reminders" of the Holocaust: Israel as the symbolic if not political representative of the Jewish people; and Germany as the originating site of Nazism (see Schmitt 1989). In the aftermath of the Holocaust and World War II, both nations have been involved in an ongoing appraisal of their past in an effort to understand their national identities and place in the world (Brunner 1997; Diner 1990). In the process the Holocaust has become fodder for domestic political disputes. It is not just disparate national contexts, however, but the international arena as well that constructs collective memory (see Nichols 1995). Indeed, the problem of Holocaust memory and the aftermath of World War II has been diffused as a cross-national phenomenon for all the participants of World War II, with important geopolitical ramifications and implications for evolving conceptions of international justice (Deák et al. 2000; Todorov 2001b; see Best 2001).[2]

In addition, this chapter will take us into the realm of "symbolic politics," that is, the process by which political actors attempt to strategically manipulate symbols to alter the balance of power among groups (Edelman 1977). Partisan politics depends in large part on the effective use of rhetoric, which may be defined as persuasive communicative activity that is intended to induce others to make preferred judgments and political decisions. Thus rhetoric is not simply a contest of words but a way of "talking" social reality into being. In our case, rhetoric becomes part of the "memory work" that constructs the memory-nation (Berger 1996; Geyer & Meyer 1994; Holstein & Miller 1990; Neuman 1998).

Symbolic politics in the postwar era has been infused with a generalized rhetorical idiom of victimization. According to Joseph Amato, "the question of who suffers what at whose hands [is] the major moral axis" of contemporary public discourse that structures claims and counterclaims about the past (1990:xxv).[3] Thus an explication of the rhetoric of victimization politics will help set the stage for our nation-state case studies and for understanding the "continuous battle over the assertion and dismissal of the victim/victimizer dichotomy" that has characterized Jewish and German discourse about the Holocaust (Krondorfer 1995:27; see also Marcuse 2001; Olick & Levy 1997).

THE RHETORICAL DISCOURSE OF VICTIMIZATION POLITICS

Victimization rhetoric is a generalized discourse that entails claims or grievances that place persons or groups into a category of those who have been harmed or wronged in some significant way (Amato 1990; Holstein & Miller 1990; Loseke 1999). As a resource used by claimsmakers to communicate about social problems, victimization discourse relies on other rhetorical idioms that bring forth images of calamity, loss, and endangerment. According to Paul Ibarra and John Kitsuse (1993), the general rhetoric of calamity evokes the specter of unimaginable and utter disaster, the rhetoric of loss expresses concern about the devaluation of cherished persons or things, and the rhetoric of endangerment conjures up threats to people's physical safety. In addition, victimization discourse typically specifies remedial or compensatory actions that are expressed through an idiom of entitlement regarding the allocation of consequent rights and resources.

Victimization discourse also designates a victim's complementary opposite, that is, a victimizer or perpetrator who is the source of harm and who incurs an obligation to compensate the victim and/or be sanctioned. Lawrence Nichols observes that social problems discourse occurs in a "dialogical" context, that is, through "an exchange of ideas and opinions among two or more speakers" (2000:56). Dialogue about social problems does not presume a commonality of interests and in fact suggests disagreement. Thus an alleged victimizer may respond to a victim's claims in varying degrees of rhetorical admission or denial regarding the facticity or disreputability of these claims as well as the responsibility to atone or make amends (Holstein & Miller 1990; Loseke 1999; Nichols 1990).

The denial elements of victimization discourse are instances of what Ibarra and Kitsuse (1993) call counterrhetorical strategies, that is, rhetorics aimed at countering other's claims. Counterrhetorics may be sympathetic or unsympathetic. The former may acknowledge the basic features of the claim but require modifications or revisions; the later may involve rejection of the claim altogether. Counterrhetorical strategies often make appeals to defeasibility (capable of being annulled or made void) through normalization or relativity claims that shift or redistribute blame by asserting that what one party has done is no worse or is less egregious than what another party has done. Counterrhetorical strategies of normalization or relativity may also entail victim contests or competitions of victimhood, that is, claims that one group has suffered more than another and hence deserves special remedial consideration (Amato 1990; Holstein & Miller 1990; Loseke 1999; Nichols 1990).

According to Amato, the Holocaust has become the "archetypical expression of the suffering innocent" (1990:183). By definition the designation "Holocaust" is a rhetorical motif that evokes past calamity and the loss of Jewish lives as well as a formerly vital European Jewish culture. Many Jews claim that a Holocaust could indeed happen again, that they are endangered without a Jewish state to protect them, and that they are now entitled to a state of their own (Novick 1999; Segev 1993).

While there may be some Germans who deny that the Holocaust occurred, more common are those who claim that Hitler and the Nazis alone, not Germany or the German people, were responsible for what happened. At issue here is the question of whether "membership in a community implicate[s] one in collective responsibility for suffering . . . [and] entail[s] some sort of obligation" not only to past victims but to future generations (Amato 1990:176). Some Germans also claim that what happened to the Jews was comparable to the persecution experienced by other minorities in other countries (including the United States) and that Communism was (and is) as great (or greater) a threat as Nazism or fascism. Some Germans claim that they too were victimized by the Nazis and by the Allied occupation after the war, and that the Jews were at least partly responsible for their own fate [Anti-Defamation League (ADL) 1993; Marcuse 2001; Olick & Levy 1997].

Moreover, both rhetorical and counterrhetorical claims about the Holocaust have been infused with general evaluative motifs involving the interrelated themes of nationalism, war and sacrifice, martyrdom and heroism. Craig Calhoun argues that "nationalism . . . remains the preeminent rhetoric for attempts to demarcate political communities, claim rights of self-determination and legitimate rule by reference to 'the people' of a country" (1993:211).[4] Amato (1990) notes that since World War I military sacrifice has occupied center stage in the national culture of all nation-states:

> Governments must justify blood spilt on behalf of the nation . . . [and] elevate the deaths of their servants beyond politics itself to the mythic level of heroes and martyrs. . . . Each nation [has] made itself a holy community of suffering by martyring so many in its name. . . . The more people paid for the war with their sufferings . . . the more they came to feel that they belonged to the nation and the nation belonged to them. (138–39, 180)

With this background in mind, I now examine ways in which Israeli and German memories have been contested, negotiated, and rhetorically constructed in domestic and international context. I begin by considering the early postwar years and then turn to other key events that helped construct these two memory-nations.

THE EARLY POSTWAR CONTEXT

Israel: Establishing a Jewish Nation-State

Recall that long before the Second World War Jewish Zionists in Europe had called for the creation of a Jewish state in their ancient homeland in Palestine (see Chapter 4). Zionists in prewar Palestine viewed the rise of Nazism in Germany as confirming their historical prognosis that the only solution to the plight of the Jewish people was an independent state. David Ben-Gurion (1886–1973) was at that time the acknowledged leader of Mapai, the largest socialist-labor Zionist party and the dominant political party in Palestine. He expected that Nazism would provide moral capital or, in his words, "a fertile force" for the Zionist movement (quoted in Segev 1993:18; see also Shapira 1995; Teveth 1996).

During the 1930s Ben-Gurion and Mapai favored negotiations with Nazi officials over emigration of German Jewry and the transfer of their financial assets to Palestine. The Nazis were receptive because they wanted to rid themselves of Jews, and they hoped that cooperation with the Zionists would ward off an anti-German economic and diplomatic boycott that had been initiated by several (mostly American) Jewish organizations (Bauer 1994; Segev 1993; see Chapter 2).

In prewar Palestine, Zeev Jabotinsky's Union of Zionist Revisionists, Mapai's principal opposition party to the right, was at first adamant in its rejection of any contact with Nazi Germany. The Revisionists supported the boy-cott as a means of ending Nazi persecution of German Jews. Mapai, on the other hand, viewed the *Ha'avarah* (transfer) Agreement that was worked out with the Nazi-German government as a means of settling German Jews in Palestine.[5] Ben-Gurion viewed the debate between *ha'avarah* and boycott as a debate between Zionism and assimilation. According to Ben-Gurion:

> The assimilationists have always declared war on anti-Semitism. . . . Now some Zionists have joined the chorus of the assimilationists. . . . But we must give a Zionist response to the catastrophe faced by German Jewry—to turn this dis-aster into an opportunity to develop our country, to save the lives and property of the Jews of Germany for the sake of Zion. (quoted in Segev 1993:27)

Ben-Gurion's opponents countered that his reference to "assimilation" was "the height of demagoguery" (quoted in ibid.:27). They claimed that Mapai was victimizing the Jewish people by playing politics with Jewish lives: "All this enthusiasm [for *ha'avarah*] from the left would not have been were insti-tutions affiliated with Mapai not benefiting" (quoted in ibid.). Jabotinsky be-gan calling for the evacuation of all European Jews to Palestine and criticized the Mapai-dominated Jewish Agency for Palestine for selectively distributing immigration certificates. Indeed, the labor Zionists envisioned themselves as creating a society of self-reliant "new men" achieving mastery of their en-vironment by returning to the land and agricultural labor. In their view, ur-ban life—as characterized by Jewish life in the Diaspora—bred social and moral degeneration.[6] Mapai immigration policies therefore gave preference to younger Zionists, particularly those with agricultural training or a willingness to work the land, who seemed best suited for their nation-building program. Those who wanted to come only because they had no other place to go were viewed with condescension. Jabotinsky forces claimed that their followers, who were primarily from the urban lower-middle class, were the chief victims of this policy. After the war, as we shall see, Herut, the offspring of the Revi-sionist movement, charged Mapai with sabotaging rescue efforts (Davidson 1992; Shapira 1995, 1997; Teveth 1996).

The establishment of the state of Israel in 1948 did not come about as a di-rect consequence of the Holocaust. Great Britain was resolutely opposed to re-linquishing control of Palestine, and after the war it became clear that the White Paper of 1939 that had limited Jewish emigration was not just a tem-porary measure implemented in the wake of World War II (see Chapter 4). Rather, it was part of a broader pro-Arab turn in British policy in the Middle East. Furthermore, the war had devastated the British economy and had made the nation even more dependent on Middle-Eastern oil. The British had no de-sire to antagonize Arab interests in the region (Johnson 1987; Reinharz & Friesel 1997).

Although the Palestinian Jews had been aligned with the Allies' war efforts in Europe, they had opposed Great Britain in the Middle East. As Ben-Gurion had said, "We must fight Hitler as though there were no White Paper, and fight the White Paper as if there were no Hitler" (quoted in Johnson 1987:520). After the war Jews responded to the need to relocate some 250,000 Jews in European displaced person (DP) camps by organizing illegal immigration transports to Palestine. They also engaged in armed resistance against the British administration in Palestine. Jewish rebels clashed with British soldiers, buildings and railways were blown up, and many people were killed. Britain eventually acquiesced and in February 1947 turned to the United Nations (UN), which had substantial Arab representation, for a resolution of the problem (Reinharz & Friesel 1997).

The UN, established in October 1945, had as its official mission the goal of saving "succeeding generations from the scourge of war" and reaffirming "faith in fundamental human rights, in the dignity and worth of the human person, in the equal rights of men and women and of nations large and small" (cited in Art 1993:52). A special committee, the United Nations Special Committee on Palestine (UNSCOP), was created to investigate the Palestine problem and recommend a solution. UNSCOP members visited the DP camps in Europe and spoke with spokespersons on all sides of the conflict. In August 1947 a report was published that recommended the partition of Palestine into a Jewish and an Arab state. While the Arabs, who were strongly represented in the UN, opposed this resolution, Jewish Zionists accepted partition as the most practical solution (Johnson 1987; Reinharz & Friesel 1997).

At the time, U.S. policy in the Middle East "was not very different from the British one . . . although [it was] not as sharply crystallized and certainly less self-assured" (Reinharz & Friesel 1997:104). According to Paul Johnson's (1987) account, President Franklin Roosevelt had been unsympathetic to the Zionist cause, but his successor Harry Truman had a more emotional and pragmatic view of Zionism:

> He felt sorry for Jewish refugees . . . [and] saw the Jews in Palestine as underdogs. He was also much less sure of the Jewish vote than Roosevelt . . . [and] needed the endorsement of [influential] Jewish organizations in such swing-states as New York, Pennsylvania and Illinois . . . [in] the coming 1948 election. (ibid.:525)

In addition, the Soviet Union had no particular objections to a Jewish state, savored the prospects of declining British influence in the Middle East, and viewed Israel as a potential socialist state (Novick 1999).

In November 1947 the UN General Assembly voted by a small margin to approve the partition plan. The Arabs were outraged. Azzam Pasha, Secretary-General of the Arab League, announced on the radio, in a rhetorical idiom that evoked the specter of endangerment and calamity: "This will be a war of extermination and a momentous massacre" (quoted in Johnson 1987:526). Between December 1947 and May 1948 Israeli forces fought a War of Independence against Palestinian Arabs, and between May 1948 and July 1949 Arab troops from Egypt, Syria, Iraq, Lebanon, and Jordan entered the fray. By the time the fighting stopped, the Israelis were victorious and had gained control of about half the land planned for the Palestinian Arab state in the initial UN resolution. About 150,000 resentful Arabs were now under Israeli control and an additional 700,000 who had fled or were driven out of Palestine became refugees in neighboring Arab countries (Penslar 1995; Shapira 1995; Teveth 1996). The Palestine problem now become the "Palestinian problem." The construction of a Palestinian national identity, as distinct from a broader Arab or pan-Arab identity, became ever more crystallized (Litvak 1994; Taraki 1990). And war and violence in the Middle East continues to this very day.[7]

According to Anita Shapira, during this initial period the Holocaust did not figure predominantly in Israelis' understanding of the events that led to the emergence of their nation-state. Rather, the nation was perceived primarily "as the outcome of immanent processes precipitated by the heroic struggle against the British" and the Arab nations (1997:77). Israeli collective memory had not yet been infused with the Holocaust, and nationalist sentiments focused on the heroic fighters who had served so valiantly in the War of Independence to establish the Israeli state. The Holocaust was not yet viewed as an appropriate memory for the advancement of Jewish national identity, for the perceived passivity and defenselessness of the European Jews stood in marked contrast to the image of the self-reliant "new men" fighting for their nation. "The only Holocaust story that seemed fit to tell was that of the Warsaw Ghetto uprising" (ibid.:76; see Chapter 4). Immigrant survivors who had been involved in armed resistance were sought after, treated as heroes, and urged to relate their experiences. Survivors who had not responded in this way, on the other hand, were often viewed as deficient and were even disdained (Cole 1999; Davidson 1992; Novick 1999).

Israeli memory of the Holocaust, however, was soon to change. As we shall see, the Holocaust was to become far more central to the Israeli memory-nation, in many respects a state-sponsored secular or "civil religion" and a principal source of national identity and cohesion. At the same time, Germany was to retain its status as Israel's complementary opposite: as a victimizer-nation that symbolized both a horrific past and a potential for future villainy if the lessons of the Holocaust were ignored or forgotten (Krondorfer 1995; Segev 1993; Wolffsohn 1993; Young 1993).[8]

Germany: The Nuremberg Trials, Denazification, and the Cold War

In June 1945 the major Allied powers—the United States, Great Britain, France, and the Soviet Union—divided a devastated Germany into four zones of military occupation (Marrus 1997). The experience of being occupied was not pleasant for Germans. Residents surrounding the liberated concentration camps were forced to view the horrors of the remains, and some were even recruited to help with burial and clean-up responsibilities. Germans were exposed to an Allied media campaign that confronted them with film footage of the camps and accusations regarding their guilt. Intended by the Allies as "educational," these experiences engendered feelings of bitterness and humiliation among Germans whose most common reaction was not to reflect on their own complicity but to say "we did not know" and to "deny having anything to do with the atrocities" (Marcuse 2001:57; see Chapter 3). Rather than being penitent for the misery their nation had wrought, they made counter-rhetorical claims about their own victimization.

Among the important tasks that lay before the Allies was the postwar adjudication of Nazi war criminals. Previously, in the Moscow Declaration of November 1943, the United States, Great Britain, and the Soviet Union had agreed to undertake joint prosecution of "the major criminals whose offences have no particular geographical location" (cited in Marrus 1997:21). Other prosecutions, it was decided, would take place independently in "the countries in which [the] abominable deeds were done in order that they may be judged and punished according to the laws of these liberated countries and of the Free Governments which will be erected therein" (ibid.). All told, the number of trials undertaken in the aftermath of World War II was historically unprecedented (Deák et al. 2000; Marcuse 2001).[9]

The International Military Tribunal (IMT) that conducted proceedings in Nuremberg, Germany, between October 1945 and October 1946 is the most well-known of the many postwar trials. The IMT was presided over by judges from the four occupying Allied powers. Nuremberg was chosen for its symbolic importance as the place where the infamous Nuremberg Laws were passed (see Chapter 2). The term "Nuremberg trials" is often used to refer to several different criminal proceedings, but it is most commonly associated with the trial of twenty-four defendants who were chosen because they were "the most important surviving principal[s] in [their] domain of responsibilities and activities" (Rosenbaum 1993:19).[10] Hermann Göring was arguably the most infamous luminary on the list of defendants. Adolph Hitler and Heinrich Himmler would have been among the most notable Nazis to be prosecuted if they had not committed suicide before they could be apprehended. After his capture Joseph Goebbels committed suicide as well.

There was some initial disagreement among the Allies as to the purpose of the trials. The British wanted to summarily execute the defendants, while the Soviets wanted to use the trial solely to establish the appropriate punishments though not to determine questions of guilt or innocence. In contrast, U.S. Supreme Court Justice Robert Jackson, who was appointed to head the U.S. prosecution team, believed that the trial should be more than a showcase for the victors to engage in collective acts of retribution. For the IMT to have moral legitimacy, he argued, it must obey the "ultimate principle" that no man should be prosecuted unless "you are willing to see him free if not proved guilty. . . . The world yields no respect to courts that are merely organized to convict" (cited in ibid.:21). Thus there were in fact three acquittals in the IMT proceedings; and two other cases were dropped, one because the defendant was too ill to stand trial and the other because he committed suicide. The remaining nineteen defendants were convicted and twelve were sentenced to death (Mushkat 1990).[11]

The IMT prosecuted individuals under three broad areas of international law: crimes against peace, war crimes, and crimes against humanity. Crimes against peace included "the planning, preparation, initiation, and waging of wars of aggression, or a war in violation of existing treaties, agreements, and assurances" (cited in Marrus 1997:122). War crimes included violations of "the laws and customs of war," including murder, enslavement, and ill-treatment of war prisoners or civilians in occupied territories (ibid.:149). Crimes against humanity included "murder, extermination, enslavement, deportation, and other inhumane acts committed against any civilian population . . . or persecutions on political, racial or religious grounds . . . whether or not in violation of the domestic law of the country where perpetrated" (ibid.:187–88). It was with crimes against humanity that the Nuremberg trials broke new ground, for it was the first time a country was held "internationally responsible for what it did to its own people . . . no matter what its own national laws . . . allowed" (Rosenbaum 1993:34; see also Simpson 1993).

While the particularity of Jewish victimization was acknowledged at the IMT, it was subsumed under the broader categories of war crimes and crimes against humanity and soon half forgotten (Hilberg 1991; Osiel 1997). And except for the defendants, Germans did not participate in the proceedings. According to Judith Miller (1990), this absence conveyed an impression of separation between Nazis and other Germans, as if Germany itself had been occupied by a foreign element that had imposed its will on a reluctant population. Thus the guilt of a select few absolved the many of their responsibility and allowed them to put the war behind them.[12] Moreover, no representative of German industry was included among the high-profile IMT defendants. Although some businessmen were convicted and imprisoned in other proceedings, they were released after a few years (Domansky 1997; Judt 2000; Rubenstein & Roth 1987).

Most of the defendants in the postwar trials pleaded not guilty to the charges against them and made appeals to defeasibility:

> They had known a little about what was happening but not too much; it was too dangerous to know more. They had only been following orders and had served their country faithfully. Besides, the conditions in the camps weren't al-

ways that bad. And they had tried their best to save as many as they could. Without them more would have been killed. Why should they be singled out? If they were guilty, who in fact was innocent?

In such claims, the myth of the "good Nazi" was born. Decent men who had done their best during difficult times now claimed to be victims of postwar injustice (Deák 2000a; Johnson 1999; Marcuse 2001).

Nevertheless, the Allies did not rest with criminal prosecutions. They also instituted a policy of German "denazification" in an attempt to cleanse Germany of its disreputable elements. Denazification was first articulated by the United States, Great Britain, and the Soviet Union at the Yalta Conference six months before the end of the war. The conference generated a joint statement whereby by the countries agreed

> to wipe out the Nazi Party, Nazi laws, organizations, and institutions, remove all Nazi and militarist influences from public office and from the cultural and economic life of the German people, and take such other agreed measures in Germany as may be necessary for the future peace and safety of the world. (cited in Ruckerl 1990a:359)

At the war's end about 240,000 Germans were placed under mandatory arrest and interned in camps. Some Germans complained, in an unsympathetic counterrhetoric of relativity, that the conditions in these camps were worse than the camps Germany had operated during the war, and that the denazification program was "an attempt to exterminate National Socialists as people with differing political opinions" (quoted in Marcuse 2001:102).

In 1946 the Allies drew up denazification guidelines that identified the "offices and positions from which former Nazis were barred" (Ruckerl 1990a:361).[13] The designees were distributed into varying categories based on their perceived degree of culpability, and different punishments were specified, which included imprisonment, loss of employment, confiscation of property, loss of pension rights, special deductions from income taxes, and restrictions on voting rights. "Had these guidelines been observed, the denazification measures would have been much harsher than they were in practice" (ibid.). In actuality, however, the program resulted in "an ever-increasing number of 'Germans'" being included on the side of the innocent and "an ever-decreasing number of 'Nazis'" being included on the side of the guilty (Domansky 1997:246; see also Marcuse 2001; Simpson 1993).

At the same time, the emerging cold war between the Western Allies and the Soviet Union dramatically changed the postwar political context and resulted in a curtailment and then a complete abandonment of denazification over the next few years. The Western Allies and the Soviets could not agree on the type of political-economic system that should be set up in postwar Germany. The United States, Great Britain and France, of course, favored a capitalist-style democracy, while the Soviets favored a Communist-style regime. The three Western nations combined forces and consolidated their control over their zones of occupation, and the Soviet Union entrenched its position in the east. In 1949 Germany was officially divided into two nations: the FRG, also known as West Germany, and the German Democratic Republic, also known as East Germany. This division lasted until the end of the cold war, when East Germany became part of the FRG in 1990 (Marcuse 2001; Ruckerl 1990a; Simpson 1993).

The Soviets were the first to abandon denazification. They viewed Nazism and fascism as logical outcomes of Western capitalism and credited German Communists with spearheading the antifascist resistance that had occurred during the Nazi era (Domansky 1997; Herf 1997; Judt 2000). East Germany was now seen as a bulwark against the resurgence of Nazism in Germany, and in the East-German collective memory that was subsequently constructed, the persecution of Jews became a minor theme in the great debates about capitalism/fascism versus communism/antifascism.[14] According to Jeffrey Herf:

> The German Communists rightly drew attention to sufferings that the Nazis inflicted on the Soviet Union, and to the enormous contribution made by the [Soviet] Army to the defeat of Nazi Germany. Yet though they presented themselves as the representatives of the persecuted and oppressed, their memories of resistance reflected the realities of [the cold war]. (1994:293)

In the West the cold war also took precedence over further attempts to denazify Germany. Up to that point U.S. Secretary of Treasury Henry Morgenthau, Jr., had been a leading proponent of dismantling the German corporate structure, which had supported the Nazis and been complicit in the Final Solution. Secretary of State George Marshall, on the other hand, placed priority on reintegrating the FRG into the postwar capitalist economy, and it was this view that prevailed. The West needed German industrialists with financial resources and technical and administrative expertise, whatever their Nazi past, to help rebuild the West German economy. In addition, the North Atlantic Treaty Organization (NATO), the military alliance of Western nations that was established in 1949, needed to count on West Germany to oppose the bloc of Eastern-European nations that were controlled by the Soviet Union. Thus there was little interest in implicating the Germany military in the crimes it had committed in the eastern territories of Nazi-occupied Europe (Bartov 1997a; Simpson 1993; see Chapter 3).

Moreover, the U.S. government even helped hundreds of Nazi war criminals avoid prosecution and escape to safe havens. Nazis from Germany and other collaborating governments who claimed expertise about the Soviet Union were recruited as intelligence agents. German scientists from the wartime armaments program that had utilized slave labor were given false identity papers and brought to the United States to work in the U.S. rocket program. Vatican officials, who were fervently anticommunist, assisted in these efforts, providing Nazis temporary refuge in Italy and helping them emigrate to South America. Adolph Eichmann was among them. It was not until 1960 when Israeli intelligence agents, aided by information about Eichmann's whereabouts that had been provided by Wiesenthal's Documentation Center, seized Eichmann in Argentina and brought him to Israel to stand trial (Rosenbaum 1993; Simpson 1988, 1993).

In the early postwar years the Allies supervised West Germany's political and economic reconstruction and provided millions of dollars in U.S. aid. With the 1949 election of Chancellor Konrad Adenauer (1876–1967), leader of the Christian Democratic Union (CDU), the new Germany began to distinguish itself from its Nazi past and seek legitimacy as an equal partner in the community of Western democratic-capitalist nations. But all this was achieved at the cost of Germans' reluctance to meaningfully confront the moral implications and broader social responsibility of their country's Nazi past. Thus very little about the Nazi period was taught in West German schools, and Germans rarely mentioned the former Nazi affiliations of major figures in business and politics.[15] Nevertheless, the tainted memory of the Nazi era continued to mar Germany's national identity and international legitimacy within the community of Western nations (Fox 2001; Herf 1997; Krondorfer 1995; Marcuse 2001).

Restitution and the Rhetoric of Reconciliation

In the early postwar years, attempts at bridging the victim-victimizer relationship between Israel and West Germany focused on the question of appropriate economic and diplomatic relations between the two nations. Many Israelis continued to equate the new Germany with the old. In their view, conscience, duty, and national honor required no contact with their former enemy. Practical considerations, however, made it difficult for Israel to boycott West Germany. Export of citrus fruit from Palestine to West Germany, for example, which had even taken place under Nazi rule, provided the nation much needed financial currency. Ben-Gurion, who became Israel's first prime minister, also felt that reconciliation with West Germany was necessary for Israel to become a viable member of the Western bloc, which had accepted West Germany as a member. Chancellor Adenauer, in turn, was persuaded that cooperation with Israel would demonstrate his country's repentance and help establish its moral legitimacy. West Germany would benefit economically from trade relations with Israel as well (Herf 1997; Segev 1993; Wolffsohn 1993).

Another point of contention emerged over Jewish proposals that Germany pay restitution for the harm it had caused to Jewish victims during the war. The major players on the Jewish side were the Conference on Jewish Material Claims Against Germany (CJMCAG), an umbrella group that represented major international Jewish organizations, and the Mapai-led Israeli government itself. In a letter of atonement to the CJMCAG, Adenauer demonstrated his willingness to negotiate on this issue: "The honor of the German people requires it do all it can to compensate the Jewish people from the injustice done to it" (cited in Segev 1993:205).[16]

Adenauer's conciliatory position provoked opposition in West Germany. In a counterrhetorical move that proffered a competing claim of victimhood, West German Transport Minister Hans-Christoph Seebohm contested Adenauer's stance and linked the willingness to make restitution to concerns about the spread of communism and the expulsion of millions of ethnic Germans who had been living in territory now under communist rule:[17]

> The question of the possibility of fulfilling the Germany obligation towards the Jews is . . . closely related to the task of securing our people and thus Europe against a further advance of the Bolshevist Asiatic tendency. . . . If I am prepared at the present time to recognize the moral duty of making restitution to the Jews, I can only do so if the other powers in the world are prepared to fulfill their moral duty to make restitution to the Germans expelled from their homeland. (cited in Wolffsohn 1993:17–18)

Nevertheless, Adenauer remained steadfast, adhering to what Michael Wolffsohn (1993) describes as *geschichtspolitik* (the politics of history) rather than to *tagespolitik* (the politics of the day or the routine). In Adenauer's view, willingness to atone and pay restitution was in West Germany's national interest, for it would send an important symbolic message to the international community. But even before negotiations over specific financial arrangements could take place, the Israelis demanded that Adenauer make a public declaration of contrition in an official ceremony of some sort. Ben-Gurion believed that such a declaration was necessary to overcome opposition within Israel. The ceremonial act that Adenauer agreed to was a speech he made before the West German Bundestag (parliament) in September 1951. The precise words that he uttered were the result of a protracted set of negotiations with representatives of the Israeli government, a series of drafts and counterdrafts that constituted an exchange of sympathetic counterrhetorics. It was important to reach rhetorical agreement on precisely how much blame and responsibility should be placed on Germany (Segev 1993).

The Israelis wanted Adenauer to acknowledge the guilt of the German people. In an early draft, Adenauer explicitly rejected the thesis of German collective responsibility, but he agreed to say that "unspeakable crimes have been committed in the name of the German people" (cited in ibid:202–4). While Adenauer was willing to admit that "people had been killed," the Israelis insisted that he say "innocent people." And when Adenauer said that "limited circles . . . engaging in anti-Semitic agitation" still existed in Germany, the Israelis had him replace "circles" with "groups." He refused but was willing to drop "limited."

The Israelis asked Adenauer to specify that Germany would make financial amends not only for property loss but for "general injury done to the Jewish people." Adenauer agreed to call "for moral and material indemnity, both with regard to the individual harm done to the Jews and with regard to the Jewish property for which no legitimate individual claimants still exist." Adenauer also said that Germany would pay within its "limited" ability. The Israelis asked that "limited" be removed. And when Adenauer admitted that "much remains to be done," the Israelis wanted him to replace "much" with "most." Adenauer agreed to "very much."

In addition, Adenauer hoped to pronounce that West Germany was part of the Western bloc that defended the world against communism. The Israelis asked him to soft-pedal this point so as not to antagonize leftist parties within Israel. An early draft had spoken of crimes committed in "territories occupied by the German army." Reference to the "German army" was removed, without Israeli objection, so as to minimize the guilt of the military.

Adenauer's speech was well received by the Bundestag. In Israel, however, reconciliation with Germany was vehemently contested. Menacham Begin, leader of the Herut party, was the most vocal opponent. (Begin was a Holocaust survivor who had emigrated to Palestine in 1942 and had been a leader of the armed opposition against the British.) In a counterrhetorical and rather melodramatic speech to the Israeli Knesset (parliament), Begin raised the specter of martyrdom and challenged Mapai as the rightful heir of Holocaust, and hence Israeli, memory:

> There are things in life that are worse than death itself, . . . for which we are ready to die. . . . Nations . . . have gone to the barricades for lesser matters. . . . [W]e the last generation of slaves and the first of the redeemed . . . are prepared to do anything . . . to prevent negotiations with our parents' murderers. . . . May God help us prevent this Holocaust of our people, in the name of our future, in the name of our honor. (quoted in ibid. 1993:219–20)

Nevertheless, Begin's moralism did not prevail over Ben-Gurion's pragmatism. Even most survivors were willing to accept the restitution money, and Israel profited from its economic ties with West Germany.

ISRAELI COLLECTIVE MEMORY

As noted earlier, during the War of Independence the Holocaust was not a central component of Israeli collective memory. Over the years, however, the Holocaust began to play an increasingly influential role. In this section I trace the construction of Israeli Holocaust memory in domestic and international political context as it evolved through the creation of the state's central Holocaust memorial, through two major postwar trials, and through postwar conflicts in the Middle East. I will also show how the Israeli memory-nation has been constructed through the rhetoric of victimization discourse.

Yad Vashem

The Jews are a people for whom memory has always been important. In his study of Holocaust memorials, James Young writes:

> Memory of historical events and the narratives delivering this memory have always been central to Jewish faith, tradition, and identity. . . . Throughout Torah, the Jews are enjoined not only to remember their history but to observe the rituals of faith through remembrance: "Remember the days of old, consider the years of ages past" (Deut. 32:7). . . . "Remember this day, on which you went free from Egypt, the house of bondage, how the Lord freed you from it with a mighty hand." (Ex. 13:3) (1993:209–10)

Thus it was easy for Israelis to view the foundation of their new state as religiously ordained, as redeeming the Diaspora Jews from a life in exile. The Jewish people, "despite spatial dispersion and temporal ruptures had preserved its common identity" and after years of suffering—most recently in the Holocaust—had finally returned home to its birth place in the Land of Israel (Ram 1995:92; see also Shapira 1995, 1997).

At the same time, it was Zionism not Jewish theology that constrained the way in which the Holocaust was incorporated into Israeli collective memory. Nowhere is this more true than with Yad Vashem ("Everlasting Name"), "The Memorial Authority for the Martyrs and Heroes of the Holocaust." Yad Vashem was first proposed by Mordecai Shenhabi at a board meeting of the Jewish National Fund (JNF) as early as 1942 (Segev 1993). Shenhabi proffered pragmatic arguments couched in a rhetoric of calamity. While attempting to persuade the JNF that it needed a new fund-raising cause to finance the absorption of immigrants and the purchase of land for settlement in Palestine, Shenhabi argued that "we are obligated to perpetuate the memory of the century's greatest catastrophe within the framework of our Zionist enterprise" (cited in ibid.:428). At that time JNF board members were concerned that the project would detract for other fund-raising efforts; and they also expressed reservations about the profitability of such an investment. They did, however, exchange views regarding appropriate ways to memorialize the Holocaust, that is, what was permitted and what was forbidden. These commemorative agents felt that a memorial should not be entirely negative but should promote the forward-looking optimism of the Zionist movement.

Plans for Yad Vashem were renewed after Israel was established. Shenhabi's argument was now less pragmatic, emphasizing instead that a memorial should be designed to establish the link between the particularity of Jewish victimization during the war and the moral entitlement of the Jewish people to a nation of their own. Shenhabi persuaded top Jewish officials that a competing proposal for a Holocaust memorial in Paris would not be in Israel's national interest. Israeli Minister of Education Ben-Zion Dunur concurred when he told Ben-Gurion that the proposed Paris memorial was an indication of "the Diaspora instinct" that would "give Paris the place of Jerusalem" and weaken Israel's international position (cited in ibid.:431).

In 1953 the Israeli Knesset unanimously passed the Yad Vashem Law, which established Yad Vashem with a mandate to explicitly link the memory of Jewish victimization with the memory of Jewish heroism. In Shmuel Spector's words, Yad Vashem was designed to

> commemorate the six million Jews murdered by the Nazis and their helpers; the Jewish communities and their institutions that had been liquidated and destroyed; the valor and heroism of the soldiers, the fighters of the underground, and the prisoners in the ghettos; the sons and daughters of the Jewish people who had struggled for their human dignity; and the "Righteous among the Nations" who had risked their lives in order to save Jews. (1990c:1683)

The law also assigned Yad Vashem the task of creating memorial projects, collecting and publishing testimonies of the Holocaust and the heroism of that period, granting commemorative citizenship to the victims, and representing Israel in international projects regarding Holocaust memory. Since the 1960s Israeli officials have taken important guests of state on a mandatory visit to the memorial; and conscripts in the Israeli army and Israeli school children are taken regularly as well (Cole 1999; Novick 1999; Shapira 1995).

However, an important subtext of this martyrdom-heroism interpretive motif was the implicit contrast between the Diaspora Jews, who had known only helplessness and destruction, and the Israeli Jews, who had fought for their independence and self-preservation. The victims of the Holocaust were to be remembered because they demonstrated the need for fighters, while the fighters were to be remembered for having secured the Jewish state that had redeemed the Jewish people (Segev 1993; Young 1993).

The Kasztner and Eichmann Trials

Two postwar trials in Israel marked the next significant events in the political construction of Israeli Holocaust memory. The Kasztner trial had primarily domestic repercussions, while the Eichmann trial had both domestic and international implications.

The Kasztner trial involved a libel suit initiated by Rezso Kasztner, the director of the Israeli Department of Public Relations in the Ministry of Trade and Industry. In 1952 Malkiel Gruenwald, a Hungarian Holocaust survivor, published a pamphlet charging Kasztner with collaborating with the Nazis when he served as head of the Jewish Rescue Committee in Hungary during the war (see Chapter 4). Gruenwald accused Kasztner of negotiating a deal with the Nazis for the release of Hungarian Jews in exchange for ransom money. Gruenwald claimed that Kasztner, who had ties with the Mapai party during the war, used his influence to save only those Jews he favored—those who were affiliated with Mapai, those who could pay their own way, and his own relatives. He also accused Kasztner of pocketing some of the money (Bauer 1994; Gouri 1994; Segev 1993; Weitz 1994).

The Herut party seized upon the accusation to resurrect prewar resentments over Mapai's selective immigration policies and its failure to rescue European Jews. Kasztner was advised by officials of the Mapai government either to agree to enter a libel suit or resign. Kasztner reluctantly agreed to the suit. At the trial Gruenwald's attorney, Shmuel Tamir, an ultraconservative lawyer, took the opportunity not only to defend his client but to attack Mapai's actions during the war. Tamir accused the Mapai leadership of having withheld the truth of the Nazis' extermination program from the Jewish people and hence of encouraging Jewish passivity and forestalling resistance efforts. In his view Mapai—like the Jewish Councils of Nazi Europe—had not done enough to save Jews and had passively complied if not actively collaborated with the enemy.

Gruenwald received a favorable ruling from the judge in the libel case, who concluded that "Kasztner [had] sold his soul to Satan" (quoted in Weitz 1994:351). Although this decision was later overturned by the Israeli Supreme Court, the whole affair was the first major blow to the Mapai leadership, and according to one Mapai official, "the first time that a large number of Israelis lost confidence in the establishment" (quoted in Segev 1993:280).[18] In the next election campaign, Herut proclaimed that Mapai constituted an enemy from within: "When you vote Mapai, you vote for a Jew who turned Jews over to the Gestapo" (quoted in ibid.:287).

Self-righteous politicians employing unsympathetic victimization counter-rhetorics were in no short supply on either side of the Israeli political spectrum. They increasingly contested the memory of the Holocaust to prove to voters that the opposition political party was the real villain of the Nazi era. However, while some criticized Mapai (and the Jewish Councils) for discouraging resistance during the war, others asked whether the Jewish partisans who had advocated resistance had not also sent Jews to their deaths. According to Tom Segev:

Many Israelis took it on themselves to judge the Jews of the Holocaust as if it were within their abilities and as if it were their right to do so. These are the heroes, these are the cowards, these are worthy of glory, these of disgrace. . . . This was a debate over the value of rebellion as a symbol to be handed down to future generations. (ibid.:290, 297)

Following the Kasztner affair, the 1961 trial of Adolf Eichmann was an opportunity for Mapai to reassert domestic political control over the legacy of the Holocaust (Osiel 1997; Segev 1993).[19] Internationally it was an opportunity to remind the world of the particularity of Jewish victimization (which had at times been obscured by the Nuremberg trials) and to build international support for Israel. Thus it was Ben-Gurion's view that the purpose of the trial was not simply to punish Eichmann but to bring the entire Holocaust before the court. It was an occasion for building national pride and for highlighting not only Jewish suffering but, more importantly, Jewish resistance. According to Attorney General Gideon Hausner, the prosecutor in the Eichmann case, "Here was an opportunity to bring before the entire world the hundreds and thousands of heroic deeds that were not generally known" (cited in Segev 1993:353). Both Jews and non-Jews would be reminded that Israel was the only country in the world that could guarantee Jewish security, that it was a nation of people who were ready and able to defend themselves, and that Jews would never again be led like "lambs to the slaughter."

When Nahum Goldmann, president of the World Zionist Organization, came out in support of trying Eichmann in an international rather than Israeli court, Ben-Gurion was outraged. Goldmann argued that "since Eichmann and the Nazis exterminated not only Jews, it would be worthwhile to invite those countries, many of whose citizens were also killed by him, to send their own judges" (cited in ibid.:329). Ben-Gurion responded in an evocative rhetoric of loss and calamity:

> The Holocaust . . . is not like other atrocities . . . [of] the Nazis . . . but a unique episode that has no equal, an attempt to totally destroy the Jewish people. . . . It is the particular duty of the State of Israel, the Jewish people's only sovereign entity, to recount this episode in its full magnitude and horror, without ignoring the Nazi regime's other crimes against humanity—but not as one of these crimes, rather as the only crime that has no parallel in human history. (cited in ibid.:329–30)

Conflict in the Middle East

Throughout Israel's history most of the Arab community has rejected the legitimacy of its existence. In 1954, for instance, the king of Saudi Arabia threatened that "Israel to the Arab world is like a cancer to the human body, and the only remedy is to uproot it, just like a cancer" (quoted in Dershowitz 1991:214). In 1956, in response to attacks from Palestinian commandos aided and financed by Egypt, Israel invaded and occupied Egyptian territory to the west in the Sinai Peninsula and the Gaza Strip. Politicians of both the Israeli left and right were united in their opposition to Egyptian president Gamal Abdel Nasser, whom they rhetorically described with "fascist" and "Nazi" motifs. In response to international condemnation for their military actions, Israeli politicians countered with memories of the Holocaust: "A million and a half young people and children were slaughtered in broad daylight, and the world's conscience was not moved. But now that the Jews are gathered in to the State of Israel, the outside world cannot give its consent" (quoted in Segev 1993:297). Israel acquiesced, however, when both the United States and the Soviet Union pressured it to withdraw from the occupied territories (Johnson 1987; Segev 1993; Wolff-sohn 1993).

Tensions in the Middle East soared again in 1967, as Arab spokesmen once again rhetorically evoked the specter of calamity and endangerment by promising to "wipe Israel off the map" and "drive the Jews into the sea" (quoted in Novick 1999:148). When Nasser began amassing Egyptian troops in the Sinai Peninsula, Israel launched a preemptive air strike. Syria and Jordan, which had signed defense pacts with Egypt, then attacked Israel. Israel emerged victorious in a war that lasted just six days, and it reoccupied the Sinai Peninsula and Gaza Strip and took control of territory in the Golan Heights (from Syria) and the West Bank (from Jordan) to the east. In Israel this Six Day War has often been compared to the six days of creation, and the Israeli soldiers' fighting spirit that led to their decisive victory has been attributed to their memory of the Holocaust (Segev 1993).

In 1973 full-scale war broke out again when Egyptian and Syrian troops attacked Israeli positions in the occupied territories on Yom Kippur, the holiest day in the Jewish year. Although Israel won the Yom Kippur War, "the victory came only after serious and terrifying early reverses and after substantial Israeli casualties" (Novick 1999:151; see also Sachar 1992). Escape from disaster was due in large measure to a massive U.S. resupply operation that provided Israel with crucial weaponry. Israel was thus left feeling vulnerable and, with the important exception of the United States, increasingly isolated in the international community. On November 10, 1975, the United Nations, whose membership was now "dominated by . . . non-European countries recently liberated from European" colonialism, passed a resolution proclaiming that Zionism was a form of "racism" (Novick 1999:154). November 10, 1938, had been the night of *Kristallnacht*, and the insult of the coincidental date enraged the Jews even more (Roiphe 1988).

This is not to say that there have not been positive developments in Israeli-Arab relations over the years. A 1979 peace treaty between Israeli and Egypt, for example, that was negotiated with the help of U.S. president Jimmy Carter, ended the conflict between these two nations and led to Israel's withdrawal from the Sinai. At the same time, the vivid experience of genuine threats to Israel's security opened the door to ever greater use of the Holocaust as a rhetorical motif in Israel (Marrus 1991). Begin, for instance, who helped build the Likud party (center-right) coalition that carried him to power as prime minister in 1977, often referred to Israel's pre-1967 borders as "Auschwitz lines." He compared Palestine Liberation Organization (PLO) leader Yasir Arafat to Hitler and the PLO's Palestinian National Covenant to *Mein Kampf*: "Never in the history of mankind has there been an armed organization so loathsome and contemptible, with the exception of the Nazis" (quoted in Segev 1993:399).[20] Just prior to Israel's controversial 1982 invasion of Lebanon, which Israel undertook in response to Palestinian terrorist attacks, Begin rhetorically characterized his view of his country's predicament: "There is no way other than to fight selflessly. . . . [T]he alternative is Treblinka, and . . . there will be no more Treblinkas. . . . No one, anywhere in the world, can preach morality to our people" (quoted in ibid.).

Ironically, the Holocaust has also become a rhetorical resource for Israel's adversaries, as Arab spokespersons and their allies have used unsympathetic counterrhetorics to turn the memory of the Holocaust back against the Jews. For example, in a 1989 issue of *El-Istiqlal*, a Cyprus-based Palestinian journal, Khalad El-Shamali claimed that the Holocaust is Zionist propaganda that is used to "legitimize the new [Israeli] Nazism" and that "Nazi camps were more 'civilized' than Israeli prisons" (cited in ADL 1993:60). According to Anne Roiphe, such counterrhetoric aims to "take away from Jews the justification of history for their new nation" (1988:166).

In Israel the rhetorical use of the Holocaust was also omnipresent during the Kuwait crisis and the Persian Gulf War of 1990–1991, when Germany resurfaced as the object of Israeli indignation (Segev 1993; Wolffsohn 1993). Saddam Hussein, whom Israelis (and Americans) equated with Hitler, had developed about 90 percent of his chemical-weapons capability with the help of German firms (Walker 1994). The Israeli press was filled with articles and letters that compared the now-unified Germany with the Nazi regime; and a demonstration was held outside the German embassy in Tel Aviv. As Iraq attacked Israel with missiles, the Israeli civil-defense authorities distributed gas masks to the citizenry. In an article in *Yediot Aharonot,* Noah Klieger accused Germany of victimizing the Jews once again: "I did not survive the Auschwitz death camp . . . in order . . . to walk around an independent Jewish state with antigas equipment, against gas developed and manufactured by Germans" (cited in Segev 1993:506).[21]

The 1992 election that brought Labor party leader Yitzhak Rabin to power as prime minister, and the subsequent 1993 Israeli-Palestinian Peace Accord negotiated in Oslo with the PLO, did not lessen the use of Holocaust memory in Israeli political rhetoric.[22] At speeches during the White House peace accord ceremony and before the Israeli Knesset, Rabin summarized the basic outlook of the Israeli memory-nation:

It is certainly not easy for the families of the victims of the wars, violence, terror whose pain will never heal; for the many thousands who defended our lives with their own and have even sacrificed their lives for our own. For them, this ceremony has come too late. . . . In one hundred years of settlement, this Land [of Israel] has known great suffering—and blood. We, who returned home after 2,000 years of exile—after the Holocaust that sent the best of the Jewish people to the ovens; we who searched for calm after the storm, a place to rest our heads, we extended a hand to our neighbors—and it was rejected time after time. And our soul did not tire of seeking peace. (quoted in Roth 1993:79–80)

Up to this point in the Israeli-Palestinian dispute, however, every movement toward peace has been accompanied by a return to violence on both sides. In addition, younger left-wing historians in Israel have launched a challenge to the traditional state-sponsored memory that claims that Palestinian intransigence and terrorism are the main obstacles to lasting peace (Arad 1995; Podeh 2000). These so-called New Historians have characterized Israel as a colonial power that has enforced its will, often brutally, on an oppressed Palestinian people whom they depict "as passive victims of Zionist aggression and manipulation" (Brunner 1997:291). They have tried "to efface the impact of the Holocaust on Israeli identity" and have called for a return to the pre-1967 borders (Shapira 1995:19). They note that the Israeli-Palestinian "controversy concerns a national conflict whose violence does not belong only to the past, but also to the present and, unfortunately, . . . its future as well" (Brunner 1997:290).

WEST GERMAN COLLECTIVE MEMORY

As the loser of World War II, Germany was stigmatized internationally and forced to endure (until 1990) the punishment of a divided nation. German national identity has been fractured by its complementary and oppositional relationship with the Jews, whom Germans once "blamed for the traumas of modernity, . . . as the signifier of ruptures and disturbances one would like to banish from the inside," but who have now been "displaced by the event of their own destruction" (Santner 1990:281–82; see also Krondorfer 1995; Olick & Levy 1997).

Like Israeli collective memory, the West German memory-nation has drawn upon the rhetoric of victimization discourse. However, German memory has been on the defensive, and Germans have been inclined to use counterrhetorical strategies that make appeals to defeasibility by normalizing or relativizing the Holocaust. Germans have also engaged in victim contests and made claims to their own entitlements. In this section I trace the construction of West German memory in domestic and international political context as the nation worked through its feelings of repentance, struggled with the legacy of resistance and postwar political dissent, and politicized academic historical debates.

Back to the Future: From Repentance to Self-Assertion

If Jewish victimization in the Holocaust was unique, as the Israelis maintained, was not German responsibility for this victimization unique as well? Shortly after Eichmann was arrested, Chancellor Adenauer contacted Ben-Gurion to express his concern that the trial would reawaken anti-German sentiment around the world. Adenauer was thus pleased when Attorney General Hausner, at Ben-Gurion's request, chose his rhetoric at the trial carefully and referred not to the "crimes of Germany" but to the "crimes of Nazi Germany" (Seger 1993:346). And when Hausner described the Holocaust as but one manifestation of a long history of anti-Jewish persecution that had begun in ancient times, Adenauer was pleased that Germany had not been singled out. However, it was events in West Germany, not Israel, that would raise controversy over the particularity of the perpetrators during the Holocaust.[23]

Adenauer's conciliatory approach toward Israel, which had prevailed against internal German opposition to restitution, had paid dividends. In 1959, when a former German intelligence officer, now a West German cabinet minister, was implicated in a murderous episode during World War II, Ben-Gurion openly declared his belief that the "new Germany" had overcome its Nazi past. Ben-Gurion even offered to appear publicly with Adenauer, who was advised by his foreign minister that the potential damage of such an appearance to German-Arab relations was more significant than any historical obligation to Israel. During the 1950s even the Western allies, who had been losing influence in the Arab world to the Soviet Union, had urged West Germany not to damage its relations with the Arab states. Adenauer, however, was also reluctant to jeopardize the improved relations with Israel. He declined the public appearance but met privately with Ben-Gurion. Yet Ben-Gurion's support was not without a price, as West Germany agreed to provide financial and military aid to Israel (Wolffsohn 1993).

In 1962 news of German rocket technicians working (as private citizens) in Egypt surfaced. Israel demanded that Adenauer force them to return to West Germany. Adenauer refused, explaining that a democratic government could not tell its citizens where they could work or live. Levi Eshkol, Ben-Gurion's successor as prime minister, retorted that "German weapons experts were once again endangering Israel's security" (ibid.:25). The technicians were eventually withdrawn—lured back to Germany with attractive job offers—but the atmosphere between Israel and Germany had become tainted once again.

By the 1960s West Germans were beginning to express an increasing self-assertiveness, what Wolffsohn describes as a "we-are-somebody-again" attitude that was indicative of Germans' desire to extricate themselves from the burden of their historical past (ibid.:26). After acceding to another request to provide assistance to Israel, the new chancellor Ludwig Erhard claimed that "we do not have a perpetual obligation to supply arms to Israel" (quoted in ibid.:27). West Germany wanted to stake out a position of neutrality in the Middle East and did not want to jeopardize Germany's export and oil interests by antagonizing the Arabs. Increasingly, West German political leaders began to steer a foreign policy with Israel without the symbolism of atonement. The victim-victimizer relationship between the two nations had to be severed. History was no longer to be used as a political instrument against what was now an unquestionably democratic and economically prosperous nation (Benz 1994; Geyer & Hansen 1994; Krondorfer 1995; Olick & Levy 1997).

The Legacy of Resistance and Critique from the Left

A 1952 public opinion poll taken in West Germany found that only 20 percent of the respondents believed that Hitler's opponents should have resisted during the war, 34 percent thought that the resisters should have waited until after the war was over, and 15 percent felt there should have been no resistance at all (Large 1994). Survivors of the German wartime resistance complained that they had not been accorded the same degree of influence in political parties and in government as those who had "wintered over" during the Nazi years (ibid.:246). Though Adenauer was included in the latter group, he had not been a Nazi supporter and understood that political capital could be gained from identifying himself with the resistance legacy. At the tenth anniversary of the 1944 assassination attempt on Hitler (see Chapter 4), Adenauer took the opportunity to enter West Germany into the international competition for postwar victimhood and martyrdom. In a speech at the newly constituted Foreign Office (FO), he declared that former FO resisters had "given their lives . . . so that the unjustifiable condemnation [of the FO] at home and abroad might be reversed" (quoted in ibid.:246–47). He also made note of FO officials who "had urged the Western powers to stand up to Hitler" and not appease him at Munich. This counterrhetorical appeal to defeasibility attempted to share or shift the blame for the "other [Nazi] Germany" onto the Allies. President Eugen Gerstenmaier added, in a speech on the same occasion, "The blood of the martyred resisters has cleansed our German name of the shame which Hitler cast upon us" (quoted in ibid.:247).

At the same time, the cold war climate significantly skewed political characterizations of the resistance movement. Domestically CDU leaders downplayed the significant resistance efforts of the political left, especially the Communists, and exaggerated the degree to which conservative institutions, like the FO and ecumenical organizations, represented the anti-Nazi resistance. The left, in turn, proclaimed its right to carry the banner of heroism and lead Germany in its quest for a positive postwar national identity. According to Kurt Schumacher, leader of the Social Democratic party until his death in 1952, "We Socialists would have been the resisters even if the Americans and the British had become fascists" (quoted in ibid.:250).[24]

Christopher Simpson (1993) adds that the German left actually played a greater role in the postwar denazification of Germany than any other German group. After the war, left-wing antifascist groups "organized local unions known as *Betriebsrats* (work councils) that took over management of hundreds of companies, particularly larger factories," driving out Nazi-era boards of directors and personnel managers, Nazi activists, and Gestapo informers (ibid.:247). However, the radical politics of the work councils disturbed the occupying Western governments, which "moved quickly to suppress" them (ibid.:248).

In the 1960s a countervailing trend in German memory construction emerged with the left-wing student protest movement that had developed in West Germany as well as other Western nations. The West German student left challenged what they perceived as their elders' silence regarding the country's Nazi past, and they called into question the older generation's commitment to democratic institutions. Employing "fascism" as a general rhetorical motif, the left claimed that the West German government was still run by "fascists," a charge that was also leveled by protesters in other Western countries against their governments, including the United States. The protesters claimed, in a rhetoric of relativity, that the "fascism" of the postwar democracies was comparable to the fascism of the 1930s, though perhaps more subtle and technologically sophisticated. Similarly, the genocide of World War II was comparable to more recent military campaigns such as the United States' involvement in the Vietnam War. Thus Germans had to remain constantly on guard against future "holocausts," especially a nuclear one that was a possible consequence of U.S. imperialism (Brunner 1997; Marcuse 2001; Markovits 1990; Miller 1990).

In another unsympathetic counterrhetorical move, the German left turned the politics of victimization back against Israel, especially after the Israeli victory in the Six Day War (Krondorfer 1995; Marcuse 2001). According to the left, perhaps "the Israelis were in fact the new 'Nazis' and their victims, . . . the Palestinians, the new 'Jews'" (Markovits 1990:271). Perhaps Zionism was a "fascist" political formation comparable to National Socialism. Thus the left (in West Germany and elsewhere) not only questioned Israel's policies but the very legitimacy of its existence. Roiphe characterizes this view:

> If Zionists are no better than Nazis, then the basis of granting the new state its legality is eroded away and all the world can join together in taking back this

gift of guilt . . . because the Jews have demonstrated that they are not victims but brutes. . . . [They] no longer have a moral club to wield over anyone else. Now they are wielding real clubs like everyone else. (1988:166, 170)

The Politics of Historiography

The political climate of the 1960s helped break the silence of West German academic historiography regarding the Nazi period. Prior to that time, West German historians generally viewed Nazism as a historical accident that was disharmonious with the general thrust of German history. Gradually a younger generation of historians initiated a scholarly inquiry into the structural and ideological dimensions of Nazism, including the role of the bureaucracy, although controversial topics such as the complicity of the German army, the professional and scientific communities, and the citizenry at large did not receive close attention until the late 1970s. Significantly, the younger historians, who identified with the liberal/social-democratic wing that dominated West German politics for a time, began to contextualize the Nazi period in terms of the evolution of German nationalism and its militaristic and antidemocratic traditions (Evans 1989; Friedlander 1993; Marcuse 2001; Miller 1990; see Chapter 1).

In 1983 West Germans commemorated the fiftieth anniversary of the Nazis' seizure of power with a plethora of media coverage, exhibitions, and conferences. But the unprecedented negative significance given to this historical event raised doubts among conservatives about the wisdom of confronting the country's past in this way, for rarely does a nation call upon itself to acknowledge its villainous side. Five years earlier historian Hellmut Diwald had published his *Geschichte der Deutschen* (History of the Germans), which advanced a competing claim of victimhood by arguing that Germany's past had been unjustifiably "morally disqualified" (cited in Evans 1989:15). Diwald sought to restore a popular history of Germany that celebrated the national glory of its pre-Nazi past and that devoted little more than two pages to the atrocities committed by the Nazi regime, especially against the Jews.

Diwald's book was not well received when it was first published, but the ascendancy of Chancellor Helmut Kohl's conservative (center-right) coalition in 1982 marked a change in West Germany's political climate. According to Kohl, West Germany had paid its debt to the Jews and to the international community. It was now time for Germans "to stand up and take their rightful place in the struggle for Western freedom and democratic values" (Miller 1990:45). Public opinion polls indicated that Germans at that time were less proud of being German, for example, than Americans were of being American. Michael Stürmer, a professor of history who advised Kohl on historical matters, wrote a series of newspaper articles arguing that Germans needed a positive sense of their historical past to provide cohesiveness to the country and that those who wished to undermine German's national self-confidence were collaborating with the Eastern bloc (Evans 1989, 1991).

In 1984 Western leaders met to celebrate the fiftieth anniversary of the landing at Normandy, France, the site of the Allied invasion of Europe that marked the beginning of the last campaign of World War II (Hilberg 1986). Chancellor Kohl, who was not invited, was compensated by being asked by French president Francois Mitterand to participate in a ceremonial observance of World War I at a Verdun battlefield cemetery in France. However, Kohl sought to redeem Germany not merely for its role in World War I but for World War II as well. For this purpose he invited Ronald Reagan, president of the United States, to a ceremony at a German military cemetery in Bitburg in May 1985. Reagan agreed to participate because he wanted to support his cold war ally, especially since Kohl had incurred criticism in his country for "allowing NATO to station Cruise missiles and Pershing II rockets on West German soil" (Marcuse 2001:360).

When the White House announced the intended visit to Bitburg "in a spirit of reconciliation, in a spirit of forty years of peace, in a spirit of economic and military compatibility" with West Germany (quoted in Miller 1990:47), it failed to anticipate the forthcoming barrage of criticism, most vocally from the Jewish community but also from U.S. veterans and congressional representatives. Bitburg, it turned out, was the site not only of some two thousand buried German soldiers but about fifty SS men as well (Hartman 1986; Marcuse 2001; Schmitt 1989).

Reagan had initially conferred with Kohl about also visiting the Dachau concentration camp but decided not to go there because he did not want, in his words, to "reawaken the memories . . . and the passions of the time" (quoted in Hilberg 1986:19). After the public outcry about Bitburg, however, he did visit the Bergen-Belsen camp to pay respect to the victims. Still, Reagan only antagonized protesters further when he claimed that the men buried at Bitburg "were victims, just as surely as the victims in the concentration camps" (quoted in Hartman 1986:xiv). Reagan described World War II as a "war against one man's totalitarian dictatorship" and asserted that the German people had an "unnecessary . . . guilt feeling that's been imposed upon them" (quoted in ibid.:xiii, 258). Thus Reagan lent his support to a counterrhetorical construction of the past based on notions of universal victimhood and military martyrdom. As Geoffrey Hartman observes, it was as if Reagan wished "to recall nothing of the past except common sacrifices and a shared code of military honor," as if the behavior of the German military during the war was no different that that of any other armed forces that were fighting for the security of their nation (ibid.:5). But the behavior of the Germany military was in fact different. German troops, as we have seen, were not simply defending the country against a hostile enemy; they helped carry out the Final Solution, turning Jews over to the SS and engaging in mass killings themselves (see

Chapter 3). And even when the troops were not directly involved in the killings, it was the army's conquest of the eastern territories that made the Final Solution possible in the first place (Bartov 1997a; Brunner 1997).

Nonetheless, Chancellor Kohl could not have been more pleased with Reagan's rendition of the past. In a rather brilliant rhetorical slight-of-hand, Kohl used the bodies of dead soldiers at Bitburg to both bury a guilty past and to exalt a noble future for Germany. As he said:

> The President of the United States . . . and I paid homage at the military cemetery . . . at Bitburg . . . to the dead buried there and thus to all victims of war and tyranny, to the dead and persecuted of all nations. . . . Our visit to the soldiers' graves . . . [is] a reaffirmation and a widely visible and widely felt gesture of reconciliation . . . [and] deep friendship . . . between our peoples. (quoted in Hartman 1986:256)

In Germany, Kohl and Reagan's "Bitburg history" did not go unchallenged. Three days later, on the fortieth anniversary of the war's end, the more moderate West German president Richard von Weizacker delivered a counter-rhetorical speech before the Bundestag that urged Germans to take a more honest look at their past:

> We need to have the strength to look truth straight in the eye—without embellishment and without distortion. . . . Who could [have remained] unsuspecting after the burning of the synagogues, the plundering, the stigmatization with the Star of David, the deprivation of rights, the ceaseless violation of human dignity? Whoever opened his eyes and ears and sought information could not fail to notice Jews were being deported. The nature and scope of the destruction may have exceeded human imagination, but in reality there was . . . the attempt . . . not to take note of what was happening. There were many ways of not burdening one's conscience, of shunning responsibility, looking away, keeping mum. When the unspeakable truth of the Holocaust then became known at the end of the war, all too many of us claimed that we had not known anything about it or even suspected anything. (cited in ibid.:262, 265)

Following the Bitburg affair, and in spite of von Weizacker's rebuttal, conservative West German historians increasingly lent their voices in the popular print media to the call for a positive national identity. One rhetorical strategy was to normalize or relativize the Nazi period and hence make the Nazis' crimes less reprehensible by equating their actions to those of dominant groups in other nations. Philosopher-historian Ernst Nolte, for instance, whose *Three Faces of Fascism* (1965) gained him an international reputation (see Chapter 1), argued that every powerful nation had "its own Hitler era, with its monstrosities and sacrifices," and that the experience of Jews under Nazism was comparable to the experience of persecuted minorities elsewhere (cited in Maier 1988:28). Moreover, Nolte argued that the Soviet Union, not Nazi Germany, was the prototype terror state, and that Hitler had been driven primarily by his resolve to prevent the spread of communism (see Mayer 1989). Nolte also claimed that Hitler's actions against the Jews in the German-occupied territories, however misguided or excessive, were taken in response to Jewish support of the Allied war effort and the threat of Jewish partisan activity behind German lines (Baldwin 1990; Brunner 1997; Evans 1989; Olick & Levy 1997).

Nolte's critics countered that the problem with his view was not that historical comparisons are illegitimate, but that Nolte undertook them to gloss over differences that painted German national identity in a negative light (Evans 1989, 1991). Thus when Stürmer, among others, argued that the absence of an integrating national identity had precipitated the rise of Nazism by undermining prewar Germany (see Chapter 1), Jürgen Habermas, Germany's most distinguished contemporary philosopher, sounded an alarm about conservatives' revision of history. According to Habermas:

> The only patriotism that does not alienate us from the West is a patriotism of commitment to constitutionalism. . . . Whoever wants to suppress the blush of shame . . . and summon the Germans back to a conventional form of . . . national identity, destroys the only reliable basis of our Western loyalty. (cited in Maier 1988:45)

Expressing implicit agreement with some of the German left's views on fascism, Habermas argued that the legacy of the Nazi era still bound the German people because they shared a common heritage that had made the Holocaust possible and that could make it possible (in other forms) again.

Thus the *Historikerstreit* (historians' dispute), as this controversy was called, emerged full bloom (Baldwin 1990; Brunner 1997; Evans 1989). Although most German historians agreed that many of the conservatives' claims lacked empirical support, the latter had "succeeded in giving some respectability to arguments previously thought beyond the pale" (Evans 1991:13).[25] In a 1988 address that was supposed to commemorate the fiftieth anniversary of *Kristallnacht,* for example, Bundestag president Philipp Jenninger reinforced the claim of German victimhood by saying:

> As for the Jews: Hadn't they in the past presumed a role—as was said back then—that they weren't entitled to? Shouldn't they have finally had to accept restrictions? Didn't they perhaps even deserve to be put in their place? And especially: Didn't the propaganda—aside from a few wild exaggerations that couldn't be taken seriously—correspond in the main points with their own suspicions and convictions? (cited in Marcuse 2001:367)

Jeffrey Olick and Daniel Levy suggest that "the delivery of the speech made it difficult to determine whether Jenninger was simply portraying how the situation might have seemed reasonable to average Germans at the time, or whether in fact he was saying that it was reasonable" (1997:931). Harold Marcuse, on the other hand, thinks the speech "contained too much Nazi vocabulary and diction . . . [and] was completely inappropriate for the occasion" (2001:367). In either case, many left-wing members of the Bundestag walked out in protest and two days later Jenninger was forced to resign.

With the end of the cold war and the reunification of the FRG, German claims and counterclaims about the past continue to mark the memory-nation. In October 1990, at the first parliamentary meeting of the reunited country, Chancellor Kohl called for a moment of silence to remember all the victims of Nazism, communism, and his formerly divided nation. According to Young, "By uniting memory of its own martyrs with those it once victimized," Kohl placed universal victimhood at the center of the unified FRG's "first nationally shared memorial moment" (1993:25–26). But without a divided Germany "as a punitive reminder," Young wonders, will the future Germany eventually recall only its own martyrs and its own triumphs? [26] In 1992, for instance, a *Der Spiegel* poll found that 62 percent of German respondents still hoped for an end to the focus on the Nazi past, 44 percent felt that Hitler had had both good and bad qualities, and 32 percent believed that the "Jews were at least partly responsible for the persecution they experienced" (ADL 1993:2).

At the same time, Marcuse observes that younger Germans are generally more interested than their elders in learning about Germans as perpetrators and less tolerant about claims of German victimhood. The older cohort's often "strident insistence on a right to ignorance is giving way to the willingness . . . to confront the question of . . . [German] responsibility" (2001:382). Moreover, in 1990 the teaching of the Nazi period (including the anti-Jewish campaign) became required in German schools. This compulsory curriculum is intended to encourage students to understand "the dangers for their own society of those things that made the Nazi regime and the Holocaust possible" (Fox 2001:308). The impact of this effort remains to be seen. What is clear, however, is that most German youths will never have contact with Jews; there are fewer than thirty thousand left in the entire country. Jews remain an abstraction, a group that is not part of Germany. Hitler has succeeded. Germany is virtually *Judenfrei* (Lerner 1994).

NOTES

1.   This is the subtitle of Wiesenthal's (1998) book, which is a symposium on this issue.
2.   In Chapter 6 I examine the construction of Holocaust memory in the United States. In Chapter 7 I address issues of human rights and international justice.
3.   Amato (1990) traces the historical construction of this sentiment through Christianity, utilitarianism, romanticism, and the rise of modern democratic states.
4.   Brunner suggests that whereas healthy forms of nationalism allow citizens the en-

joyment of "the 'quiet pride' of being part of a nation which can be emphatic to others," unhealthy nationalism expresses "the need to persecute and exclude [others] from the national self" (1997:262).

5.   The Ha'avarah Agreement functioned until the middle of the war. About twenty thousand Jews were assisted and about $30 million was transferred from Germany to Palestine (Segev 1993).

6.   The Diaspora refers to the spatial dispersion of Jews, as a result of religious persecution, since ancient times.

7.   Historical accounts lay blame on different parties for the origins and perpetuation of the "Palestinian problem" (Arad 1995; Brunner 1997; Johnson 1987; Podeh 2000). Pro-Israeli historians claim that the Palestinians were ordered, misled, or panicked into leaving by Arab radio broadcasts, hoping to return when the fighting was over. Pro-Palestinian accounts claim that they were forcefully and brutally expropriated from their land and that they fled to avoid being killed by the Israelis. Johnson (1987) adds that over 567,000 Jews living in Arab states were encouraged or forced to flee their homelands. But whereas Israel resettled these Jews, the Arab countries did not resettle Palestinians and kept them in refugee camps.

According to Litvak's (1994) review, Palestinian historians associate the emergence of Palestinian nationalism to the rising tide of Jewish immigration in the early twentieth century and especially to the fragmentation of Arab pan-nationalism and the dismemberment of Syria by Britain and France, which occurred after World War I. He argues that "the need to refute Zionist claims of Jewish historical links to Palestine prompted a historiographical effort to prove the continuous 'Arabness' of Palestine from antiquity to the present," a view that the Israelis dispute (ibid.:27). Prior to 1948, he adds, the notion of a distinct Palestinian identity was a view fostered by the elite but was not widely held by the masses until they suffered the experience of rejection by the neighboring Arab states and of living as a minority within Israel.

8.   Bresheeth notes that in Israel there was even "a certain cultural 'ban' on German music," including a total ban on Wagner's work, that remains "almost unchanged" to this very day (1997:198).

9.   According to one estimate, the Allied tribunals alone convicted some sixty thousand German and Austrian war criminals (Ruckerl 1990b).

10.   Nuremberg was also the site of twelve other trials involving 177 defendants, including Nazi party officials, business executives, judges, and doctors (Jones 1990).

11.   Göring managed to commit suicide the night before he was to be executed.

12.   Osiel (1997) notes that criminal trials quite naturally focus on the intentions and motivations of defendants and, in the case of Nuremberg, contributed to the focus in Holocaust historiography on the Nazi elite. He also suggests that prosecutors' arguments at Nuremberg framed the crimes not as a rupture from the past but as in violation of "longstanding doctrines in the law of war" (ibid.:117).

13.   Under the denazification program, adult Germans were classified as "major offenders," "offenders," "lesser offenders," "followers," or "exonerated." Some 12,753,000 people were processed in the U.S. zone alone (Marcuse 2001).

14.   Eastern-bloc collective memory also ignored the Hitler-Stalin pact that preceded the German and Soviet occupation of Poland (see Chapter 2, note 8), as well as the atrocities (including rapes) committed by Russians against civilians during its westward advance and military occupation. The hypocrisy of ignoring these actions dur-

ing the postwar trials did not go unnoticed by many Germans (Deák 2000a; Judt 2000; Nesaule 1995).

15.   A study of West German politicians in 1956 found that about a quarter had been active Nazi supporters (Marcuse 2001).

16.   In contrast, East Germany "felt no obligation to make restitution to Jewish survivors living abroad or to refrain from Soviet-bloc attacks on Israel" (Herf 1994:287).

17.   Bell-Fialkoff (1999) places the number at ten to fourteen million.

18.   Kastner was murdered by a Jewish-nationalist extremist in 1957 while the Supreme Court was debating his appeal.

19.   The controversy over Jewish collaboration and resistance emerged once again in the Eichmann trial and will not be restated here. Eichmann was convicted and executed in 1962. For discussions of the controversy generated by Arendt's (1963) observations of the trial, see Alexander (1994), Hilberg (1996), Novick (1999), Segev (1993), and Chapter 6.

20.   The PLO was founded in 1964.

21.   Germany responded to Iraq's attack by sending anti-SCUD missiles, and money, to Israel. This was no mere act of sympathy, for Germany perceived Hussein's actions as a threat to its strategic interests in the Middle East (Segev 1993; Wolffsohn 1993).

22.   Just as Egyptian president Anwar Sadat was assassinated by religious militants in his own country for negotiating the 1979 peace accord with Israel, Rabin was killed by a Jewish extremist in 1995.

23.   In 1955 Adenauer succeeded in getting Alain Resnais's *Night and Fog* banned from the Cannes Film Festival, fearing that "such a well-publicized screening would damage the image" of the FRG abroad (Weissberg 1997:179).

24.   Schumacher had been imprisoned for ten years in the Dachau concentration camp (Marcuse 2001).

25.   Several articles of the FRG's constitution (the "Basic Law") and evolving doctrines established by the Federal Constitutional Court and the Criminal Code allow for the suppression of pro-Nazi speech and actions on the grounds that it undermines "the free democratic basic order" or "constitutional order"; and freedom of expression in the FRG is weighed against "the right to inviolability of personal honour." In 1985 a revision of the Criminal Code was passed that made denial of the Holocaust a crime. This law also criminalized denial of the postwar Soviet expulsions of Germans from Eastern Europe (which the legislature regarded as comparable to the Holocaust) (Kommers 1989; Osiel 1997; Stein 1986).

26.   One of Kohl's pet projects has been the creation of a national victims' memorial that would broadly construe the notion of victimhood, but he has also supported a memorial specifically devoted to the murdered Jews (Marcuse 2001). Nevertheless, conservative historians have generally dominated the official commissions that oversee the development of historical museums in the FRG (Baldwin 1990; Brunner 1997; Geyer & Hansen 1994; Maier 1988).

6

The Americanization
of the
Holocaust

In this chapter we will continue our inquiry into the postwar context of the Holocaust and the construction of collective memory as a social problem. In the previous case study of Israel and the Federal Republic of Germany (FRG), we saw that Holocaust memory is a contested terrain involving competing claims and counterclaims about victims and perpetrators. But as also suggested earlier, the problem of Holocaust memory is not just a matter of disparate domestic contexts but of the international arena as well, a phenomenon involving the cross-national diffusion of social problems (see Best 2001).

Increasingly the United States, a nation that might seem to have little stake in disputes about Holocaust memory, has moved to center stage, contributing to what some analysts characterize as the "Americanization" of the Holocaust (Berenbaum 1987; Rosenfeld 1997). The Americanization of the Holocaust involves a process by which the United States has turned an event that was not of its own making into an event of its own, a process by which the genocide has become popularized and made "far more accessible . . . to increasingly larger audiences" (Rabinbach 1997:230). In addition, it involves capitalizing on the Holocaust for making commercial profit and fund-raising, what some refer to as the "selling of the Holocaust" or the "Holocaust industry" (Cole 1999; Finkelstein 2000; Novick 1999).

To a large extent the Americanization of the Holocaust has occurred through the "Hollywoodization" of the Holocaust, for what is popularly known about this event has been significantly shaped by what has been shown on television and the theater screen. Peter Novick points to the 1978 airing of the Emmy Award winning miniseries *Holocaust,* written by Gerald Green, as "the most important moment in the entry of the Holocaust into general American consciousness" (1999:209). The over nine-and-a-half hour miniseries was shown over four nights as part of NBC's *The Big Event,* "the network's regularly scheduled series of movies, concerts, and other special broadcasts" (Shandler 1997:154). It was preceded by much advance publicity, the publication of a paperback novelization of Green's screenplay, and the distribution of educational viewing guides; and it was seen in part or in whole by an estimated 120 million viewers around the country. Through the story of two fictional families—one of assimilated German Jews and the other of a highly placed SS official—most of the principal historical landmarks were covered, including the Nuremberg Laws, *Kristallnacht,* the Wannsee Conference, the Warsaw ghetto uprising, and Auschwitz. The miniseries was in many respects a "minisurvey course" on the Holocaust, and more information was imparted to more people in just these four nights than in all of the preceding postwar years. When it was shown in Germany, in January 1979, the *Holocaust* prompted an unprecedented confrontation with the subject that, in the words of one German journalist at the time, "has shaken up post-Hitler Germany in a way that German intellectuals have been unable to do" (cited in Novick 1999:213).[1]

Many critics, however, decried the crass commercialization of the miniseries. For Elie Wiesel, turning the Holocaust into what he called a "cheap . . . soap-opera" was a sacrilegious act (cited in ibid.:211). Media critic Molly Haskell wrote that "the Holocaust is simply too vast, . . . too incomprehensible, to fit into . . . the reductive context of the small screen" (cited in Shandler 1997:158). Others found the interruption of commercials for products such as air deodorizers and panty shields offensive. Media critic John O'Connor questioned whether a "story that includes victims being told that the gas chambers are only disinfecting areas" should be used to promote Lysol for "killing germs" (ibid.).

The *Holocaust* miniseries was followed by many other (mostly television) films that in the aggregate (supplemented by imported foreign films) "served to firmly affix the Holocaust on the American cultural map" (Novick 1999:214; see also Insdorf 1989). Arguably the culmination of these cinematic events was Steven Spielberg's *Schindler's List,* which was released in 1993. This was also the year in which the U.S. Holocaust Museum in Washington, D.C., was opened, thus placing the Holocaust squarely within the official state-sponsored memory of the United States (Linenthal 1995).

In this chapter I examine the central role of the United States, and Jewish Americans in particular, in constructing a collective memory of the Holocaust that is not only suitable to the American context but capable of being recycled abroad. I will show how various claimsmakers appropriated the Holocaust as a cultural resource that can be used to advance their interests, and how the Americanization of the Holocaust itself has been viewed as a social problem.

POPULARIZATION AND AMERICAN FILM MEMORY

The French-Jewish filmmaker Claude Lanzmann is often credited by film critics as producing the definitive documentary about the Holocaust, the 1978

Academy Award winning *Shoah*. Over nine hours in length, *Shoah* is relentless in its "presentation of the core of the horrors" and its "attention to the details of the mechanism of genocide" (Avisar 1997:40). The very length of the film places a heavy "demand on the viewer to appreciate the enormity of the historical trauma" (ibid.). It does not use any archival footage but relies instead on the dramatic unfolding of painful memories. We see the existential torment "of the survivors, the immoral evasion of former perpetrators, and the lingering . . . anti-Semitism . . . of the complacent bystanders" (ibid.:41). The pace of the film is slow, and the mood solemn, with long takes and "pauses that maintain a sense of wonder toward the incredible and incomprehensible" events. Lanzmann spends a good deal of time filming "old sites of atrocity" as they look in the postwar years and showing us survivors who are struggling to come to terms with their emotional pain, thus rendering "the Holocaust as a past that is still present" (ibid.).

According to Simone de Beauvoir, *Shoah* is "neither fiction nor documentary" but a work of "art" (1985:iii). Moreover, it is a film about "witnessing," about different testimonial stances—the victims, the perpetrators, the bystanders—that "can neither be assimilated into, nor subsumed by, one another" (Felman 1994:93). Above all, it is a film against silence, a film aimed at insuring that "the story will go on."

The story that goes on, however, will be told in many ways, and in many languages. (*Shoah* itself uses English, French, German, Hebrew, Polish, Sicilian, and Yiddish.) But arguably the most widely disseminated story that will be told will be the American story of the Holocaust, a story that accommodates the needs of the American nation, a story that involves "the 'colonization' of the Holocaust by American culture" (Loshitzky 1997:4).

Representing Anne Frank

As many as a quarter of the six million Jews who died during the Holocaust were children. All of these children have come to be symbolized by one name: Anne Frank (1929–1944). The diary she wrote while hiding from the Nazis in an attic with her family in Amsterdam, Holland, is "the most widely read book of World War II" (Rosenfeld 1991:243). Anne "is the most famous child of the 20th century," and with the exception of Hitler himself, the most famous figure of the Nazi period (ibid.: 224). It was her story that first introduced the Holocaust into American culture, as it evolved "from a European document of World War II into an Americanized representation" (Doneson 1987:149).

The diary, which was first published in Dutch in 1952 under the title *Het Achterhuis,* had an inauspicious beginning. (*Het Achterhuis* means "behind" or "in back of" the "house" and is sometimes translated as "The Annex.") Although the initial print run consisted of just fifteen hundred copies, the early reviews were uniformly favorable. The book was described as "a moral testament," "a human document of great clarity and honesty," and an account that "transcends the misery" it records (cited in Rosenfeld 1991:248). The first English translation was published in the United States and Great Britain in 1952. A popular Broadway play based on the diary—*The Diary of Anne Frank*—written by Frances Goodrich and Albert Hackett, a wife-husband writing team from Hollywood, opened in 1955. It was a box-office smash that won a Pulitzer Prize, the Tony Award, New York Drama Critics Circle Award, and the Antoinette Perry Award. The 1959 film version based on the Goodrich-Hackett script proved to be equally popular and was followed by several television adaptations (Novick 1999; Rosenfeld 1991).

Many analysts attribute the success of *The Diary of Anne Frank* to the story line that downplays Anne's Jewishness and turns her into a universal figure who represents all martyred innocents (Doneson 1987). Anne's longer mediations on Jewish persecution and anti-Semitism are not included, and instead remarks are substituted that do not even appear in the original diary: "We're not the only people that've had to suffer. There've always been people that've had to . . . sometimes one race . . . sometimes another" (quoted in Rosenfeld 1991:257). Thus one reviewer wrote that *The Diary of Anne Frank* was "not in any important sense a Jewish play" (cited in ibid.:254). Edward Alexander (1994), on the other hand, notes a passage from the diary that offers a different impression:

> Who has inflicted this upon us? Who has made us Jews different from all other people? Who has allowed us to suffer so terribly up til now? It is God that has made us as we are, but it will be God, too, who will raise us up again. If we bear all this suffering and if there are still Jews left, when it is over, then Jews, instead of being doomed, will be held up as an example. Who knows, it might even be our religion from which the world and all peoples learn good, and for that reason only do we have to suffer now. We can never become just Netherlanders, or just English, or representatives of any country for that matter, we will always remain Jews, but we want to, too. (Frank 1952:186–87)

Nonetheless, the mass appeal of *The Diary of Anne Frank* is also due to the limited circumstance of the attic, for it allows audiences a safe entry into the Holocaust by shielding them from the horrors of the ghettos, concentration camps, and mass killings (Rosenfeld 1991).[2] In addition, the script emphasizes the uplifting elements of the Holocaust insofar as the Frank family was aided by altruistic "Good Samaritan" Christians who risked their lives to help people in need (Doneson 1987; see Chapter 4). And it highlights the portions of the diary that reveal Anne as a buoyant and optimistic girl who is resolved to maintain her ideals: "In spite of everything, I still believe that people are really good at heart" (Frank 1952:237). Unlike Simon Wiesenthal (1998), who could not forgive his persecutors (see Chapter 5), Anne offers forgiveness and hope for the future. As Garson Kanin, the play's first director, remarked at the time of the play's opening:

> I have never looked on it as a sad play. I certainly have no wish to inflict depression on an audience; I don't consider that a legitimate theatrical end. I never thought the original material depressing. . . . Looking back, Anne Frank's death doesn't seem to me a wasteful death, because she left us a legacy that has meaning and value to us. (quoted in Rosenfeld 1991:253)

Thus the audience viewing the play is not subjected to that portion of the diary that would convey a different message:

> I don't believe that the big men, the politicians and the capitalists alone, are guilty of the war. Oh no, the little man is just as guilty, otherwise the people of the world would have risen in revolt long ago! There's in people simply an urge to destroy, an urge to kill, to murder and rage, and until all mankind, without exception, undergoes a great change, wars will be waged, everything that has been built up, cultivated, and grown will be destroyed and disfigured, after which mankind will have to begin all over again. (Frank 1952:201)

Importantly, *The Diary of Anne Frank* became an American export, as the European story, now Americanized to create broad appeal, was diffused back into Europe (Doneson 1987; Marcuse 2001). Germans were especially receptive to this somewhat sanitized version of the Holocaust. As one German reviewer wrote, "The persecution and murder of Jews seems to be merely a peculiar external circumstance—secondary in importance to the personal tragedy of the heroine" (cited in Rosenfeld 1991:266). Another observed, "We see in Anne Frank's fate our own fate—the tragedy of human existence per se" (ibid.).

Anne Frank died in the concentration camp at Bergen-Belsen, where she was sent after her family had been discovered in the attic by the Dutch police. While her legacy endures, just what that legacy entails remains a matter of dispute. Some analysts, for example, believe that Anne is a questionable Jewish symbol since the Franks were assimilated Jews for whom religious observance was inconsequential (Novick 1999). Others appropriate her as a Zionist symbol, even though she did not express a desire to go to Palestine herself. As one writer noted, in the aftermath of the 1967 Six Day War between Israel and its Arab neighbors (see Chapter 5):

> Hitler killed [Anne] and six million others. But the events recorded in her diary became part of the national memory that built the State of Israel—and the spirit behind its six-day war last June. No longer would Jews try only to survive. There would be no more martyrs. Dead heroes, if need be, but no more Anne Franks. That is her living legacy. (cited in Rosenfeld 1991:276)

Above all, however, Anne Frank will remain a peculiarly American symbol, for she is faithful to the spirit of optimism that is celebrated in American culture (Doneson 1987). In 1979, twenty-five years after the opening of the Broadway play, director Kanin compared Anne to Peter Pan, writing that she "remains forever an adolescent. . . . She reminds us that the length of a life does not necessarily reflect its quality. . . . Anne lives on" (cited in Rosenfeld 1991:253).

Spielberg's Holocaust

Alvin Rosenfeld notes that *The Diary of Anne Frank* has a narrative structure that is characteristic of other American films on the Holocaust that "are likely to end . . . on a note of redemptive promise" (1997:143). This is certainly true of Spielberg's *Schindler's List,* the 1993 Academy Award winning movie based on the novel by Thomas Keneally, that has been described "as the 'definitive' Holocaust film . . . [that] may actually do more to educate vast number of people about the . . . Holocaust than all the academic books on the subject combined" (ibid.:139–40). But there is a drawback to this popularity as well, for the film transforms a relatively minor event into a matter of extraordinary significance as if it were "a representative segment" of the Holocaust when in fact it was not (Bartov 1997b:46).

Oskar Schindler (1908–1974), who is credited with saving some eleven hundred Jews from certain death, would appear to have been an unlikely hero or "righteous Christian" (see Chapter 4). A flamboyant, hard-drinking womanizer, gambler, and black marketer, Schindler served as a Nazi military intelligence officer and became a wealthy factory owner. He came to Krakow, Poland, in late 1939, where he operated an enamel kitchenware factory that utilized Jewish slave labor provided by the Nazis. Although he was willing to exploit Jews as slaves, Schindler treated his workers humanely and successfully lobbied with Nazi officials to prevent hundreds of them from being sent to extermination camps.

Schindler's List is indisputably a finely acted and well-crafted film, and it fulfills what Omer Bartov considers to be the two major ingredients necessary to satisfy the American public's "taste for representations of the past": (1) "the quest for authenticity, for a story that 'actually' happened, though retold according to accepted [Hollywood] conventions"; and (2) "the demand for a 'human' story of will and determination, decency and courage, and final triumph over the forces of evil" (1997b:46).

Several elements of *Schindler's List* make it appear authentic, give it a documentary character (Avisar 1997). Spielberg used black-and-white photography and shot much of the film in Krakow, the area where most of the events actually took place. The historical narrative covers many of the important stages of the genocide, portraying the ghetto, deportations, labor camps, selections, and death camps.

The central dramatic confrontation in the film takes place between Schindler, played by Liam Neeson, and Anon Goeth, the commander of the Plaszow labor camp, played by Ralph Fiennes. According to Ilan Avisar, Goeth is one of "the most vicious villain(s) ever to appear on the screen. He kills people for breakfast, practices shooting on living targets, murders 25 prisoners in cold blood after an attempted escape, and exercises the terror of a menacing maniac in his treatment of a helpless [Jewish] maid" (1997:51). While the beginning of the film shows Schindler's negative traits, as the film progresses this side abates as he outmaneuvers Goeth in a heroic struggle between "the good guy and the bad guy" (Bartov 1997b:54). Finally, *Schindler's List* has a happy ending, and thus allows us to enter the dark world of the Holocaust without feeling there is no escape (Rosenfeld 1997).

In the film, the fate of "Schindler's Jews" hangs in the balance. But in elevating Schindler to the level of a saint, the Jews are diminished, for they remain passive beneficiaries of his charitable deeds. According to Judith Doneson, this theme, which also informs *The Diary of Anne Frank,* resonates with Christian audiences whose religion has historically viewed the "Jews as condemned eternally for rejecting Jesus as the Messiah but whose continuing existence is necessary . . . to test the qualities of mercy and goodness incumbent upon good Christians" (1997:140). At the end of the film this theme is brought home as "the camera pans lovingly over the crosses in Jerusalem's Latin Cemetery, coming to rest on the gravesite where Schindler himself is buried" (Avisar 1997:142). Thus what many regard as the definitive Hollywood Holocaust film is in many respects less about Jews and more about a Christian man who saved Jews.

Like *The Diary of Anne Frank, Schindler's List* was an American export. In Germany, according to Avisar (1997), pitting a good German against a bad German on balance mitigated a blanket condemnation of the German people. This helps explain the generally favorable reaction to the film in spite of complaints about American cultural imperialism (Loshitzky 1997). Spielberg's *Holocaust* "does not show what 'Germans' did but what *individual* Germans did, offering hope that one of them—Schindler—would become the many" (Weissberg 1997:178).

Some critics have noticed a parallel between Spielberg's own development as a filmmaker and that of Schindler's character. Spielberg, the man who made Hollywood millions with fantasy films, invested $42 million of the profits he earned from *Jurassic Park* in order to move himself up to the next level and become a "serious" filmmaker (Avisar 1997; Bresheeth 1997). Previously he had had little interest in his Jewish heritage and had even tried to deny or forget about it (Weissberg 1997). Spielberg says that his involvement in *Schindler's List* caused him to take religious instruction and "reconvert" to Judaism. Thus, in film critic Janet Maslin's words, Spielberg had succeeded in making "sure that neither he nor the Holocaust would ever be thought of in the same way again" (cited in Avisar 1997:55). His contribution to Holocaust memory was further solidified by his creation of the Survivors of the Shoah Visual History Foundation, which has recorded over fifty thousand videotape testimonies, making it the largest such collection in the world (see www.vhf.org).

In Israel the release of *Schindler's List* (along with the opening of the U.S. Holocaust Museum that same year) signified that Israelis had lost their hold on this element of Jewish collective memory.[3] Indeed, the Diaspora Jews in America were confronting the Holocaust on their own terms, constructing their own representation of the past, and diffusing this representation to the rest of the world (Bresheeth 1997).

POPULARIZATION AND AMERICAN HISTORIOGRAPHY

Films such as *The Diary of Anne Frank* and *Schindler's List* have a much greater impact on the public's understanding of the Holocaust than do works by professional historians. Few historians ever make their way into the popular media in a way that would have much impact on public consciousness. How many people, for instance, have ever read or heard of Raul Hilberg's ground-breaking magnum opus, *The Destruction of European Jews,* first published in 1961, which outlined the details of the Nazi bureaucratic destruction process?

Hilberg (1996)—an Austrian Jew who emigrated to the United States as a youth, and who served in the U.S. armed forces during the war—began studying the Holocaust in 1948 while he was a graduate student in political science at Columbia University. In his autobiography, Hilberg recalls how virtually alone he was in his scholarly pursuit of the subject. For hours upon hours he poured over thousands of German documents available from the Nuremberg trials before he understood and was able to describe the bureaucratic processes that culminated in the Final Solution (see Chapters 1–3).

Hilberg recounts his difficulty finding a publisher for *The Destruction of the European Jews.* His Ph.D. dissertation, which was the basis of the book, had won him Columbia University's prestigious Clark F. Ansley Award in 1955, which entitled Hilberg to have the work published by Columbia University Press. The dissertation, however, was not the completed work, and Columbia University Press would not agree to finance publication of the entire manuscript, which by 1957 had grown to some sixteen hundred typewritten pages. In addition to Columbia University Press, other publishing houses turned down the opportunity to publish the book. Reviewers complained, among other things, that Hilberg had relied too exclusively on German documents, that he was too critical of the Jewish Council's passive complicity with Nazi edicts, and that, as one publisher said, it did not "constitute a sufficiently important contribution as a case study in public administration to stand alone on that ground" (cited in ibid.:114).

Hilberg eventually published his manuscript with Quadrangle Books, a small independent company in Chicago, but only after a Jewish-survivor family agreed to subsidize the project with $15,000 "in payment for copies that were to be shipped as donations to libraries" (ibid.:117). When *The Destruction of the European Jews* was finally published in 1961, Hilberg "could not help noticing the cheapness of the paper and the binding, which seemed to be an announcement that the book was not made to last" (ibid.:118). Such was the state of American Holocaust historiography at the time.[4]

The Goldhagen Controversy

Thirty-five years after the publication of Hilberg's *The Destruction of the European Jews,* another political science dissertation on the Holocaust was published by the Alfred Knopf company: Daniel Jonah Goldhagen's *Hitler's Willing Executioners: Ordinary Germans and the Holocaust.* Goldhagen, a Jewish-American son of a Holocaust survivor, had already won the Sumner Dissertation Prize at Harvard University and the American Political Science Association's Gabriel A. Almond Award for best dissertation in the field of comparative politics (Shandley 1998). The book was released with a flurry of "publicity that is not unusual for a commercially listed book but that is quite rare for a first book based on a dissertation" (ibid.:3). Goldhagen also wrote an op-ed piece that appeared in the *New York Times* and immediately set out on a well-promoted book tour.

Advance praise from reviewers appeared on the book's back cover and hailed *Hitler's Willing Executioners* as an "astonishing, disturbing, and riveting book, the fruit of phenomenal scholarship and absolute integrity, [that] will permanently change the debate on the Holocaust." The *New York Review of Books* called it "a tour de force," an "original, indeed brilliant contribution to the . . . literature of the Holocaust" (see reviews at www.amazon.com). The *Philadelphia Inquirer* anointed it as the "most important book ever published about the Holocaust. . . . Eloquently written, meticulously documented, impassioned. . . . A model of moral and scholarly integrity." *Kirkus Reviews* deemed it an "explosive work that shatters many of the assumptions and commonly accepted myths concerning the Holocaust," noting that its "documentation will make refutation nearly impossible." The book quickly became a national and international best-seller and made Goldhagen a widely sought after public speaker in the United States and abroad.

The positive reviews of *Hitler's Willing Executioners* tended to be written by nonhistorians, that is, by journalists or newspaper/magazine columnists (Markovitz 1998). Many professional historians and Holocaust scholars, on the other hand, were highly critical of the book, for reasons I will explore shortly (see Browning 1998; Finkelstein & Birn 1998; Shandley 1998).

Goldhagen basically advances two main theses in his book. One is that ordinary Germans, such as the rank-and-file Order Police, played a major role in the actual killing of Jews (see Chapter 3).[5] In mustering evidence for this proposition, Goldhagen adds to the research on the Order Police that first appeared in Christopher Browning's book, *Ordinary Men: Reserve Police Battalion 101 and the Final Solution in Poland,* published in 1992 with much less attention from the lay public. This is the part of Goldhagen's book that makes for the most dramatic reading, for it includes graphic descriptions (as well as photographs) of the atrocities that occurred. Goldhagen also argues, as did Browning, that there is no evidence of significant dissent among the troops or of punishment for those who were unwilling or unable to participate in the killings. Therefore, Goldhagen contends, the killers had a choice, and most did not choose to abstain.

Goldhagen's thesis that ordinary people participated in the Holocaust stands on solid ground. But this is hardly a new or original insight. Part of the negative reaction to the book among scholars was due, in part, to the hype surrounding the book's claims to charting a new course in Holocaust historiography, which many dismissed as a marketing strategy to sell more books (Browning 1998; Shandley 1998). The most severe criticism, however, was levied at Goldhagen's second thesis, which characterized the German people as adherents to a uniquely virulent and "eliminationist" form of anti-Semitism that predated the rise of Nazism.

Many historians dispute Goldhagen's contention that Germans were more anti-Semitic than the peoples of other European countries, and they note that Goldhagen presents no comparative evidence to support his proposition (Shandley 1998). Scholars also argue that a variety of anti-Semitisms existed in Germany and that the "eliminationist" strain was not typical of most Germans, who were attracted to Nazism for other reasons, for example, their economic program, appeal to nationalism, or anticommunist stance (Augstein 1998; Browning 1998; see Chapter 2). In fact, as Hilberg and others have shown, it took time even for Nazi anti-Semitism to evolve into the Final Solution (Mommsen 1998b).

Goldhagen also puts some scholars off with the seemingly haughty tone in which he dismisses the way others have explained Germans' behavioral motivation, writing as if he seems bent on "picking a fight with everyone who has previously had a scholarly engagement" with the Holocaust and as if only he has discovered the essential truth (Schoeps 1998:81; see also Shandley 1998). Browning (1992), for instance, offered a multicausal explanation of the Order Police troops' motivations, including careerist ambitions, unquestioned obedience to what was perceived as legitimate governmental authority, group pressures to conform, and masculine values of toughness—all of which Goldhagen found wanting.

In his book, Goldhagen focuses on cases where the German Order Police "displayed a special cruelty toward their Jewish victims," making them run a gauntlet and beating them before they were killed, or making them strip naked and crawl to mass graves that awaited them (Riemer 1998:178; see Chapter 3). He also notes how often the Germans "struck mocking, proud, or boastful poses over defenseless old Jewish men," how they "were eager to hunt down Jewish women and children hiding in forests," and how they took photographs as souvenirs so they could boast of their achievements (ibid.). Browning, on the other hand, notes that different groups within the battalion he studied behaved in various ways and that their reactions ranged from "enthusiastic participation, through dutiful, nominal, or regretful compliance, to differing degrees of evasion" (1998:221). While Browning is sympathetic with many of Goldhagen's points, he believes that Goldhagen has selectively interpreted the evidence to advance a narrow thesis: that a single factor—anti-Semitism—can account for the complexities of behavioral motivation and response.

Josef Joffe wonders whether there was some resentment toward Goldhagen on the part of historians "who have labored hard in the field . . . for decades without producing a worldwide best-seller" (1998:220). He acknowledges, however, that the Goldhagen controversy involved very legitimate scholarly disputes over questions of historical methodology, of the relationship between theory and data in historical research, and of the need for accuracy regarding the details of the historical record (Finkelstein & Birn 1998; Shandley 1998).

These questions aside, Jeremiah Riemer notes that Goldhagen's book made people aware of how novel it actually was for a Holocaust scholar to emphasize anti-Semitism as a causative factor and that many, if not most, of the ordinary "perpetrators believed it made sense to kill Jews" (1998:179). As I noted earlier, Goldhagen argues that many explanations treat the perpetrators as if they were "people lacking a moral sense, lacking the ability to make decisions and take stances," as if they were simply automatons following orders (1996:13; see Chapter 1). Hence Goldhagen was more willing than other scholars to morally indict his subjects and point his finger, so to speak, at "the Germans" (Joffe 1998:224). As Jan Philipp Reemtsma suggests:

> For every other great historical outrage, for every other mass killing or genocide, we assume that the murderers did what they did out of conviction that their actions were just—only for the Holocaust do we look for explanations that might make it plausible that the Germans perpetrated, allowed, or intentionally overlooked something they fundamentally did not wish. (1998:257)

In Reemtsma's view, Goldhagen reminded readers that:

> [Germans'] obsession with Europe's Jewish population as a problem that had to be solved was extremely widespread and that both the formulation of this phantasmal problem and its possible solution resulted in an increasingly murderous [policy]—and that the circle of those willing to participate actively was far larger than had previously been assumed. (ibid.:258)

Arguably the release of *Hitler's Willing Executioners* in the FRG provoked more controversy than elsewhere (Shandley 1998). The German historians' dispute of the 1980s had barely subsided (see Chapter 5). The book reignited "discussion of painful problems that [were] far from having been conclusively resolved" (Wehler 1998:94). Perhaps Germans still wanted to glory in their past, to recapture a positive national identity by normalizing or relativizing the Holocaust or by acting as if they suffered as much as anyone else. The press seemed to react defensively, perceiving Goldhagen as "really writing about Germany today, or about the 'eternal German,' and not specifically about the very different Germans who set out to destroy the Jews of Europe" decades ago (Reimer 1998:177). Some of the attacks were rather personal. It was pointed out that Goldhagen was Jewish, a son of a Holocaust survivor no less. Who was he to indict Germans with such dribble? Was this "yet another act of Jewish aggression against the German people?" (Markovits 1998:123). The message seemed to be: Don't even bother to read the book (Joffe 1998).

But there was a positive response in Germany as well. After all, people were reading the book in droves. Those on the other side of the historians' dispute accused Goldhagen's opponents of being "in the camp of the normalizers or even the deniers, at least [on the side] of those denying that ordinary Germans participated" in the Holocaust (Shandley 1998:22). Goldhagen, they said, should be celebrated as a friend of the FRG, reminding Germans that they should look to the Western democracies, not to their predemocratic past, to construct a positive national identity. Indeed, this was the point Jürgen Habermas had made just a few years earlier. And when the *Blatter für Deutsche und Internationale Politik* (Journal for German and International Politics) decided to award its prestigious Democracy Prize to Goldhagen, Habermas was invited to make some laudatory remarks at the award presentation. Habermas praised Goldhagen for having shook Germans "naive trust in our own traditions" (1998:265). As he said:

> On the present occasion we are evaluating the contribution that an American, a Jewish historian, has made toward Germans' search for the proper way to come to terms with a criminal period of their history. . . . [I]n an ethical-political discourse, the question is not primarily the guilt or innocence of the forefathers but, rather, the critical self-assurance of their descendants. . . . [Those who] were born later, who cannot know how they themselves would have acted, are trying to [reach] some clarity about the cultural matrix of a burdened inheritance . . . to decide what is to be continued, and what revised, from those traditions that had earlier formed such a disastrous motivational background. . . . Goldhagen's work . . . refers to very specific traditions and mentalities, to ways of thinking and perceiving that belong to a particular cultural context—not something unalterable to which we have been consigned by fate but factors that can be transformed through a change of consciousness and that in the meantime have actually been transformed through political enlightenment. (ibid.:267, 271–72)

Indeed, upon accepting the award Goldhagen (1998) acknowledged that the FRG had in fact become an "internationally responsible" democratic nation-state and that this had been due in large part to Germans' ability to develop a "remarkably self-critical national history," responsive to critiques from abroad and outsiders such as himself (ibid.:277).

> That I am being . . . [honored] in Germany for writing a book with the unsettling and painful content that mine has is the strongest testimony to . . . the character and democratic promise of contemporary Germany, and to the fact that it is really all the people in Germany, responsible for making the Federal Republic the democratic country that it has become, who deserve the prize. (ibid.:285)

Historical Revisionism and the Problem of Holocaust Denial

At the beginning of this book I noted some people's concern that scholarly disputes about the Holocaust—disagreements regarding the facticity of certain events and competing interpretations of the empirical record—would encourage Nazi apologists and lend legitimacy to those who would deny that the Holocaust occurred. Even reputable historians have been accused of heresy, as Hilberg was when both American and Israeli Jews deemed his observations about the complicity of the Jewish Councils impious and "defaming of the dead" (cited in Guttenplan 2000:60; see also Hilberg 1996; Novick 1999).

Hannah Arendt was met with similar disdain when she reported on her observations of the 1961 trial of Adolf Eichmann in Israel (see Chapters 1 and 5). Arendt, an eminent Jewish-German philosopher and political scientist who had emigrated to the United States in 1941, was commissioned by the *New Yorker* magazine to write a series of articles that were published in 1963 and compiled in a book, *Eichmann in Jerusalem: A Report on the Banality of Evil,* that same year. The publicity surrounding the trial and Arendt's work gave the Holocaust more exposure in the United States and sparked more debate among historians, journalists, and the public than any previous postwar event (Cole 1999; Novick 1999).

In characterizing Eichmann as a banal figure, Arendt was perceived by some as an apologist for his deeds. She also suggested, as did Hilberg, that the Jews were complicit in their own demise. The Anti-Defamation League (ADL) called her book "evil," and she was described by others as a "self-hating Jewess" who lacked "love for the Jewish people" (cited in Novick 1999:134; see also Wolin 1996:10).[6]

The passage of time has tempered negative judgments of *Eichmann in Jerusalem,* which in spite of its faults is now generally recognized as a valuable contribution to the Holocaust literature, as stimulating serious debate, thought, and scholarship (Alexander 1994; Arad 1996; Novick 1999). However, the negative reactions to Arendt's and Hilberg's work, as well as Gold-hagen's, raises important questions about "ownership" of history, that is, about what can and cannot be legitimately said, about who can say it, and about the criteria that are used to construct legitimate historiography (Lipstadt 1993; Linenthal 1995; Shermer & Grobman 2000).

All this leads us to the problem of Holocaust denial, to the organized at-tempt to establish denial of the Holocaust as a legitimate scholarly enterprise. The two leading critical exposés of Holocaust denial in the United States were written by historians Deborah Lipstadt (1993) and Michael Shermer and Alex Grobman (2000). These scholars make a distinction between historical revi-sionism and denial. Revisionism, in their view, entails refinement of existing knowledge about an historical event, not a denial of the event itself, that comes through an examination of new empirical evidence or a reexamination or rein-terpretation of existing evidence.[7] Legitimate historical revisionism acknowl-edges a "certain body of irrefutable evidence" or a "convergence of evidence" that suggests that an event—like the black plague, American slavery, or the Holocaust—did in fact occur (Lipstadt 1993:21; Shermer & Grobman 2000:34).

Denial, on the other hand, rejects the entire foundation of historical evi-dence, and with respect to the Holocaust entails three basic claims: (1) "[The] gas chambers and crematoria in the concentration camps were used . . . [only] for delousing clothing and disposing of people who died of disease and over work . . . [and] not for mass extermination"; (2) Only about 600,000 Jews rather than six million actually died; and (3) The deaths that occurred were "nothing more than an unfortunate by-product of the vicissitudes of war" rather than a result of an intentional program of mass extermination (Shermer & Grobman 2000:3).[8]

In the United States deniers take advantage of their First Amendment right to freedom of speech and press. The First Amendment protects everyone's right to question the existence of whatever they like—of God, of Elvis Presley's death, of O.J. Simpson's guilt or innocence, or of the Holocaust. Bradley Smith, for example, gained considerable media attention in the 1990s when he took out full-page ads in U.S. college newspapers and widely distributed a pamphlet he wrote, "The Holocaust Controversy: The Case for Open Debate" (ADL 1993; Lipstadt 1993; Shermer & Grobman 2000). Smith, who is based in California, publishes a newsletter, "The Smith Report," which according to its subtitle is "America's only monthly Holocaust revisionist newsletter." He also operates a Web site, the Committee for Open Debate on the Holocaust (www.codoh.com). Smith appeals to students' natural skepticism and naivete when he writes:

No subject enrages campus Thought Police more than Holocaust Revisionism. We debate every other great historical issue as a matter of course, but influential pressure groups with private agendas have made the Holocaust story an exception. . . . Students should be encouraged to investigate the Holocaust story the same way they are encouraged to investigate every other historical event. (cited in Shermer & Grobman 2000:62)

In many other countries around the world—including the democratic nations of Australia, Austria, Belgium, Canada, France, Germany, Israel, Italy, New Zealand, Sweden, and Switzerland—the legal system allows for the suppression of speech and printed material that denies the Holocaust (Shermer & Grobman 2000).[9] Neither Lipstadt nor Sherman and Grobman favor legal restraints on Holocaust denial in the United States. But neither do they think, as some suggest, that the deniers should simply be ignored. Rather, they wrote their books to subject the Holocaust denial movement to critical scrutiny.

Holocaust deniers attempt to don the mantle of legitimacy by publishing professional-looking books and monographs, replete with footnotes and bibliographic citations. These writers are in fact very knowledgeable about particular aspects of the Holocaust and try to exploit ambiguities of historical detail, making it difficult for anyone who is not well-versed in these specifics to properly respond to their claims.

The Institute for Historical Review (IHR), based in California, presents itself as a "think-tank" of sorts, which holds pseudoacademic conferences and publishes the pseudoacademic *Journal of Historical Review*. It was founded in 1978 by a right-wing extremist, Willis Carto, and first achieved notoriety in 1980 when it offered $50,000 to anyone who could prove that the Nazis had gassed Jews at Auschwitz. Holocaust survivor Mel Mermelstein accepted the challenge and provided the IHR with evidence in the form of his own and other survivors' testimony. When the IHR refused to pay him the money, Mermelstein filed a civil lawsuit. The judge ruled in favor of Mermelstein, noting that the court had taken "judicial notice" that Jews had been gassed at Auschwitz (cited in Shermer & Grobman 2000:43). Mermelstein was awarded the $50,000 and an additional $40,000 for "personal suffering" (ADL 1993; Lipstadt 1993).

More recently, in 2000, the Holocaust was on trial (and in the news) again in the British libel case of *David Irving v. Penguin Books Ltd. and Deborah Lipstadt* (Greif 2000; Guttenplan 2000). David Irving, best-selling author of some thirty popular history books, is perhaps the most knowledgeable and sophisticated Holocaust denier. In what is arguably his most oft-cited book, *Hitler's War* (1977), he portrayed Hitler as a harried executive who was unaware of the campaign against the Jews that his minions had undertaken in the East. While most historians disagree with this contention, they do not characterize it as outlandish (Guttenplan 2000; Marrus 1987).

Nevertheless, throughout his career Irving has moved increasingly closer to the denial camp. Although he is British, he has forged ties with Holocaust deniers throughout Europe and North America, including the IHR. Irving is a self-described "moderate fascist" who has a great fondness for Germany (cited in Lipstadt 1993:161). He has written that Great Britain made a mistake in going to war against Germany and that the Allies and Germany committed comparable atrocities. In the late 1980s he began claiming that gas chambers had never been used for extermination (ADL 1993; Shermer & Grobman 2000).

Irving chose to sue Lipstadt and Penguin Books (the publisher of her book in the United Kingdom) in Britain rather than the United States because libel laws in that country place the burden of proof on defendants to show that they did not libel plaintiffs. Lipstadt's side was required to demonstrate that the evidence that Irving was a denier was "so clear-cut that only a willful misreading or conscious distortion of the facts could account for [his] positions" (Guttenplan 2000:47). Lipstadt felt that it was not just she and her publisher who were on trial but the history of the Holocaust itself. As she said, "If I hadn't fought this, [Irving] would have won by default. He could have said—it would have been said—the High Court in London recognizes his definition of the Holocaust" (quoted in ibid.:51). During the trial the defense amassed piles of Nazi documents and submitted lengthy reports by experts, including Christopher Browning, who when given an opportunity to testify in court "quickly made rubble of Irving's arguments" (Greif 2000:36). The judge ruled in favor of the defense. History had won, yet Holocaust denial does not go away.

Holocaust deniers are an amalgam of discontented types. Some are simply attracted to conspiratorial theories and a cause that unifies them against an external enemy. Others are also white supremacists who support right-wing if not fascist politics. They are anti-Semitic and harbor resentment that Jews have gained recognition of their suffering and have been able to use the memory of the Holocaust to advance their interests. They are decidedly pro-German and think Germany should stop apologizing for things it did not do. Some are outright neo-Nazis who seek to rehabilitate the reputation of National Socialism by decoupling it from the Holocaust. They appeal to young people who are attracted to the skinhead movement, and they fill the Internet with their propaganda of hate (ADL 1993; Hamm 1993; Lipstadt 1993; Shermer & Grobman 2000).

At times there appears to be a fine line between outright Holocaust denial and the normalization or relativization of the Holocaust that has been expressed by some mainstream intellectuals and political leaders, such as what occurred in Germany during the Bitburg affair and the historians' dispute. Lipstadt (1993) is concerned that in the future the deniers will increasingly adopt this approach in an effort to achieve more credibility.

David Duke is currently one of the most well-known Holocaust deniers in the United States (see www.davidduke.com). In the late 1980s this former neo-Nazi and Ku Klux Klansman tried to remake himself as a mainstream Republican conservative when he was elected to the Louisiana State Senate. In 1990 he received 44 percent of the vote (and a majority of the white vote) in a losing bid as the Republican nominee for the U.S. Senate. On the political stump, Duke sounds no different from Patrick Buchanan, the former White House official, newspaper columnist, television commentator, and perennial presidential candidate. Although Buchanan has never denied the Holocaust, he has been attracted to some of the deniers' issues. He has written that it was a mistake for the United States to have gone to war against Germany and that Jews were not gassed at the Treblinka concentration camp. Buchanan received his information about Treblinka from the IHR (Dershowitz 1991; Lipstadt 1993; Shermer & Gorbman 2000; Turque 1991).[10]

THE HOLOCAUST AND THE POLITICS OF VICTIMIZATION

Obviously Holocaust denial is especially offensive to survivors, for it constitutes a searing affront to their own experiences and to their memories of the murdered dead. But after the war survivors had experienced another, more subtle, form of denial, that of silence or indifference, a reaction that was even forthcoming from Jews. Earlier I noted that in Israel survivors who had not been involved in armed resistance were viewed as deficient and even disdained (see Chapter 5). In the United States the reaction was no more supportive. Michael Berger, for instance, recalls that Jewish Americans (even relatives) were sometimes willing to hear "a little bit" about his or other survivors' experiences.[11]

> [But then] they didn't want to hear any more. Or they would tell you that "we suffered, too. Did you know that we couldn't get any sugar [during the war] and that gasoline was rationed?" It was as if they were comparing their suffering with ours. Perhaps they felt guilty about what happened to their European relatives—that they either didn't do enough to help them or didn't dare to protest strongly. So we actually stopped talking about it. We felt that nobody understood us or wanted to understand us. (Berger 1995:14)

In his study of Holocaust survivors in the United States, Aaron Hass (1995) found that most did not speak at any length about their experience for at least thirty years after the war, if they spoke of it at all. Up until that time the world was not quite ready to hear them, to say nothing of embracing them as revered figures. They were seen as "displaced persons," "refugees," or "greenhorns," and were not yet celebrated as "survivors" (Novick 1999). This state of affairs, however, was eventually to change.

Jewish Americans and the Rise of Holocaust Consciousness

Eliezer Ben-Rafel (1982) defines an ethnic group as a collective entity whose members share some primordial attributes such as history, religion, language, or physical appearance (often referred to as "race") as well as particular socio-cultural characteristics and an awareness of themselves as constituting a distinct group.[12] Mitch Berbrier (2000) notes that ethnicity is a social construction, less an objective category than a subjective perception or collective representation. While ethnicity may be an externally imposed label used by those in power to oppress a particular group, it may also be self-imposed and used by members as a resource to promote social solidarity and advance a cause or claim (Nagel 1994).

According to Berbrier (2000), the social agents of ethnicity often comprise an "ethnicity industry," that is, a heterogeneous network of people and institutions involved in promoting, maintaining, and/or modifying particular constructions of ethnicity and the interests of their ethnic group.[13] An ethnicity industry includes ethnic associations and fund-raising organizations, ethnic libraries and museums, ethnic studies programs in schools and universities, ethnic diversity or multicultural programs, ethnic festivals and rituals of ethnic commemoration, and government agencies dealing with ethnic-group issues. Norman Finkelstein (2000) refers to Jewish-American activities regarding the Holocaust as constituting a "Holocaust industry." But this was by no means the case until the late 1960s.

While World War II had united Americans, the Vietnam War and Watergate scandal undermined the nation's sense of collective identity and eroded the government's political legitimacy. According to Novick, by the 1970s the United States had come "to be seen as an inappropriate (and unworthy) object of 'we' feelings," and people began looking elsewhere for a sense of group identity and feeling of connection to a moral community (1999:189). The "melting pot" vision of a universal American culture that would assimilate disparate ethnic groups and diminish particularistic identities gave way to a multicultural vision of ethnic pluralism that would preserve diversity (Parrillo 1997). For socially disadvantaged nonwhite groups, however, ethnic heritage or ancestry proved to be a weaker basis of group solidarity than a shared sense of disadvantage or "victim identity." Victimhood was embraced and victimization rhetorics were used to mobilize efforts to gain access to the "American dream" (see Chapter 5).

Prior to the multicultural movement, Jewish Americans had tried to downplay their ethnicity and present themselves as "just like everybody else, [even] more so" (Novick 1999:7). Jews were one of the most economically successful and culturally assimilated ethnic groups in the country. High rates of interfaith marriages and declining religious observance led to a loss of ethnic cohesion and group identity. In many respects Jewish ethnicity mirrored that of other white ethnic groups (e.g. Irish, Italians, Poles) for whom ethnicity has become a rather shallow and amorphous experience, tied more to feelings about family and family lineage than about membership in a larger social group (Alba 1990; Freedman 2000; Lipset & Raab 1995; Nagel 1994).

Moreover, until the 1967 Six Day War the Holocaust had remarkably little impact on the ethnic identity of American Jews (Finkelstein 2000). Jewish-American elites supported the U.S. position in the cold war and its pragmatic approach to reconciliation with the FRG. Holocaust survivors, as already noted, were not held in high esteem and were urged to keep silent about their experiences. Whereas nowadays victim status has become appropriated as a political resource, in earlier periods "it evoked at best the sort of pity mixed with contempt. Few wanted to think of themselves as victims, and even fewer to be thought about that way by others" (Novick 1999:121). Most Jewish Americans "regarded the victimhood symbolized by the Holocaust as a feature of the Old World that they . . . were putting behind them" (ibid.).

The Six Day War, however, began to change Jewish-American's complacency toward the Holocaust. Previously the United States government had not been an undisputed ally of Israel. It had been concerned about some Israeli leaders' socialist leanings and had pressured Israel to return land it occupied after the 1956 military conflict with Egypt. Secretary of State John Foster Dulles urged President Dwight Eisenhower to pay more attention to the Arab states as "potential allies against the Soviet Union" (Sachar 1992:724). Nonetheless, relations between the United States and Egypt deteriorated as Egyptian president Gamel Abdel Nasser tried to expand his territorial empire, to undermine pro-Western governments in the Middle East, and to turn to the Soviet Union for economic aid.

During the 1960 presidential campaign, John Kennedy sought the Jewish vote in key states that helped him secure victory, and his administration introduced a more favorable tilt in U.S. foreign policy toward Israel. Although Kennedy did not support Israel on every issue, he made a point of explaining his policies to Jewish Americans and of "displaying sensitivity to their concerns" (Sachar 1992:731). Kennedy was the first U.S. president to approve the sale of weapons to Israel, providing an assurance of support that had not been forthcoming in either the Truman or Eisenhower administrations. Subsequently, Israel's military success in the Six Day War solidified the state's position as a capable U.S. ally and an important strategic asset in the Middle East. Jewish Americans felt increasingly self-confident in voicing political support and providing financial assistance for Israel (Miller 1990; Novick 1999).

Still the Six Day War, along with the Yom Kippur War of 1973, left Israelis and their Jewish-American supporters uneasy about Israel's security and made fears of a renewed Holocaust more imaginable (see Chapter 5). According to Novick, for some Jews, thinking about Israel's situation in the Middle East in terms of the Holocaust was "spontaneous and unstudied" (1999:165). But others saw the Holocaust as an ideological resource that could be used to mobilize support for Israel by imbuing complex contemporary disputes "with the moral clarity of the Nazi period" (ibid.). The newly heightened status of victims brought about by the "victim identity" movement helped remove inhibitions that had previous led Jewish Americans to shun the victim label. Jewish-American leaders discovered that the Holocaust drew more Jews to public events than any other subject and was capable of appealing to Jews who had only marginal Jewish affiliations. They also recognized that the Holocaust could be used as a fund-raising resource for Jewish causes, particularly for support of Israel and for Holocaust-related organizations and activities themselves (Finkelstein 2000; Freedman 2000).

Some Jews hoped that "Holocaust consciousness" would become a vehicle for Jewish Americans to rediscover the religious core of Judaism. Instead, however, it became a sort of secular or "civil religion," much like what had occurred in Israel (Freedman 2000; Prosono & Brock 1996; Vital 1991). It was the Holocaust, not Judaism, that gave Jews their sense of ethnic identity. Now all could be united in their common "knowledge that but for the immigration of near or distant ancestors, they would have shared the fate of European Jewry" (Novick 1999:190). In doing so they advanced a claim about the Holocaust's uniqueness that, as we shall see, led to hostile reactions from other ethnic groups with whom Jews have engaged in competitions of victimhood (Linenthal 1995; Rosenbaum 1996; Rosenfeld 1999). At the same time, Jewish Americans constructed a collective memory of the Holocaust that would speak to their concerns and not just to the concerns of Israelis. Israelis in turn became anxious that the Diaspora Jews were no longer accepting the primacy of an Israel-centered Holocaust memory, of the exclusive right of Israelis to speak for the Jewish dead, or for that matter, the Jewish people of the world (Bresheeth 1997; Rabinbach 1997).[14]

The United States Holocaust Memorial Museum

In many respects the United States Holocaust Memorial Museum (USHMM), which opened in April 1993, represents the ultimate American usurpation of Holocaust memory. Located on the Washington Mall in Washington, D.C., the "ceremonial center" that holds the country's other national monuments, the USHMM places the Holocaust squarely within the official memory of the United States (Linenthal 1995:2). According to Edward Linenthal's account, the museum was the outcome of years of deliberation and planning that began in 1978, when President Jimmy Carter established the President's Commission on the Holocaust (PCH). Carter's decision to create the commission took place amid the attention given to NBC's *Holocaust* miniseries and was motivated by a desire to appease Jewish concerns about the president's pro-Arab tilt in the Middle East, particularly his linkage of aircraft sales previously promised to Israel to aircraft sales to Egypt and Saudi Arabia, as well as his willingness to include the Palestine Liberation Organization in peace talks that recognized the legitimate rights of the Palestinian people.

Carter's chief of domestic policy, Stuart Eizenstat, who himself had numerous relatives who were killed in the Holocaust, helped persuade the president that the creation of a memorial would send an important symbolic message, on the occasion of Israel's thirtieth anniversary: that the administration remained a staunch supporter of the Israeli state. In an executive order Carter empowered the PCH to make "recommendations with respect to the establishment and maintenance of an appropriate memorial to those who perished in the Holocaust" (cited in ibid.:23).

Holocaust survivor Elie Wiesel was appointed to head the commission. Wiesel was characterized by various Carter advisors as an "undisputed expert on the Holocaust period," a "non-political appointment [that would be] virtually free of attack from most sources," and the "one candidate who would be undisputed by the Jewish community" (cited in ibid.:21).[15] Wiesel's rise to prominence reflects not only his own accomplishments as a prolific author and Nobel Peace Prize winner, but the elevated status of survivors more generally. Once the Holocaust was embraced, however belatedly, the designation "survivor" evoked not just sympathy but honor and admiration, even awe. Wiesel was especially revered, acquiring what some characterize as a saintlike (even Christ-like) status, as a man who returned from the citadel of death and whose suffering carried with it a prophetic obligation to remind people of what had occurred and to warn them of what might happen again if the Holocaust were to be forgotten (Novick 1999; Sachar 1992).

While President Carter would have been satisfied with a monument to the Holocaust, Wiesel and other members of the PCH wanted it to be a "living memorial" that would include a museum, archive, and educational/research institute. Some discussion took place as to whether the memorial should be located in New York City or Washington, D.C. One member, historian Lucy Dawidowicz, spoke in favor of New York, arguing that it was the "center of the Jewish population in the United States and the cultural crossroads of the modern world. A site facing or near the United Nations would be particularly suitable" (quoted in Linenthal 1995:57–58). According to Linenthal, however, others felt that a "museum built in New York, even if national in intent, would . . . be perceived as a Jewish museum built in the heart of the Jewish community in America. Memory of the Holocaust would [thus] remain the province of American Jews" (ibid.:59). Locating the memorial in Washington, D.C., on the other hand, would more clearly situate the Holocaust within the nation's collective memory.[16]

The government's decision to sponsor a Holocaust memorial, especially on the Washington Mall, raised the ire of other victimized groups. Why privilege the Holocaust, which was largely a European tragedy, when African Americans or Native Americans had no such national memorial of their own? The argument, therefore, had to be made as to why the Holocaust was an event central to American memory, why it offered valuable "lessons" for Americans themselves. According to commission member Michael Berenbaum, "we see in [the Holocaust] a violation of every essential American value, . . . [of] in-alienable rights of all people, equal rights under the law, restraint on the power of government, and respect for that which our Creator has given and which the human community should not take away" (1993:2–3). Thus the Holocaust "clarified the importance of adhering to democratic values, and offered a stark historical example of what happened when such values failed" (Linenthal 1995:67).

But there was another side to Holocaust memory that provided lessons for Americans as well: the indifference to human suffering near and afar. Here the PHC decided that an American museum should not simply represent the Al-lie's role in defeating Nazism and liberating victims from the death camps, but of failing to do more, of failing to enact rescue efforts in a timely manner in order to save more lives (see Chapter 4). While it is counterintuitive to think that a government would sponsor a memorial that characterized its history in a negative light, PCH historical consultant Sybil Milton noted that this mes-sage would underscore the contemporary "commitment of the United States to an active participatory role in the world" (cited in Rabinbach 1997:241). Similarly, historian David Wyman asserted that "an American consensus had been reached on . . . the need for the United States to intervene to stop po-tential future genocides or at the minimum to act to alleviate the impacts of any such catastrophes" (cited in ibid.). In the words of political columnist George Will, "No other nation has broader, graver responsibilities in the world. . . . No other nation more needs citizens trained to look life in the face" (cited in Linenthal 1995:65).

The Bystander Narrative   Anson Rabinbach notes that state-sponsored narra-tives of the Holocaust "in different countries vary markedly in the proportion of attention given to perpetrators, victims, and bystanders" (1997:240). He be-lieves that the emphasis on the bystander in the USHMM "subtly shifts the moral weight of the story from the crimes of the perpetrators to the offence of the bystanders," as if the bystanders are as guilty as the perpetrators themselves (ibid.:242). At the dedication of the museum in 1993, President Bill Clinton gave credence to this view when he said: "Far too little was done. . . . Before the war even started, doors to liberty were shut, and even after the United States and the Allies attacked Germany, rail lines to the camps within miles of mili-tarily significant targets were left undisturbed" (quoted in Novick 1999:48).

Since the late 1960s a series of historical works have been critical if not outright condemnatory of the United States' response to the Holocaust (see Rubenstein 1997).[17] In a review of this literature, Frank Brecher (1990) iden-tifies Wyman's 1984 book, *The Abandonment of the Jews,* as the culmination of these efforts. Wyman's account, having "achieved a certain canonical status," became the basis for much of the bystander narrative in the museum (Novick 1999:48). This narrative contains three basic elements of a morality tale that indicts "the United States for complicity in the Holocaust" (ibid.):

(1) a restrictive prewar immigration policy, which prevented European Jews from escaping before the trap closed; (2) the failure to pursue various prospects for threats, reprisals, or negotiations to alleviate the situation of Jews within Hitler's grasp; and . . . (3) the unwillingness of the U.S. Air Force to bomb the rail lines leading to Auschwitz or the killing facilities themselves. (ibid.:48–49)

In Chapter 4 I tried to present a balanced account of the first two elements, reserving discussion of the bombing issue until now. I avoided a moralizing tone and informed the reader of scholarly disagreements regarding events that did (and did not) transpire. The narrative in the Holocaust museum, however, was constructed to tell a story of the indifferent bystander and thus avoided any ambiguities and complexities of historical interpretation and evidence that might leave visitors with a sense of doubt or uncertainty about the understanding they should take away with them (Linenthal 1995).

Wyman's narrative of the bombing issue—first advanced in a 1978 article and later in his 1984 book—has been singled out by analysts as the central and most emotionally laden symbol of American indifference to the Holocaust (Neufeld & Berenbaum 2000; Rubenstein 1997; see Chapter 4, note 21). Novick suggests that in the museum it is in some ways the dramatic climax of the narrative, for "after walking through graphic representations of death camps, the visitor encounters a floor-to-floor display condemning the refusal to bomb Auschwitz—as if to say, 'The American government could have, but chose not to, put an end to this'" (1999:54). Linenthal describes the exhibit this way:

[The visitors] come to a photomural of a U.S. Air Force intelligence photograph of Auschwitz-Birkenau, taken on May 31, 1944. The text . . . [reads], "Two freight trains with Hungarian Jews arrived in Birkenau that day; the large-scale gassing of these Jews was beginning. The four Birkenau crematoria are visible at the top of the photograph." Next to the photomural is an artifactual indictment of American indifference, the August 14, 1944, letter from Assistant Secretary of War John J. McCloy in which he "rejected a request by the World Jewish Congress to bomb the Auschwitz concentration camp." Explaining to visitors that the U.S. Air Force "could have bombed Auschwitz as early as May 1944," since bombers had "struck Buna, a synthetic-rubber works relying on slave labor, located less than five miles east of Auschwitz-Birkenau," the text notes that the death camp "remained untouched." And, it concludes, "although bombing Auschwitz would have killed many prisoners, it would also have halted the operation of the gas chambers and, ultimately, saved the lives of many more." (1995:217–18)

According to Wyman's (1984) account, the United States War Department rejected several appeals, mostly from Jewish sources, regarding the bombing of Auschwitz. McCloy claimed that "such an operation could be executed only by the diversion of considerable air support essential to the success of our forces now engaged in decisive operations elsewhere and would in any case be of such doubtful efficacy that it would not warrant the use of our resources" (cited in Wyman 1984:296). Wyman rejects both rationales, noting the proximity of the Buna bombing raids and the fact that the War Department never actually investigated the feasibility of such bombing missions. Rather, it acted on the basis of an a priori policy of noninvolvement in rescue activities. Wyman goes on to explain why, in his estimate, such bombing would have been possible and how it would have saved lives.

The museum's narrative of the bombing issue ignores the complex literature that has developed around this question. Several analysts have offered evidence to dispute Wyman's assessment of the feasibility and potential effectiveness of bombing, and have noted that it was even opposed by some Jewish leaders, who feared it would cost more lives than it would save. Others, however, have supported the basic thrust of Wyman's assessment with additional empirical evidence, or they have at least granted Wyman's position more credence than his critics are willing to concede (Neufeld & Berenbaum 2000; Rubenstein 1997; Teveth 1996).

The point here is not to evaluate this literature but to note that the museum's portrayal is one-sided. One view has been "elevated from interpretive stance to historical truth" (Linenthal 1995:224). Moreover, as Rabinbach observes, the "lesson" of the museum's bystander narrative is "morally ambiguous" because it does not help the visitor evaluate the circumstances that might compel a bystander to act or the conditions that would make such actions productive, futile, or even harmful (1997:241). Instead, the museum offers an apparently "universal principle of intervention . . . to be followed in all circumstances where crimes against humanity occur, when in effect it presents only the most extreme case of inhumanity as the criterion for action" (ibid.:241–42). Novick wonders whether this "lesson" will be interpreted as justifying humanitarian intervention *only* when contemporary atrocities parallel the Holocaust, and whether horrors that do not meet this criterion will "seem insufficiently dramatic, even a bit boring" (1999:257).

Linenthal (1995) suggests that the United States' sporadic and selective interventions in recent global affairs shows how Holocaust memory cannot provide a clear direction for foreign policy, for in the political sphere such memory is to be taken seriously when it is in the interest of the powerful to do so and ignored when other priorities intrude. Writing of the 1990's "ethnic cleansing" of Muslim Bosnians by the Serbian government in the former Yugoslavia, which included mass murders of civilians and the systematic rape of women, Linenthal asks:

Was the appropriate analogy the Holocaust, which damned indifference and demanded intervention? Was it Vietnam, which cautioned against becoming trapped in a quagmire? Should the events be understood as a civil war, lending support to those who claimed America had no stake in the fighting? Was the fighting an expression of ancient ethnic hatreds, which implied an endless course of blood-letting impervious to outside intervention. Expressing his own confusion three days after the museum opened, Secretary of State Warren Christopher asked, "[How am] I able to sort out which of these things are possible situations like the Holocaust?" (ibid.:264)

Linenthal's observations point to the ambiguity of framing a particular event as an instance of "genocide" that would construct the problem as a matter of sufficient concern so as to justify government intervention (Gamson 1995). Perhaps the question asked by Carter's national-security advisor Zbigniew Brzezinski on the day of the museum's dedication most aptly describes the bystander legacy of the Holocaust: Is Holocaust remembrance a "proclamation of a moral imperative . . . [or a] pompous affirmation of hypocrisy?" (cited in Linenthal 1995:266).

The Politics of Uniqueness and Competitions of Victimhood

A common axiom of the Holocaust industry, a view that is reflected in the USHMM and in much Jewish scholarship about the Holocaust, is that the Jewish genocide is unique and that attempts to compare it with other events constitute, in Lipstadt's words, "immoral equivalencies" (1993:212). Such claims entail an attempt to resist what social problems theorists refer to as "domain expansion," the process by which the boundaries of an accepted social problem are expanded to include a broader array of circumstances (Best 1990; Loseke 1999). As suggested earlier, Jewish resistance to domain expansion has raised the ire of other ethnic groups.

Controversy over the so-called uniqueness doctrine emerged early in the deliberations of the PCH. President Carter favored a broad definition of the Holocaust that included both six million Jews and five million non-Jews (e.g., Gypsies, Poles, Soviet POWs) who were killed.[18] Wiesel, on the other hand, was among those who were adamant about maintaining the Jewish core of the museum. Any attempt to extend the boundary of this core would diminish, trivialize, and efface the memory of the Jewish dead. Other groups could be included, but they had to be kept at the periphery "in a carefully managed hierarchy of victims" (Linenthal 1995:113). Wiesel seemed to fear that if eleven rather than six million victims were given prominence, the non-Jews would receive 5/11 of the museum's space (Novick 1999).

Berenbaum tried to broker a compromise in the PCH by arguing that there was "no conflict between describing the uniqueness of the Jewish experience and the inclusion of other victims of Nazism" (cited in Linenthal 1995:228). In fact, he insisted that "the examination of all victims is not only politically desirable but pedagogically mandatory if we are to demonstrate the claim of uniqueness" (ibid.). In the end, however, the Wiesel position won out, as the "other victims" of the Holocaust received "little more than perfunctory mention in the museum's permanent exhibition," although it was agreed that more flexibility would be allowed in "temporary" museum displays and in the museum's other educational and research activities (Novick 1999:220).

The uniqueness controversy was also prominent in PCH deliberations over questions of how (or if) the museum would portray historical precedents to the Holocaust, particularly the 1915 Turkish genocide of over one million Armenians, a Christian minority in Muslim Turkey (see Rosenbaum 1996). Berenbaum was among those who favored a substantial Armenian presence, wanting to present the Armenian genocide as a "prelude" to the Holocaust while at the same time showing that "unlike the Turkish clash with the Armenians during which Armenians living in Constantinople and other cities were safe—and only those living in the East were at risk—all Jews in Europe were targeted" (cited in Linenthal 1995:236–37). In this way, Berenbaum argued, the comparison would still portray the Holocaust "as a unique, hitherto unprecedented event" (ibid.).

Nonetheless, resistance in the PCH to this sort of inclusion remained strong. And when the Turkish government (which to this day has refused to acknowledge that a genocide rather than mere wartime casualties took place) stepped into the fray, the political pressure to marginalize the Armenians grew (Novick 1999). One member of the PCH was even warned by the Turkish ambassador to the United States that "the well-being of Jews might be threatened were Armenians included in a federal Holocaust museum" (Linenthal 1995:232). Israeli officials also lobbied PCH members to exclude the Armenians, noting that Turkey was a NATO ally and "served as an escape route for Jews from Iran" (ibid.:239). In the end Berenbaum succeeded in salvaging only one reference to the Armenians for inclusion in the permanent exhibit, and this was an oft-quoted remark of Hitler: "I have issued the command . . . that our war aim does not consist in reaching certain lines, but in the physical destruction of the enemy. . . . Only thus shall we gain the living space which we need. Who, after all, speaks today of the annihilation of the Armenians?" (cited in Berenbaum 1993:62).[19]

Troubled by the PCH decision and the political lobbying that influenced it, Berenbaum told the members that such constraints on the boundaries of memory would evince "the politicization of our mission" and diminish "our ability to reach out and to include groups who naturally can see in the Holocaust a sensitive metaphor to their own experience" (cited in Linenthal 1995:235). Unlike other PCH members, Berenbaum was quite comfortable with an Americanization of the Holocaust that would expand the boundaries of memory and thus appeal to a broader audience.

Gavriel Rosenfeld (1999) notes that Jewish advocacy of the uniqueness doc-

trine emerged in the late 1970s and was in part a defensive reaction to the initial postwar indifference to Jewish survivors, to the attempts to relativize the
Holocaust with unwarranted comparisons (including those made by Israel's
Arab adversaries), and to outright Holocaust denial.[20] Alexander, for example,
complained that the world had initially reacted as if "the enormity of the Holocaust could be recognized . . . only if it were universalized, [only] if its victims
were recast, as we have seen [with] Anne Frank, . . . as 'human beings' rather
than as Jews" (1994:195).

It was quite natural, however, that Jewish claims of uniqueness and the
growing public interest in the Holocaust would provoke envy if not hostility
from other ethnic groups who were competing for media attention and political and economic resources to address their own social problems (see Gusfield
1981; Hilgartner & Bosk 1988; Loseke 1999; Neuman 1998). Armenians and
Gypsies were offended by being relegated to the periphery of the USHMM;
and African Americans, Native Americans, and other ethnic groups felt that
it was just as important—in some cases more important—to remember their
tragic histories (Linenthal 1995; Novick 1999). In advancing a claim that the
Holocaust was unique and unsurpassed by all other atrocities, were not Jews
trivializing or discounting the experiences of other groups? And were not Jews
in fact one of the most privileged ethnic groups in American society? Who
were they to claim that their suffering has been (is) worse than all others? Perhaps claims regarding the Holocaust's uniqueness have supplied the United
States with a convenient pretext for ignoring its own murderous past. Perhaps
it is propaganda intended to divert attention from the ongoing Israeli genocide of the Palestinians. These are some of the charges that were levied by
opponents of the Jewish-American Holocaust industry (Finkelstein 2000;
Rosenbaum 1996; Rosenfeld 1999).

Arguably one of the most publicized ethnic-group conflicts over the Holocaust has taken place between Jewish and African Americans (Novick 1999).[21]
Blacks' objections to Jewish claims to preeminent victim status were explained
by the critically acclaimed writer James Baldwin in 1967:

> One does not wish . . . to be told by an American Jew that his suffering is as
> great as the American Negro's suffering. It isn't, and one knows that it isn't from
> the very tone in which he assures you that it is. . . . The Jew's suffering is rec-
> ognized as part of the moral history of the world and the Jew is recognized as a
> contributor to the world's history: this is not true for blacks. . . . The Jew is a
> white man, and when white men rise up against oppression, they are heroes:
> when black men rise, they have reverted to their native savagery. . . . [I]t is not
> here, and not now, that the Jew is being slaughtered, and he is never despised,
> here, as the Negro is, because he is an American. The Jewish travail occurred
> across the sea and America rescued him from the house of bondage. But Amer-
> ica is the house of bondage for the Negro, and no country can rescue him.
> ([1967] 1994:34–35, 37)

Years later, in 1987, Nai'm Akbar, a president of the National Association of Black Psychologists, expressed a similar sentiment:

> [It is a] simplistic notion of slavery which makes it easy for people to compare their holocaust to our holocaust. They don't understand that going to the ovens knowing who you are, is damn well better than walking around for 100 years not knowing who you are. . . . Our holocaust in America is worse than the holocaust in Europe. (cited in Amato 1990:159–60)

More recently, in 1993, Khalid Abdul Muhammad, who at the time was Minister Louis Farrakhan's "national assistant" in the Nation of Islam, delivered a well-publicized speech at Kean College in New Jersey in which he demonized Jews as Christ killers, slaveholders, bloodsuckers of black people—the worst of the world's exploiters, agents of the devil, who "everywhere they go . . . undermined the very fabric of society" (quoted in Berman 1994:2). It was the kind of speech that might have been given in the Middle Ages. Farrakhan himself, who has a popular following among some segments of the African-American community, and whom mainstream African-Americans leaders are reluctant to criticize, added heat to the fire by (falsely) claiming that "75 percent of the black slaves in the Old South were owned by . . . Jews!" (quoted in Berman 1994:3; see also Lipset & Raab 1995).[22]

A few months later, in an attempt to promote reconciliation, then New Jersey governor Christie Todd Whitman proposed showing *Schindler's List* at a forum on racism at Trenton College in which Muhammad was a keynote speaker. Upon seeing the film Muhammad remarked: "That was a Holocaust but African Americans pay a hell of a cost" (quoted in Loshitzky 1997:6). Some time later he referred to the film as "swindler's list." Such remarks not only illustrate the depths of resentment that some blacks hold toward Jews—a resentment that is returned in kind by some Jews as well—but also the precarious nature of trying to use one group's oppression to gain insight into the oppression of another (Berman 1994; Lipset & Raab 1995; Loshitzky 1997).

In the middle of the Muhammad controversy, in January 1994, another widely reported incident made the news. A well-intentioned teacher in Oakland, California, had arranged for a group of black and Latino high-school students to attend a screening of *Schindler's List* on Martin Luther King Day. The teacher had hoped to expose the "students to the Holocaust as a paradigmatic lesson of the evils of racism on a national holiday honoring one of America's champions of civil rights and racial harmony" (Shandler 1997:163). However, when the students disrupted the showing by responding to some of the most violent scenes with raucous laughter and "in a manner reminiscent of audience participation in Rambo-style films," they were asked to leave the theatre (Bartov 1997b:49).

The Simon Wiesenthal Center's Museum of Tolerance (MOT) in Los Angeles, which opened two months before the USHMM, represents one of the most ambitious efforts to bridge the ethnic-oppression divide. The MOT boasts of an annual visitation of 350,000, including 110,000 children who are regularly bused in for school field trips. The theme of the museum departs significantly from the uniqueness doctrine by situating the Holocaust in a broader context of "bigotry and racism" while also characterizing the Jewish genocide as "the ultimate example of man's inhumanity to man" (see www.wiesenthal.com).

The MOT describes itself as "a high tech, hands-on experiential museum that . . . challenge[s] visitors to confront bigotry and racism, and to understand the Holocaust in both historic and contemporary contexts." In addition to its "Holocaust Section" the museum also includes several exhibits in its so-called "Tolerancenter." "The Point of View Diner" re-creates "a 1950's diner, red booths and all, that 'serves' a menu of controversial topics on video jukeboxes" such as drunk driving and hate speech that are intended to covey the "message of personal responsibility." "The Millennium Machine" is a "high-tech 'time machine'" that covers "a series of human rights abuses throughout the world, such as the exploitation of women and children, the threat of terrorism, and the plight of refugees and political prisoners." The section on "Ain't You Gotta Right?" presents a "16-screen video wall detailing the struggle for civil rights in America." And "In Our Time" is a film on "Bosnia, Rwanda and contemporary hate groups that pinpoints contemporary human rights violations going on throughout the world today."

Some observers have complained about the "Disney" quality of the high-tech exhibits and the MOT's promiscuous comparisons of the Holocaust with such a wide range of events (Rabinbach 1997; Rosenfeld 1997). On the other hand, there is no doubting that the Holocaust is the MOT's primary focus, and together with the Simon Wiesenthal Center (SWC), it is arguably one of the most successful institutions of the Holocaust industry. The SWC, which was founded in 1977, describes itself as "an international Jewish human rights organization" that is involved in a wide range activities related to: "the prosecution of Nazi war criminals; Holocaust and tolerance education; Middle East Affairs; and extremist groups, neo-Nazism, and hate on the Internet" (www.wiesenthal.com). Its mailings, like those of other Jewish organizations, regularly remind Jews of the dangers of anti-Semitism, both in the United States and abroad, and of their obligation to send money. The statements of African Americans such as Muhammad and Farrakhan have been good for the SWC's fund-raising efforts (Novick 1999).

Contemporary Compensation Claims

Earlier I noted that the Holocaust has been recognized by Jewish-American leaders as a fund-raising resource for Jewish causes. In the 1990s organizations such as the World Jewish Congress (WJC) headed by wealthy businessman Edgar Bronfman began focusing on the issue of compensation from European business interests that had capitalized on Jewish suffering during the war. The case that has received the most attention involves the Swiss banking industry, which was negligent if not capricious in withholding monies due to Jewish depositors or their heirs after the war (Bowers 1997; Chesnoff 1999; Finkelstein 2000; see Chapter 3). In this effort Bronfman enlisted the political clout of Alphonse D'Amato, then senator from New York and chairman of the Senate Banking Committee, as well as President Bill Clinton and Hillary Clinton, to pressure Swiss banks to agree to a $1.25 billion settlement. The Swiss controversy was also a catalyst to other settlements and ongoing litigation with corporations in various countries that exploited slave labor during the war (including U.S. companies that did business in Germany), as well as insurance companies that failed to compensate Jews for their loses (Herman 1999; Hirsch 1999; Jelinek 2000; Petropoulos 2001).[23]

Although many (if not most) people commend the lobbying on behalf of Holocaust survivors, some feel that the demand for compensation has been excessive and even constitutes a form of "blackmail" of companies, which fear losing even more if they contest the claims and subject themselves to civil lawsuits (Chesnoff 1999; Finkelstein 2000). Moreover, foreign financial institutions wishing to do business in the United States are vulnerable to political pressure from the U.S. government. As Congressman Benjamin Gilman of the House International Relations Committee remarked, "It is extremely important that the countries involved in the issue understand that their response . . . is one of several standards by which the United States assesses its bilateral relationship" (quoted in Finkelstein 2000:133–34).

Finkelstein (2000) is one of the most strident critics of the Holocaust industry, which he describes as a network of Jewish elites and organizations (and their gentile lawyers/consultants) that he thinks are seeking self-aggrandizement from the Holocaust.[24] According to Finkelstein, the problem is not that survivors are undeserving of compensation. Rather, it is that so much of the money will in fact not go to the victims of the Holocaust but to high-priced lawyers and Jewish organizations led by men earning lucrative six-figure salaries. Lawrence Eagleburger, for instance, who served as secretary of state under President George Bush, enjoys an annual salary of $300,000 as chair of the International Commission on Holocaust-Era Insurance Claims. D'Amato, no longer a senator, earns $350 hour plus expenses for his work in mediating Holocaust-related lawsuits. Other Holocaust-industry lawyers earn even more.

At the same time, various Jewish leaders claim that their organizations deserve a substantial portion of the settlement monies, much of which involves heirless assets, which they intend to spend on their own Holocaust and Jewish education projects. The WJC, for example, has amassed about $7 billion for its efforts on behalf of Holocaust survivors seeking compensation for their suffering (ibid.). In addition, different religious denominations have fought over their right to use the money to promote their particular branches of Judaism. All the scrambling for the proceeds has led survivor Abraham Foxman, who is also the National Director of the ADL, to complain that the restitution controversy is "desecrating the memory of the Holocaust" (quoted in Chesnoff 1999:279).

Finkelstein also decries what he sees as the hypocrisy of the Holocaust industry. He notes, for instance, that for a lecture fee of $25,000 Wiesel will talk about how the truth of the Holocaust "lies in silence," that it "defies both knowledge and description" and "cannot be explained nor visualized" (cited in ibid.:45). Or he disparages the Holocaust industry for shamelessly currying favor with politicians when, for example, the Simon Wiesenthal Center honored Ronald Reagan with its 1988 "Humanitarian of the Year" award in spite of the earlier Bitburg debacle that so many viewed as an insult to Holocaust memory. Finkelstein also wonders, along with African-American Congresswoman Maxine Waters, why efforts to compensate Holocaust survivors are celebrated while those who have been seeking reparations for the descendants of slave laborers in the United States "have literally been ridiculed" (quoted in ibid.:106–7). Thus, according to Finkelstein, the Holocaust industry's exploitation of victims' suffering constitutes a social problem in its own right.

On the other hand, Robert Chesnoff points out that the actions of the Holocaust industry have led to the declassification of countless invaluable documents and to investigations in many countries that have contributed greatly to our knowledge of the "whereabouts of stolen Nazi booty" and to the complicity of international businesses during the war (1999:272). And although the battles over the money at times appear unseemly, he reminds us that it is not the Jews but the perpetrators and their accomplices who exploited the Holocaust, and it would be a greater injustice to allow these profiteers to continue to enjoy the spoils of their misdeeds.

NOTES

1. Avisar (1997) notes that since the airing of the miniseries in Germany, German filmmakers have portrayed World War II as if it were like any other war (e.g., the Vietnam War), and hence they have relativized the Holocaust through counterrhetorical narratives that are either silent about Jewish victimization or that portray the German people as equal victims of that unfortunate period. All told, these films try to come "to grips with the past" by expunging the shameful parts of it (ibid.:47). For discussions of pro-German films about wartime military heroics, anti-Nazi resistance, and the innocence of everyday life removed from the Holocaust, see Avisar (1997), Marcuse (2001), and Santner (1990).
2. The latest version, an ABC miniseries that was aired in May 2001, was the first to continue the story by taking Anne into the concentration camps at Bergen-Belsen where she and her sister Margo died (Peyser 2001).
3. At the end of the film, Schindler's Jews are shown walking over the hills of Jerusalem as the song "Jerusalem of Gold" plays in the background. This song was

made popular during the 1967 Six Day War (see Chapter 5). However, in Israel the closing soundtrack was changed to "Eli, Eli," a musical version of a poem written by Hannah Senesh in 1941. Senesh was a Jewish commando who parachuted into occupied Hungary in 1944 to aid the Jewish underground. Cole (1999) thinks this change was an attempt by the Israelis to displace the heroic gentile (Schindler) with a heroic Jew.

4.   The second edition of the nearly eight-hundred-page book was published by Quadrangle in 1967, and the "revised and definitive" nearly thirteen-hundred-page version was published in three volumes by Holmes and Meier, along with an abridged version, in 1985.

5.   Goldhagen's book also covers the extermination camps and the death marches, the German westward evacuation of the camps to flee the advancing Soviet army. For other discussions of the latter, see Benz (2001), Berger (1995), and Krakowski (1990b).

6.   See Hilberg (1996) for a discussion of his own disputes with Arendt.

7.   The original notion of historical revisionism (in its legitimate guise) is credited to the historian William Appleman Williams, who reinterpreted dominant views regarding U.S. foreign policy, particularly as it relates to the cold war (Lipstadt 1993).

8.   In their valuable book, Shermer and Grobman dismantle each of these claims in some detail.

9.   See Chapter 5, note 25.

10.   Buchanan, a man of the political right, often complains that Jews have unduly influenced U.S. foreign policy toward the Middle East, leading to accusations that he is in fact anti-Semitic (Buckley 1992; Dershowitz 1991).

On the other side of the political spectrum, Noam Chomsky has drawn criticism for coming to the defense of French Holocaust denier Robert Faurisson. While Chomsky cannot be faulted for defending Faurisson's right to free speech, according to Dershowitz's account, he also "signed a petition that characterized Faurisson's falsifications of history as 'findings' and said that they were based on 'extensive historical research'" (1991:174). Chomsky also wrote an essay that he allowed to be used as a foreword to one of Faurisson's books (Lipstadt 1993; Shermer & Grobman 2000; Vidal-Naquet 1992).

11.   I use the term Jewish Americans, rather than American Jews, to emphasize this group's primary citizenship in the United States and to suggest comparability in this regard to other ethnic groups such as Italian Americans, Mexican Americans, and Polish Americans.

12.   According to Brodkin, the term "'ethnicity' did not come into use until after World War II, when it became the word of choice in academic and public-policy vocabularies to describe those who had been formerly discussed as members of a less-than-white white, nation or people" (1998:144).

13.   The "ethnicity industry" is a subset of what Loseke (1999) describes as the "social problems industry."

14.   Although Israeli officials have welcomed financial contributions from Jewish Americans, they have cautioned their U.S. brethren to take a back seat in Israeli affairs. As Ben-Gurion announced a few years after World War II: "I would propose that all Zionists in the Diaspora should have a voice in the affairs of the State of Israel . . . but only on the condition that they pay taxes to the State of Israel and become sub-

ject to military service" (quoted in Sachar 1992:719). Clearly the message was that only Israelis should speak for Zionism and for the Jewish people of the world.

15. In actuality, Wiesel is a more controversial figure than he was made out to be. Hitchens (2001), for instance, lambastes Wiesel for his uncritical support of Israel and apparent lack of sympathy for the plight of the Palestinians in the Middle East.

16. Cole reports that officials of the Israeli Yad Vashem memorial/museum (see Chapter 5) expressed concern "that their authoritative position in exhibiting the 'Holocaust' was seriously threatened" (1999:146). In an attempt to reassert Israel's dominant position in Holocaust memory, Yad Vashem has begun a major restructuring and expansion of its facilities.

17. This view has been accepted by many U.S. politicians. In 1985, for example, then vice president George Bush promised that "never again will the cries of abandoned Jews go unheard by the United States government" (quoted in Novick 1999:48).

18. See Chapter 1, note 2, on the claim that only five million non-Jews were killed.

19. Berenbaum and Milton had proposed that the Armenians also be included in a film *Nazi Rise to Power and Genocidal Precedents,* through reference to the fact that Secretary of Treasury Morgenthau had been moved to confront President Roosevelt about American indifference to the Holocaust because his father had been U.S. ambassador to Turkey during the Armenian genocide (see Chapter 4), and through reference to the inspiration that Jewish partisans from Bialystok drew from Franz Weferl's *The Forty Days of Musa Dagh,* a novel about Armenian resistance (Linenthal 1995).

20. For instance, some believe that the memory of Nazism and the Holocaust is trivialized when these experiences are used as metaphors to advocate for animal rights, prohibition of abortion, and opposition to gun control, as well as to draw attention to the AIDS epidemic, women's oppression, the dangers of "big government," and the suffering of adult children of alcoholics (Berger 1995; Novick 1999).

21. For historical accounts of the political alliances and divisions between Jewish and African Americans, see Berman (1994), Brodkin (1998), Kaufman (1994), and Salzman (1992).

22. A more accurate figure is probably closer to 0.3 percent (Lipset & Raab 1995).

23. U.S. banks also withheld assets of Holocaust survivors (Finkelstein 2000; Jalinek 2000).

24. See Steinweis (2001) for a critique of Finkelstein's polemical excesses.

7

Jews, Christians, and the Humanity of Difference

In his book *Night,* Elie Wiesel recalls "the little faces of the children whose bodies I saw turning into wreaths of smoke . . . which consumed my faith forever" (see Chapter 1). Yet Wiesel, who was deeply religious before the war, retained his beliefs, though he remains angry with God and perplexed about God's relationship to the Holocaust (Wiesel 1995).

Elsewhere, Wiesel tells the story of an eight-year-old girl and her mother who have arrived at a concentration camp. On the way to the gas chamber the girl questions her mother about where they are going. The mother replies, "to the end of the world." The daughter then asks if their destination is near and complains that she is tired. "Everyone is tired," her mother says. "Even God?" asks the girl. The mother responds, "You will ask Him yourself" (1978:144–45).

What God's answer might be, we will never know. Still, many a devout person has pondered God's silence during the Holocaust and engaged in genuine soul-searching over what are arguably unanswerable questions. Was He watching and He did nothing? Did He intend it to be, to have a higher purpose for the senseless deaths and suffering? As one Jewish survivor has said:

> My life is a running, nagging dialogue with God. . . . He is always on my mind. Why? Why? I sometimes find I have been walking the lonely, crowded streets . . . wandering aimlessly, conducting a question and answer session with him—with no satisfactory answers forthcoming. . . . I find I want very much to keep after Him and try to the best of my ability to overcome the obscurity of His ways. . . . I will do this to my last breath. . . . I believe this is precisely what a Jew must do, to keep after Him for answers. (Brenner 1980:98)

Whatever our religious inclinations, most of us remain confounded by the Holocaust, continue to search for ways to fathom its meaning, to untie the proverbial Gordian knot. But as we have seen throughout this book, the development and unfolding of claims and solutions to social problems is an on-going process, and thus the natural history of the "Jewish problem" and its so-lution continues to evolve. In dialectical fashion, each resolution of the problem breeds new problems, and so forth, as history marches on. The prob-lem of collective memory in particular is never really solved. The construction of the past, and its meaning for the present, is never completed.

In this chapter I conclude our examination of the social construction of the Holocaust by considering a set of interrelated issues that have emerged as sig-nificant problems in the postwar period. These include the problem of reli-gious faith after the Holocaust, the problem of Jewish continuity and of Christian-Jewish reconciliation, and the general problem of "difference" that underlies various forms of exclusionary social practices that deny people their right to be human.

JEWISH FAITH AND THE PROBLEM OF CONTINUITY

In the previous chapter I noted that ethnicity is a social construction, a prod-uct of both externally imposed labeling and internal self-definition. As such, ethnic identity is subject to ongoing dispute, negotiation, and redefinition; and ethnic history becomes a resource that is used by groups in their "collec-tive quest for meaning and community" (Nagel 1994:163). Throughout Jewish history religiosity has constituted the core of Jewish identity. The Holocaust, however, brought this religious faith into question by posing the dilemma of God's silence during the genocide.

The Silence of God

In many respects the theological problem of God's silence is no different than the one posed by the more general problem of unjust human suffering or, as one contemporary observer has asked, why "bad things happen to good peo-ple" (Kushner 1981). Even Jews who view the Holocaust as unique in its mag-nitude may see it as part of a longer history of Jewish martyrdom. And some Jews—following the biblical accounts of Abraham and Isaac and of Job—con-sider it to be God's ultimate test of their faith (Berkovits 1973; Katz 2001; Maybaum 1965).

Nevertheless, according to Richard Rubenstein and John Roth (1987), there is no escaping the conclusion that Biblical Judaism purports God to be the ultimate author of the Jews' fate and hence of their misfortune and expe-rience during the Holocaust. In traditional Jewish theology, God is believed to have entered into a special covenant with the Jews at the time He delivered the Ten Commandments to Moses at Mount Sinai following the Hebrews' de-liverance from Egyptian slavery. At the same time, God is said to have warned of dire consequences for his "chosen people" if they failed to obey divine law.

Moreover, some Orthodox Jews even hold non-Orthodox Jews responsible for their own misery, believing that the latter have erred in their ways and beliefs (Bauer 2001).[1]

In his postwar interviews with Holocaust survivors, Reeve Robert Brenner (1980) found that about 70 percent believed in God prior to the Holocaust. Among these individuals, only a third remained unwavering in their belief, while about a tenth lost faith in God's existence altogether. Regardless, most of the believers rejected the idea that "those who perished in the Holocaust were being punished by God for their own sinfulness" or that God may have had some other purpose such as a test of their faith or a desire to "purify moral character through suffering" (Rubenstein & Roth 1987:295).

Thus there was little agreement among Brenner's subjects with the traditional Jewish belief in a deity who actively intervenes in the affairs of humanity and who punishes those who ignore His commandments. Rather, most of the religiously inclined survivors believed in a God who granted people freedom of action and responsibility for their own actions. According to this view, as expressed by some Jewish theologians, God "created an imperfect world awaiting perfection. If we are to be full partners with God in perfecting the world's shortcomings, God must, of necessity hide Himself . . . so that we can bring about our own redemption" (Hass 1995:145; see also Katz 2001). As Arthur Cohen puts it, "God is not the strategist of our particularities or our historical condition, but rather the mystery . . . [and] hope of our futurity" (1981:97).

But Yehuda Bauer (2001) asks, if God has hidden Himself, is He not a callous God who chose to be absent and who could have stopped the Holocaust if He wanted? Hasn't He thus become irrelevant to humanity's affairs? Irving Greenberg (1990) suggests that perhaps God is no longer all-powerful, even if He once was, and that He now requires human cooperation to redress the ills of the world. Although "God is no longer in a position to command, . . . the Jewish people are so in love with the dream of redemption that [they have] volunteered to carry out the mission" (cited in Berenbaum 2001:628).

Other Jewish theologians try to skirt the issue of God's responsibility for the Holocaust by claiming that God's ways are mysterious and beyond the realm of human comprehension. Or they assert that the Holocaust, like the flood of Noah's time, was an act of creative destruction designed to bring the Jews and the world into a new and better age. Still others argue that the Holocaust challenges Jews to resist the logic of destruction represented by the genocide and engage in acts of resistance and restoration that mend or restore humanity, what in the Jewish tradition is known as *Tikkun* (Bauer 2001; Berenbaum 2001; Maybaum 1965; Rubenstein & Roth 1987).

Emil Fackenheim (1972) is among those who think that the biblical God of the Jews is not just a commanding God but a God of deliverance, and that the ultimate act of deliverance was the creation of the state of Israel. In turn,

Fackenheim believes that Jews are obligated to hold fast in their faith or they will grant Hitler another posthumous victory:

> We are . . . commanded to survive as Jews, lest the Jewish people perish. We are commanded . . . to remember in our very guts and bones the martyrs of the holocaust, lest their memory perish. We are forbidden . . . to deny or despair of God, however much we may have to contend with Him or with belief in Him, lest Judaism perish. We are forbidden, finally, to despair of the world as the place which is to become the kingdom of God, lest we help make it a meaningless place in which God is dead or irrelevant and everything is permitted. (1969:150)

Michael Berenbaum, on the other hand, thinks that Fackenheim's view is less a theological observation than an expression of "his fear of consequences"—that without their religious faith Jews as a people will cease to exist (2001: 627).

The Americanization of Judaism

Today about a third of the world's Jews, over 4.6 million people, live in the state of Israel, a nation that did not exist during the time of the Holocaust (World Almanac 2001). However, an even larger number of Jews live in the United States, about six million or about 42 percent of the world's Jewish population (U.S. Census Bureau 2001). Consequently, the circumstances of Jewish Americans is no mere aside but is in fact central to the problem of Jewish continuity in the post-Holocaust world. While most Jewish Americans view Israel as central to this continuity, they are increasingly asserting their right to chart their own course and construct their own identities as Jews, a process that can be characterized as the Americanization of Judaism.[2] In principle, the European Enlightenment of the eighteenth century called for Jews to receive formal citizenship rights as members of nation-states (see Chapter 2). But emancipation came with a price, for Jews were expected to pledge their primary loyalty to the country in which they lived and not to their religious group; better yet they were encouraged to divest themselves entirely of their inherited faith and assimilate into the dominant culture. Jewish integration into American society, however, came with fewer strings attached, and no homeland other than Israel has been more rewarding for Jews and accepting of them than the United States. While Jews have suffered anti-Semitism in America, ironically it is this country's acceptance of Jews, rather than its rejection, that poses the greatest threat to Jewish continuity (Freedman 2000; Lipset & Raab 1995; Tiryakian 1993).

Historians of the Jewish-American experience attribute this "favorable position of Judaism" to the special character of American Protestantism, which lacks a centrally organized structure and is composed instead of a plethora of individual denominations (Lipset & Raab 1995:29). The competition among these groups "enabled the Jews to fit in from the start of the republic as one religious entity out of many, rather than as the only or principal deviant group. . . . In fact, most Protestants tended to view Roman Catholics . . . more negatively than they did Jews" (ibid.:31).

The affinity of American Prostestantism for the Hebrew Bible goes back to the original Puritan founders. According to Jerold Auerbach (1990), the first Pilgrims who sailed from England in the seventeenth century interpreted their quest in terms of the Bible's account of the Hebrews' deliverance from Egyptian slavery. The Puritans believed that the Hebrew Bible was "the anticipatory text" for their own salvation and that "America was the promised land of biblical prophecy" (ibid.:7).

Auerbach adds that the initial Jewish immigrants from Germany took a page from their Puritan predecessors in their belief that America not Palestine was also *their* anticipated promised land. These immigrants, who arrived in the 1830s, constituted the first large wave of Jewish immigration. They were for the most part *Reform* Jews who were modern in outlook (Freedman 2000; Lipset & Raab 1995).

Reform Judaism first took hold in Germany in the early nineteenth century. This tradition asserts that many of the ritualistic practices and dogmas of the past are outmoded, and that Jews must make certain adjustments to living in a changing and predominantly non-Jewish world. Reform Jews assumed a prerogative to choose which Biblical laws were worthy of their allegiance and which were not. They placed greater emphasis on the moral teachings of Judaism, rather than on the sacred law per se, and drew inspiration from the Biblical accounts of the ancient Jewish Prophets, who preached a message of social justice that was consistent with rational ethical principles. Reform Jews wanted to remain connected to their Jewish heritage but were not interested in maintaining ethnic exclusivity. They were more oriented toward assimilation and blending into the mainstream (Auerbach 1990; Ausubel 1964; Carmody & Carmody 1993; Lipset & Raab 1995).[3]

The identification of *Orthodox* Judaism as a distinct denomination is associated with the emergence of the reform movement, for previously Judaism was Orthodox Judaism. Orthodox Jews adhere to a literal interpretation of the Hebrew Bible and continue to observe all the traditional Jewish laws, including the obligation to engage in daily prayer, follow special dietary rules, and abstain from working on the Sabbath. Men and women are required to remain separated during synagogue religious services, and females are denied the full rights to the religious education that is afforded to males (see note 1).

A third major variety, *Conservative* Judaism also emerged in the nineteenth century, at first in Germany but most influentially in the United States, where it became the largest Jewish denomination. Conservative Jews forged a compromise between the Reform and Orthodox camps. They were more traditional in their religious practices than the Reformed, but less likely than the Orthodox to accept the infallibility of sacred texts, asserting that "the divine origin of Jewish law . . . [was subject] to human development and application" (Auerbach 1990:74). Conservative Jews were also more inclusive of women than the Orthodox and more accommodating to the demands of modern society (e.g., they allow the driving of automobiles, or turning light switches off and on during the Sabbath) (Ausubel 1964; Carmody & Carmody 1993; Lipset & Raab 1995).

Irrespective of religious orientation, the early German immigrants as well as the mostly Eastern-European immigrants who followed them were disproportionately Jews with craft backgrounds, primarily in the garment trade (Lipset & Raab 1995). Many had experience as independent artisans or small businessmen. America's industrial economy, however, left little room for individual entrepreneurship and most immigrant Jews entered working-class occupations upon their arrival. They lived in ghettoized communities in the nation's urban centers. But unlike the ghetto experience in Europe, it seemed imminently possible to get out, at least for subsequent generations who were inculcated with a Jewish cultural tradition that emphasized education and literacy. Although Jews in America faced discrimination in institutions of higher education, they were first among European "immigrant groups to enter college in significant numbers" (Brodkin 1998:30). And although discrimination persisted in the corporate sector of the economy, the children of Jewish immigrants moved relatively unimpeded into the middle class through the pursuit of professional occupations like law, medicine, dentistry, pharmacy, and teaching.

Karen Brodkin (1998) points out that for a while the cultural tradition of *Yiddishkeit* played a significant role in the Jewish-American experience. As a language, the origins of Yiddish go back several centuries, but it is primarily a blend of Hebrew and German, with a smattering of other linguistic elements (Ausubel 1964). In Europe of the late nineteenth century it "provided a common link between Jews from different villages, regions, and nations" (Brodkin 1998:106). Yiddishkeit was nurtured by its religious heritage but was essentially a secular folk culture that "infused Jewish life with the intellectual, political, and artistic excitement of urban modernism" (ibid.). It drew attention to elements of Biblical Judaism that were compatible with a socialist vision of economic equality and social justice. In some urban communities of the United States in the years before World War II, Yiddishkeit inspired Jews to become major contributors to the politics of the American Left (Bershtel & Graubard 1992; Freedman 2000). According to Brodkin:

> This does not mean that all Jews were socialists, or even that Jewish socialism was the only recognized way of identifying oneself as a Jew within these communities. It does mean that part of being Jewish was being familiar with a work-

ing-class and anticapitalist outlook . . . and understanding this outlook as being particularly Jewish. It also meant that other versions of Jewish identity maintained a respectful dialogue with Jewish socialism. (1998:105)

The cultural tradition of Yiddishkeit showed "a way to be Jewish . . . without being religious" (Freedman 2000:37). Some contemporary Jews of the political left still view their Jewish heritage as providing the raw material for the expression of universally benevolent values such as equality and justice and the belief "that human worth [is] measured by service to the community rather than by wealth or recognition in the wider world" (Brodkin 1998:187). They note that Jews, though by no means a homogeneous political bloc, remain consistently more liberal than Americans of similar socioeconomic status, and that they have a noble history of principled alliances with other groups (e.g., African Americans) in the struggle for civil rights.[4] However, Jewish identity for them is a way of connecting their religious heritage to broader ethical commitments that are universally applicable to all. These commitments may have been derived from their ethnic upbringing or from the larger secular society, but their expression of these values represents a significant departure from Biblical Judaism, which did not aspire "to bring social justice" to anyone but Jews (Bershtel & Graubard 1992:252; see also Auerbach 1990; Lipset & Raab 1995).

Regardless, Yiddishkeit as a cultural force did not last much longer than the initial generation that brought it to the United States, for in the post–World War II period the conditions for its persistence began to unravel. As the proportion of Jews in white-collar jobs rose dramatically, Jewish affluence increased and interest in socialism subsided. Moreover, as Jews flocked to the suburbs, the close-knit Jewish communities that nourished the prewar Yiddishkeit urban scene disbanded. Anti-Semitism started a downward spiral that continues to this day, and Jews began intermarrying with Christians in ever-increasing numbers. "From the early twenties to the late fifties, the share of such marriages crept up only from 1.7 to 6.6 percent" (Freedman 2000:72). By the early 1970s, however, the rate of interfaith marriages grew to about a third, and by the early 1990s to over half. Less than 15 percent of interfaith couples are affiliated with any branch of Judaism, and only a small minority of their children receive any Jewish education. Only about 10 percent of children from mixed marriages end up marrying Jews, leading to the joke: "What do you call the grandchildren of intermarried Jews?—Christians!" (Lipset & Raab 1995:73).

Overall, only about half of Jewish Americans today remain affiliated with a Jewish organization or synagogue, and Jews spend less time in houses of religious worship than do Christians (Bershtel & Graubard 1992; Freedman 2000). As Seymour Martin Lipset and Earl Raab observe:

Jewish knowledge and education are, for most Jews, thin at best and becoming thinner. Some religious customs, such as attendance at an annual family Passover seder dinner, continue to be observed by as many as three out of four Jews, but rituals are often driven more by nostalgia and family attachment than by deep religious commitment. Even those practices can be expected to diminish as older generations disappear and as intermarriages rates increase even further. (1995:46)

Although the majority of Jews view the rituals and community with which they are connected as having "a long and distinguished history in which they take pride," even many affiliated Jews retain only marginally attached to their religion (ibid.:66).

Still, Sara Bershtel and Allen Graubard note that it is rather remarkable how much *unaffiliated* Jewish Americans remain "concerned with questions of Judaism" (1992:29). Lipset and Raab, too, are impressed that the majority adhere to at least some "Jewish practice into the fourth generation" (1995:205). These individuals are proud of their Jewish heritage and do not seek to avoid identification with it. They feel a sense of loss, perhaps some vague guilt connected to their inability to muster genuine religious faith. As one man observes, "I don't believe in God, so that's a problem. It is the underlying problem. To learn the blessings and light the candles and all that if one doesn't believe in God seems just like putting on a costume, nothing more" (Bershtel & Graubard 1992:21). Some secular Jews view this predicament in a benign light, attributing positive value to the fact that being Jewish is now a matter of choice, not of coercion or obligation, and that the freedom to choose one's religious and communal affiliation marks a "great moral advance" (ibid.:14). On the other hand, some Jews believe that the unaffiliated jeopardize the very survival of the Jewish people, that Jewish continuity is under threat of a "silent Holocaust" (Freedman 2000:74).

In the current vacuum of religious observance, many Jewish Americans adopt what Lipset and Raab (1995) describe as a "defensive" identity, whereby kinship with other Jews is based on a perception of shared victimization from anti-Semitism. This defensive identity typically includes a pro-Zionist and pro-Israel outlook, and as we have seen, it increasingly relies on the Holocaust as an ideological resource for mobilizing support for Jewish causes and participation in Jewish organizations (see Chapter 6). However, the unifying thread of anti-Semitism is rather thin in a country where positive images of Jews have become "more widespread than negative ones" and where a large majority of non–Jewish Americans view Jews as a warm, friendly, and unusually hardworking people who have a deep faith in God (Bershtel & Graubard 1992:65). These images may be stereotypes, but they are not derogatory.[5]

Many analysts believe that without a saving remnant of religious adherents, Jewish Americans as a distinct ethnic group will cease "to exist in any meaningful way" (Freedman 2000:339). Without the signifying mark of color that restrains some groups' freedom to assimilate, Jewish Americans will continue to follow the way of other white ethnics whose group identity is tied more to interest in family history and nostalgia for a world long gone than to a desire to exclude themselves from the larger integrated society.[6] Indeed, American society has shown a rather unique capacity to absorb and co-opt diverse ethnic cultures. For Jews this leaves only religion as the last vestige of ethnic exclusivity (Alba 1990; Lipset & Raab 1995; Nagel 1994).

Samuel Freedman (2000) argues that the most conflictual sphere impacting contemporary Jewish Americans is occurring *between different Jewish groups* rather than between those groups and the larger society. And with the decline of secular Judaism as a viable force, the various religious factions are positioning themselves in a "hierarchy of credibility" as they fight over which group is the legitimate heir to the historical tradition of Judaism, which group offers the most authentic version of Jewish identity, and which group is entitled to speak for the Jewish people as a whole (see Loseke 1999:34).

The debate over matrilineal and patrilineal descent as a basis for Jewish status is a case in point. Historically, Biblical Judaism accepted anyone born of a Jewish mother as Jewish, regardless of the father's faith. However, someone born of a gentile mother was not considered Jewish even if the father was, unless he or she underwent an official process of conversion. In 1982 an influential organization of Reform rabbis, the Central Conference of American Rabbis (CCAR), adopted patrilineal descent as a criterion for membership, which in effect "created a caste of Jews whom neither Conservative nor Orthodox authorities recognized" as legitimate (Freedman 2000:105).[7]

Freedman finds the resiliency of Orthodox Judaism to be "the most striking and unexpected phenomenon in modern American Jewish history" (ibid.: 217). Although Orthodox Jews constitute less than 10 percent of the Jewish population in the United States, their very refusal to assimilate gives them a claim to authenticity that the other groups lack. Politically they tend to be among the most conservative of Jews, and many have aligned themselves with those Israelis who believe that the Bible, not pragmatic political arrangements, should govern territorial claims in the Middle East. They support further expansion of Israeli settlements into territory claimed by Palestinians, and they reject the principle of trading "land for peace," which is supported by about two-thirds of Jewish Americans. Moreover, Orthodox Jews have deep pockets and their commitment to Israel is more passionate than those of other Jewish Americans. They thus have influence that extends beyond their numbers.[8]

On the other hand, Orthodox Jews are not a homogeneous group. The *ultra-Orthodox,* who are often referred to as *Haredim* (which roughly means God-fearing), are more zealous and uncompromising in their beliefs, desiring to isolate themselves from full engagement with the larger secular society (Bauer 2001; Freedman 2000).[9] As one adherent says:

We want isolation . . . [W]e don't want to expose our kids to the entire society. . . . We are not like the Amish. We have electricity. We have cars and other
things the modern world gives. But we want to live like our forefathers did—
dress like them, speak the same language. (quoted in Lipset & Raab 1995:206)

To this end the ultra-Orthodox emulate the distinct physical appearance characteristic of their European ancestors, with men wearing long black coats, hats,
beards, and side curls. Their children are "isolated from other groups, from the
cultural influences of television, and, after age eighteen, their marriages are
arranged by the parents" (ibid.).

In contrast, the *Modern Orthodox*, who comprise about half of the American
Orthodox, have accommodated themselves more to the modern world. With
the exception of wearing yarmulkes in public, they maintain a mainstream appearance. They have responded to the feminist movement and the demands of
Jewish women by extending the privilege of full religious education to females, as have Conservative and Reform Jews. Freedman (2000) predicts an
eventual realignment between Modern Orthodoxy and the right wing of the
Conservative movement. What keeps the Modern Orthodox apart from Conservatives at this time is the former's resistance to the ordaining of women
as rabbis, to allowing women equal participation in religious services, and to
abandoning the requirement that women sit separately from men as they
worship.

Freedman also expects the gay-rights movement to effect the relationship
between Conservative and Reform Jews. In 2000 the CCAR agreed "to bestow
formal, theological approval on gay marriage, calling same-sex relationships
'worthy of affirmation through appropriate Jewish rituals'" (ibid.:356). Although the CCAR used the term "union" rather than "marriage" and supported the right of member rabbis to abstain from this practice, "the sanction
for homosexual wedlock was self-evident" (ibid.). Freedman believes that the
left wing of the Conservative movement may soon find this issue moving them
closer to the Reform camp.

According to Lipset and Raab (1995), devoutly religious Jews will constitute an increasingly small part of the Jewish-American population in the future. Without them the maintenance of ethnic boundaries that would clearly
demarcate Jews from the rest of the population would arguably disappear, but
it will be difficult for the devout to sustain American Judaism on their own.
The Jewish community will need to engage the larger number of peripheral
Jews who are likely to "retain some sense of Jewish identity or at least some
knowledge of their ancestry" (ibid.:204). These "shadow Jews," as Lipset and
Raab call them, may be removed from the organizational structure of Judaism
but are not indifferent to the cultural values or proscriptions for living that
they associate with their Jewish heritage. At the same time, these shadow Jews
are people who have multiple allegiances and universal commitments beyond

the Jewish community, and they cherish the freedom of choice that has "so beneficently created [the contemporary] dilemma of Jewish continuity" in the United States (ibid.:207). They assert their right to construct a Jewish ethnic identity of their own making, and they resent being told by the devout that they are not "real" Jews (Bershtel & Graubard 1992; Freedman 2000).

Freedman cautions, on the other hand, that being Jewish is not simply a state of mind. "It demands a pattern of obligations and responsibilities, a web of mutuality that many modern American Jews find imprisoning and choose to reject" (ibid.:359). It is not be enough to say, as does one unaffiliated Jew, "I am still not clear why I am, but I know I am a Jew" (Bershtel & Graubard 1992:85). Perhaps the greatest bond that holds Jewish Americans together is the fact that they are Americans, that they live in a land where freedom of choice "requires perpetual efforts of self-definition" and the need to justify these choices to each other and to others (Auerbach 1990:206).

CHRISTIANITY AND THE PROBLEM OF RECONCILIATION

Earlier we saw that Christianity and Judaism were each other's disconfirming other—whereby belief in the veracity of one required belief in the falsity of the other (see Chapter 2). As such, according to Zygmunt Bauman, Jews posed a problem for the Christian church, which "could not reproduce itself . . . without guarding and reinforcing Jewish estrangement" (1989:37). However, the postwar memory of the Holocaust helped construct Christianity itself as a social problem, for the church faced a dilemma regarding its own theology as well as its own complicity in the genocide of the Jews.

Christian Theology and Jewish Suffering

Hans Jonas suggests that Christian theologians who confront the Holocaust are actually in less "theoretical difficulty" than their Jewish counterparts because the former are more inclined to attribute evil in the world to the work of the devil (2001:261). Nevertheless, Christian theologians have struggled with the religious implications of the genocide. Some agree with those who think that Jews were in fact being punished for disobedience to God, although for these Christians the nature of the Jews' sin was fundamentally different— their rejection of Jesus Christ as their Lord and Savior (Boyer 2001; Rubenstein & Roth 1987). Paul van Buren, on the other hand, advances a Christian theology that consists of a loving God who created us as free and responsible beings. Thus God is unable to intervene in our lives "without ceasing to be the God of love and freedom," leaving Him with no choice but "to sit still and . . . suffer in agony . . . [and] in solidarity with His people" (1980:116, 119).

According to Rubenstein and Roth, van Buren's view, like some Jewish formulations, deviates from traditional Scripture, which postulates that "God's divine power far exceeds anything that humans can do. God is not bound by human freedom unless he chooses to be" (1987:298). In this view "God is the One who ultimately sets the boundaries in which we live and move and have our being," and hence He is responsible for worldly events (ibid.:299). Alan Dershowitz finds any religious doctrine capable of this kind of "moral mischief" unacceptable, and he considers such precepts "reminders of the fallibility of religious texts, and of the right—indeed the obligation—of every generation of religious adherents to reevaluate their scriptures" (1991:132– 33). John Pawlikowski adds that "the fundamental challenge of the Holocaust lies in our altered perception of the relationship between God and humanity" and of the capacity of religion to serve as the basis of morality (1997:102–3).

Still, some Christians reject these admonitions and believe that Jews will continue to suffer if they continue to reject Christ. In the United States, for example, denominations such as the "Southern Baptist Convention, America's largest Protestant church, and the rapidly growing Assemblies of God church and other Pentecostal and charismatic groups," predict an ominous future for the Jews (Boyer 2001:5). In the prophetic doctrine of "dispensationalism" that is preached in these groups, the dawning of a divinely inspired new age will be preceded by "an Armageddon battle between Jesus and the Antichrist" in which the persecution of Jews will be far worse than what they experienced during the Holocaust (ibid.:6).

Toward Christian-Jewish Reconciliation

In the previous two chapters we saw how collective memory is a disputed terrain subject to challenges, alternatives, or countermemories that serve groups with competing interests and needs. In the postwar years Jewish and Christian memories have not only clashed over biblical interpretations of the Holocaust but over questions of Christian complicity in the genocide (see Chapters 3 and 4).[10] Arguably some of the most noteworthy postwar controversies have occurred between Catholics and Jews. Catholics are, of course, the oldest Christian denomination and the only one that has an international organization with a clearly defined central leadership, embodied in the Pope and the Vatican. And as the original Christian denomination, Catholicism is implicated in the origins of Christian anti-Semitism (see Chapter 2).

In 1965 the Second Vatican Council under the leadership of Pope John XXIII adopted a landmark document aimed at improving relationships between Catholics and Jews. In the *Declaration on the Relationship of the Church to Non-Christian Religions,* also called the *Nostra Aetate* (In Our Age), the church acknowledged the common heritage of Christians and Jews, recommended that "biblical and theological studies and brotherly dialogues" be undertaken to foster mutual understanding and respect, admitted that Christ's death "cannot be blamed upon all the Jews then living . . . nor upon the Jews of today," and deplored "hatred, persecutions, and display of anti-Semitism directed against the Jews at any time and from any source" (cited in Braham 1999:223).

At the same time, however, *Nostra Aetate* contained two negative references to Jews, thus repeating some doctrinal positions that have historically given rise to anti-Semitism. It reminds readers that Jewish leaders of the time did in fact press for Jesus' death and that large number of Jews today not only fail to accept Christian gospel but oppose the spread of Christianity. Many Jews as well as Christians regretted both the inclusion of these passages and the absence of an official apology for the church's inaction during the Nazi period. Nonetheless, the document was followed by additional Vatican and national Catholic church pronouncements that removed anti-Jewish references from religious textbooks, liturgy, and teachings. Many of these initiatives were undertaken during the tenure of John Paul II, who became pope in 1978 (ibid.).

More than any of his predecessors, Polish-born Pope John Paul II has "openly talked about—and asked forgiveness for—the sins, crimes, and errors committed in the Church's name" (ibid.:224). His acts of reconciliation with Jews have included the establishment of diplomatic relations between the Vatican and the state of Israel in 1994 and the hosting of a concert at the Vatican that commemorated the victims of the Holocaust that same year.

Pope John Paul II's papacy, however, has not been without controversy with Jews. In a 1979 visit to Auschwitz, for instance, he called the camp "the Golgotha of the modern world" (cited in Prosono 1994:177). The Golgotha is the place of Christ's crucifixion, and reference to it suggested that the Holocaust was to be understood as a site of Christian suffering. To be sure, many Christians died at Auschwitz, but most of the deaths were Jews. The Pope also called attention to the death of two Christian figures, Father Maximilian Kolbe and Edith Stein, who died at Auschwitz. To Jews, both Kolbe and Stein are dubious symbols of Holocaust martyrdom. Kolbe had edited an anti-Semitic newspaper before World War II, and Stein was a Jew who had converted to Catholicism. A gauntlet was thus thrown down for a competition of Christian versus Jewish victimhood.

Then in 1984 a group of Catholic Carmelite nuns moved into and renovated a building adjacent to the first Auschwitz camp that they used as a convent. Many Jews were offended by this move, especially when a Catholic priest began a fund-raising drive to help convert "our strayed brothers," a not-too-veiled call to convert Jews (cited in ibid.:178). By 1986 pressure mounted from both Jewish and Catholic circles to relocate the convent "as a gesture of respect and sympathy for the feelings of world Jewry" (ibid.). A number of European Jewish and Catholic leaders signed a declaration establishing Auschwitz as a special place of Jewish grief and as a symbol of the Final Solution. In 1987 another document was signed to establish an interfaith center where the convent could be housed.

Two years later construction on the new building had not yet begun and the conflict escalated. Rabbi Avraham Weiss of New York led a small group of demonstrators who climbed over the gate surrounding the convent and knocked on the convent door. They wanted to confront the nuns about their occupation of what Weiss characterized as "the world's largest Jewish cemetery" (quoted in ibid.:179). The protesters were greeted instead by Polish workmen who threw buckets of water mixed with paint (and purportedly also urine) on them and who beat and kicked them while the nuns and Polish police looked on. A few weeks later Cardinal Jozef Glemp, the primate of Poland, delivered an inflammatory speech before some 150,000 faithful at Czestochowa, the holiest Christian shrine in Poland, where he accused Jews of using their clout in the media to spread anti-Polish sentiments. He also blamed Jews for causing Polish anti-Semitism. Other Polish Catholic officials followed with similar statements. Pope John Paul II, hoping to squash the controversy, called for the nuns to move into a building that was completed a few years later (Dershowitz 1991; Prosono 1994).

The Auschwitz convent controversy was a battle of collective memories embodied in what Marvin Prosono describes as "symbolic territoriality"—the struggle to maintain or gain control over physical sites to which "symbols may become or are attached" (ibid.:174).[11] Official documents, as we have seen, can play a similar role in collective memory disputes, but they can become a source of conflict resolution as well. In this regard, *We Remember: A Reflection of the Shoah,* a 1998 Vatican statement reflecting the sentiments of Pope John Paul II, is a landmark document in Catholic-Jewish reconciliation. *We Remember* acknowledges the "erroneous and unjust interpretations of the New Testament regarding the Jewish people" and admits to anti-Semitic measures that historically stemmed from "some Christian quarters" (cited in Braham 1999: 225). Importantly, it deeply regrets the silence of Christians during the Holocaust and commits itself to preventing "the evil seeds of . . . anti-Semitism [from ever again] taking root in any human heart" (cited in ibid.).

Critics of *We Remember* remain unsatisfied, however, for the document blames followers rather than church doctrine for anti-Semitism, and asserts that Nazi "antisemitism had its roots outside of Christianity" rather than emanating from it (cited in ibid.:226).[12] But as Jules Isaac notes, "Without centuries of Christian catechism, preaching and vituperation, the Hitlerian [ideology and policies] . . . would not have been possible" (1959:508). Nor does *We Remember* admit to the failings of church officials, including the pope's, during the Nazi era (see Chapter 4).

These issues aside, Randolph Braham believes that *We Remember* is a document that portends well for the future and has already led to more positive developments in Christian-Jewish relations. In 1995, for example, the German Catholic bishops issued a declaration "deploying the failure of Catholics to act against Nazism or speak out against the crimes committed against the Jews, and acknowledging that they consequently bore a special responsibility to fight against antisemitism" (1999:241). Similarly, in 1997 the French Catholic Church pronounced:

> It is important to admit the primary role, if not direct, then indirect, played by the constantly repeated anti-Jewish stereotypes wrongly perpetuated among Christians in the historical process that led to the Holocaust. . . . In the face of the persecution of Jews, especially the multi-faceted anti-Semitic laws passed by Vichy, silence was the rule, and words in favor of the victims the exception. . . . Today we confess that silence was a mistake. We beg for the pardon of God, and we ask the Jewish people to hear this word of repentance. (cited in ibid.:242)

Even Cardinal Glemp recently issued an apology for a 1941 massacre of some sixteen hundred Jews by Poles in the town of Jedwabne in which he said, "We would like to apologize to God and also to all the victims, for all Polish citizens who harmed the citizens of the Jewish religion" (Stylinski 2001:A6; see also Gross 2001).

The Catholic church, of course, has not been alone in issuing formal decrees denouncing Christianity's role in the history of anti-Semitism. In 1990, for instance, the United Church of Christ's Theological Panel released a statement entitled "Message to the Churches" that acknowledged that "the Holocaust has sent Christians back to their texts and traditions to re-examine their theology and to ask about their own complicity in the anti-Semitism that gave rise to the horror" (cited in Eckardt 1997:142). And several Christian theologians have urged their Christian brethren to deemphasize if not repudiate the doctrine of supersession, that is, the belief that Christianity has superseded or supplanted Judaism (Berenbaum 2001). As Eva Fleischner asserts:

> Our willingness to confront the Christian past may bring us to a truer, more realistic, and humble understanding of the church: an institution divinely instituted, we believe, but rooted in human hearts and minds, shaped by history, hence subject to all its vicissitudes; frequently denying the very love it claims to embody; yet somehow continuing to struggle to give witness to this love. I do not see how, in the face of the Holocaust, we can continue in our arrogant Christian claim to superiority. What is called for are compunction of heart and confession of our sinfulness, in knowledge that God's love and mercy are infinitely greater yet, and can indeed transform our hearts of stone into hearts of flesh. (2001:436)

Alice Eckardt, on the other hand, remains concerned that the Christian community is still "either largely ignorant . . . or disinterested" in the downside of its history and the challenge that history poses to Christians' claims to moral righteousness (1997:141). Indeed, according to Eckardt, "some Christians are . . . incensed at any challenge to the absolute primacy of the Christian faith and its obligation to convert all other peoples . . . [and] anti-Jewish preaching can still be heard from some clergy in all branches of the Church" (ibid.). As long as Christianity and Judaism remain each other's "disconfirming other," the problem of Christian-Jewish reconciliation will go unresolved.

HUMAN RIGHTS AND THE PROBLEM OF DIFFERENCE

Today it is common to speak of human beings as being part of an interdependent global community where it becomes difficult to detach oneself from what is happening to others throughout the world (Gamson 1995). Most of us, however, are in fact detached and think of our common humanity only in the abstract. We may adhere to the adage, "Love thy neighbor as thyself," but rarely do we extend our universe of moral obligation to those who are not our neighbors. Rather we are like Cain, who when asked by God of his brother's whereabouts replied, "Am I my brother's keeper?" And we remain especially indifferent to the fate of those we perceive as different from ourselves (Fein 1979; Rubenstein & Roth 1987).

Andrew Bell-Fialkoff suggests that it is rather ironic that the modern impulse toward "freedom, self-determination, and representative democracy" has created a situation that pulls people apart, as particular collectivities seek either complete political sovereignty and independence or a distinct social identity within the boundaries of their nation's borders (1999:49). The end of the cold war, for example, has been accompanied by a resurgence of ethnic-group conflicts in the former Soviet Union and the nations of Eastern and Central Europe. For several decades after World War II the transethnic ideology of communism had masked and suppressed (but did not eradicate) prewar conflicts that have now come to the surface. According to Bell-Fialkoff, it was ethnic-group nationalism itself that helped to erode "the Communist cocoon from within," and in a reconstituted Europe this nationalism has revealed itself to have an ugly face (ibid.:33). In the name of democracy and representative government, different ethnic communities now demand the right to self-government that solidifies the political power of ethnic majorities. At the same time, these societies lack a historical ideology of egalitarianism that protects ethnic minorities. Since the 1990s the term "ethnic cleansing" has been used to describe the process by which nationalist governments—most notably in the former Yugoslavia—attempt to remove minorities populations who are perceived as the enemy from within (Gross 2000; Judt 2000).[13]

It is of course unfortunate, to say the least, that the processes of group individuation often mitigate social solidarity with others. However, Michael Ignatieff (2001) asks a provocative question that is rarely considered: Why should we in fact care about others who are not like us? The answer to this question is often sought in the view—which is itself a recent historical invention—that we all share a common humanity, that we are all part of the brotherhood and sisterhood of humankind. But is this really the case? Take the Judeo-Christian religious tradition, for instance, which in spite of proclamations about prophetic social justice rarely extends its universe of obligation to nonbelievers. Or take the founding fathers of the U.S. Constitution, who failed to see "any contradiction between the . . . claim that all men are created equal and the . . . claim that slavery was . . . a legitimate exercise of a constitutional right to property" (ibid.:25). In fact, it was not until the Civil Rights Act of 1964 that legal discrimination based on race came to an end in the United States. Thus Rubenstein and Roth observe that a "human being" is in many respects a social construction, for individuals who do not belong to a community that is "willing or able to protect their rights may be biologically human but politically they are nonpersons" (1987:192).

Genocide and the Construction of Human Rights

World War II was undoubtedly a turning point in the history of the world. While the war was unprecedented in the devastation it unleashed, it also marked a step forward in the construction of an international conception of universal human rights (Todorov 2001b). The postwar human-rights movement built on the groundwork that had been laid in the earlier part of the century. A clause of the Fourth Hague Convention of 1907 on land warfare articulated the idea of "laws of humanity" that would prevail among "civilized nations" and make murder of civilians during times of war an international crime (cited in Marrus 1997:185). At the Preliminary Peace Conference in 1919, France, Great Britain, and Russia denounced the Turkish genocide of the Armenians as "a crime of humanity and civilization for which all members of the Turkish government will be held responsible together with its agents implicated in the massacres" (cited in Fein 1993:2). The failure of the subsequent Versailles Treaty to follow through on this call for sanctions did not go unnoticed by Hitler who, you will recall, said, "Who after all, speaks today of the annihilation of the Armenians?" (cited in Berenbaum 1993:62; see Chapter 6).

Following World War II, as noted earlier, the United Nations (UN) articulated its official mission to save "succeeding generations from the scourge of war" and reaffirm "faith in fundamental human rights, in the dignity and worth of the human person, in the equal rights of men and women and of nations large and small" (cited in Art 1993:52; see Chapter 5). During the next year the International Military Tribunal at Nuremberg advanced what many consider "the central concept in the postwar moral imagination: the idea of crimes against humanity" (Ignatieff 2001:27). Crimes against humanity was a notion that stood for "grave maltreatment or atrocities committed against persons who were unprotected by law because of their nationality, . . . [including] acts . . . at the hands of their own government" (Marrus 1997:185 –86). In 1948 the UN also passed the Universal Declaration of Human Rights, which asserted that "the inherent dignity and . . . equal and inalienable rights of all members of the human family is the foundation of freedom, justice, and peace in the world" (www.un.org).

Then came the UN Convention on the Prevention and Punishment on Genocide, often referred to as the Genocide Convention (GC), which established "genocide, whether committed in time of peace or in time of war, [as] a crime under international law" (cited in Chalk & Jonassohn 1990:44).[14] The GC definition of genocide included "any of the following acts committed with intent to destroy, in whole or in part, a national, ethnical, racial or religious group":

> (a) Killing members of the group; (b) Causing serious bodily or mental harm to members of the group; (c) Deliberately inflicting on the group conditions of life calculated to bring about its physical destruction in whole or in part; (d) Imposing measures intended to prevent births within the group; (e) Forcibly transferring children of the group to another group. (cited in ibid.)

In 1948 the GC treaty was signed by thirty-three nations, not including the United States, which did not ratify the GC until 1986, when it became the ninety-seventh nation to do so. Leo Kuper has questioned the United States' reluctance to sign the treaty. Did U.S. leaders fear that their country "might be held responsible, retrospectively, for the annihilation of Indians in the United States or its role in the slave trade, or its contemporary support for tyrannical governments engaging in mass murder" (1990:422–23).

The United States' reluctance attests to a central problem of the GC treaty: It requires the signatories responsible for enforcing it to sanction their own members. Since governments are the most typical perpetrators of genocide, for one state to accuse another of genocide means undermining the ability of all states to act as they deem fit. Without an effective system of international law enforcement and prosecution, the GC has been honored more in the breech than in the observance. In the late 1970s, for example, the Khmer Rouge led by dictator Pol Pot murdered one to two million Cambodians who were perceived to be politically hostile or socially incompatible with the government's goals. No international sanctions were imposed, and the Khmer Rouge was even allowed to keep its seat in the United Nations. In this case, China's support for the Khmer Rouge was a deterrent to sanctions. In the UN only weaker states that are unaligned with more powerful governments are at risk of being punished (Chalk & Jonassohn 1990; Fein 1993; Todorov 2001b).[15]

Still, in spite of its practical limitations, the UN has been at the forefront of forging a new international consciousness of growing dimensions that subjects the denial of human rights to international scrutiny and places countries on notice that they may no longer act with impunity (Chalk & Jonassohn

1990; Fein 1993). Although most of what has occurred has involved words more than deeds, words can in the long run have the power to transform. As Tzvetan Todorov suggests:

> If we recall . . . the public debates of one hundred years ago, we can measure how far we have come: in those days, a good number of the best minds of the time displayed a perfectly serene racism. . . . [P]arallel transformation has taken place in the role of women, who have become for the first time in history political subjects on an equal footing with men. . . . [And] governments voluntarily acknowledge having acted badly in the past, and try to repair the damages for which they feel responsible. (2001b:29)

Moreover, victimized groups are not disparaged as they once were. They now enjoy our sympathy, and as we have seen, are able to use their victimization to advance their own interests (see Chapters 5 and 6).

Toward a Humanity of Difference

Genocide, of which the Holocaust is a paradigmatic case, constitutes the most extreme form of human-rights violation. While some analysts justifiably complain that the term is often misused to refer to much lesser evils, William Gamson (1995) encourages us to situate genocide at one end of a behavioral continuum that ranges from active exclusion to indirect exclusion. To attempt to annihilate another group is, of course, an example of active exclusion, whereas indirect exclusion involves the ignoring of difference that makes some groups invisible to others and hence puts them outside their universe of concern.[16] Indirect exclusion entails indifference to other's suffering that is based on their difference and denies people the ability "to make a difference" in the world (Henry & Milovanovic 1996:116). To institute a "Don't ask, don't tell" policy of dealing with gays and lesbians in the U.S. military, for instance, is to accept the indirect exclusion of others by forcing them to remain silent and unseen. Or, to fail to modify the physical structure and social organization of society to meet the needs of the disabled is to exclude that population from full participation in the life of that nation (Wendell 1996).

Gamson does not in any way equate the experiences of active and indirect exclusion; the former is clearly worse than the latter. His point is that all other-creating processes share a common character based on "the creation of an 'other' who is outside one or more universes of obligation. . . . The consequences of these other-creating processes are [of course] much more lethal when the agents are despots who control the repressive apparatus of the state" (1995:17). But there are consequences to indirect exclusion as well.

Amartya Sen (2000) notes that it is a natural and potentially benign part of social development to identity with some people and not others. This process is in fact integral to the creation of a subjective sense of self. A problem arises, however, when others become the objects of our experience in a way that involves typifying or constructing them as persons endowed with negative symbolic meaning, as people to be feared and rejected, even removed from our midst (Wendell 1996; see Chapter 2).

Sen (2000) does not think that to reverse the other-creating process of exclusion it is necessary that we identify our subjectivity with all people. Rather, we merely need to become capable of tolerating others and considering their interests and claims regardless of whether we can, as some say, "feel their pain." Ignatieff (2001), on the other hand, believes it is crucial to locate an identity of interests based on our common humanity. He understands that humanity, however, not as a humanity of sameness but as a humanity of difference. A humanity of difference must first acknowledge, as Sen suggests, that members of socially defined groups are not a homogeneous lot. Although they may share a common experience, they are themselves constituted by an internal diversity of attitudes, beliefs, and aspirations. In other words, they are unique human beings, and in that uniqueness they are like us.

According to Ignatieff, "No other species differentiates itself in [such] individualized abundance" (ibid.:28). It is our religion, our race/ethnicity, our sexual orientation, our physical ability, and so forth, that constitutes "the very basis of the consciousness of our individuality, and this consciousness, based in difference, is a constitutive element of what it is to be a human being" (ibid.). To make any one of these differences the object of active or indirect exclusion is to deny "the shared element that makes us what we are as a species" (ibid.).[17] Thus Ignatieff wants us to:

> understand humanity, our common flesh and blood, as valuable to the degree that it allows us to elaborate the dignity and the honor that we give to our differences—and that this reality of difference, both fated and created, is our common inheritance, the shared integument that we might fight to defend whenever any of us is attacked for manifesting it. (ibid.)

Throughout this book I have shown that the general processes of claims-making and responding activities that constructed the Holocaust paralleled those that construct other social problems. At the same time, I do not wish to suggest that the Holocaust was constituted by nothing distinct, for the Final Solution "happened to a particular people for particular reasons at a particular time" (Bauer 2001:67). In the future it is likely that efforts to fathom the Holocaust will be situated within larger constructions of human rights and human difference. In many respects this is as it should be. But this process of universalization will require ongoing scrutiny to guard against polemical excesses and political manipulations that trivialize and distort the memory of the genocide that destroyed the European Jews.

NOTES

1.   Neither Orthodox nor non-Orthodox Jews constitute homogeneous categories. Variations within these groups will be discussed later in this chapter.

2.   The United States is also central to the fate of international Jewry insofar as Israel's security is significantly dependent on America's continued political and financial support. Also see Chapter 6, note 11, on use of the term Jewish Americans rather than American Jews.

3.   Auerbach credits Jewish lawyers such as Louis Marshall and Louis Brandeis with locating a common emphasis on the rule of law and quest for social justice in the Jewish and American traditions (1990). In 1914 Brandeis wrote, "There is no inconsistency between loyalty to America and loyalty to Jewry. The Jewish spirit . . . is essentially modern and essentially American" (cited in ibid.:18). Brandeis's appointment to the Supreme Court, where he served from 1916 to 1939, is of particular significance not merely because he was the first Jew to serve in this capacity, but because it was the first time "a Jew was empowered to determine the final meaning" of the U.S. Constitution (ibid.).

4.   Jewish leftists have faced a particular dilemma because of the Left's critical position on Israel since the late 1960s (Bershtel & Graubard 1992; Lipset & Raab 1995; see Chapter 6). Also see Chapter 6, note 21, on the relationship between Jewish and African Americans.

5.   Lipset and Raab (1995) add that today the Jewish backgrounds of national political figures and judicial appointees provoke little public comment. Even the highly Germanic state of Wisconsin has two Jewish senators (Herb Kohl and Russell Feingold) who have enjoyed multiple electoral victories in their Senate races. If anything, the Jewish faith of Joseph Lieberman was viewed as an asset to the Democratic ticket in the 2000 presidential race. And Pat Buchanan's anti-Semitism has been a detriment rather than an asset to his political aspirations (see Chapter 6). Quite clearly the greatest sin in American politics is not to be Jewish but to be an atheist (Foer 2000; Willis 2001).

6.   Amato thinks that the family is in fact "the first religion of the majority" of Americans (1990:191).

7.   In Israel the Law of Return, which was passed by the Knesset in 1950, guarantees Jews "the right to immigrate to Israel and receive immediate citizenship there" (Freedman 2000:75). Thus the criterion of who is a Jew significantly affects someone's ability to emigrate to that country.

8.   Ironically, before the 1967 Six Day War many Orthodox Jews considered Zionism to be blasphemy, and they refused to recognize the legitimacy of what was essentially a secular Jewish state (Bauer 2001; Teveth 1996).

9.   *Hasidism,* a denomination that emerged in eighteenth-century Europe, is arguably the most well-known ultra-Orthodox group. Hasidism subordinates theological knowledge or intellectualism to an emotional devotion to God and a celebration of this depth of feeling through music and dancing. Hasidism also entails a greater degree of asceticism or renunciation of worldly things (Botwinick 1996).

10. German Christian clergy have also drawn complaints about their willingness to offer mitigating testimony on behalf of accused Nazi war criminals in postwar legal proceedings (Buscher & Phayer 1988; Marcuse 2001; Phayer 2000; Webster 2001).

11. More recently, Jewish organizations have complained about a discotheque that opened in a building that had been used for slave labor at Auschwitz (Cooper 2001).

12. *We Remember* postulates a difference "between anti-Semitism, based on theories contrary to the constant teaching of the Church on the unity of the human race and on the equal dignity of all races and peoples, and the long-standing sentiments of mistrust and hostility that we call anti-Judaism, of which, unfortunately, Christians also have been guilty" (cited in Mitchell & Mitchell 2001:323).

13. Judt notes that ethnic-group nationalism was superimposed on such religious antecedents, and of all the old prejudices that have now rushed in to fill the void left by communism's collapse, "anti-Semitism is the most striking. It is almost irrelevant that there are hardly any Jews left" in the former Soviet-bloc nations, for anti-Semitism in this part of the world "has long had a central political and cultural place; it is as much a way of talking about 'them' and 'us' as it is a device for singling out Jews in particular" (2000:312).

14. See Chapter 4, note 15.

15. Recently the UN has taken criminal actions in international courts against leaders in the former Yugoslavia and in Rwanda (Deutsch 2001; Gutman & Nordland 2001). See Todorov (2001b) for a discussion of the advantages and disadvantages of three general types of responses to genocidal injustice: criminal tribunals, reparations, and "truth and reconciliation" commissions.

16. Ralph Ellison (1952) wrote perceptively of the problem of invisibility in his novel *Invisible Man*.

17. Conservative political columnist George Will takes an entirely different tact, viewing the common character of mass atrocities not in exclusionary practices but in the "disorder" that arises in the absence of "social restraints" (2001:68).

References

Abraham, David. 1981. *The Collapse of the Weimar Republic: Political Economy and Crises*. Princeton, NJ: Princeton University Press.

Adam, Uwe. 1989. "The Gas Chambers." In F. Furet (ed.), *Unanswered Questions*. New York: Shocken.

Adam, Uwe. 1990. "Anti-Jewish Legislation." In I. Gutman (ed.), *Encyclopedia of the Holocaust*. New York: Macmillan.

Alba, Richard D. 1990. *Ethnic Identity: The Transformation of White America*. New Haven, CT: Yale University Press.

Alexander, Edward. 1994. *The Holocaust and the War of Ideas*. New Brunswick, NJ: Transaction.

Alexander, Jeffrey C. 1984. "Social-Structural Analysis: Some Notes on Its History and Prospects." *Sociological Quarterly* 25:5–26.

Alexander, Jeffrey C. 1989. *Structure and Meaning: Relinking Classical Sociology*. New York: Columbia University Press.

Allen, William Sheriden. 1984. *The Nazi Seizure of Power: The Experience of a Single German Town, 1922–1945*. New York: Watts Franklin.

Amato, Joseph A. 1990. *Victims and Values: A History and a Theory of Suffering*. New York: Praeger.

Améry, Jean. 1998. "Symposium." In S. Wiesenthal, *The Sunflower*. Edited by H. Cargas & B. Fetterman. New York: Schocken.

Anheier, Helmut K., & Friedhelm Neidhardt. 1998. "The Nazi Party and Its Capital: An Analysis of NSDAP Membership in Munich, 1925–1930." *American Behavioral Scientist* 41:1219–36.

Anheier, Helmet K., Friedhelm Neidhardt, & Wolfgang Vortkamp. 1998. "Movement Cycles and the Nazi Party: Activities of the Munich NSDAP, 1925–1930." *American Behavioral Scientist* 41:1262–81.

Anti-Defamation League. 1993. *Hitler's Apologists: The Anti-Semitic Propaganda of Holocaust "Revisionism."* New York: ADL.

Arad, Gulie Ne'eman (ed.). 1995. "Special Issue: Israeli Historiography Revisited." *History and Memory* 7(1).

Arad, Gulie Ne'eman (ed.). 1996. "Special Issue: Hannah Arendt and Eichmann in Jerusalem." *History and Memory* 8(2).

Arad, Yitzhak. 1987. *Operation Reinhard Death Camps: Belzec, Sobibor, Treblinka.* Bloomington: Indiana University Press.

Arendt, Hannah. 1963. *Eichmann in Jerusalem: A Report on the Banality of Evil.* New York: Viking.

Aronson, Shlomo. 1990. "Reichssicherheitshauptamt." In I. Gutman (ed.), *Encyclopedia of the Holocaust.* New York: Macmillan.

Art, Robert. 1993. "United Nations." *World Book Encyclopedia.* Chicago: World Book.

Askenasy, Hans. 1978. *Are We All Nazis?* Secaucus, NJ: Lyle Stuart.

Auerbach, Jerold S. 1990. *Rabbis and Lawyers.* Bloomington: Indiana University Press.

Augstein, Rudolf. 1998. "The Sociologist as Hanging Judge." In R. Shandley (ed.), *Unwilling Germans?* Minneapolis: University of Minnesota Press.

Ausubel, Nathan. 1964. *The Book of Jewish Knowledge.* New York: Crown.

Avisar, Ilan. 1997. "Holocaust Movies and the Politics of Collective Memory." In A. Rosenfeld (ed.), *Thinking About the Holocaust.* Bloomington: Indiana University Press.

Baldwin, James. [1967] 1994. "Negroes are Anti-Semitic Because They're Anti-White." In P. Berman (ed.), *Blacks and Jews.* New York: Delta.

Baldwin, Peter (ed.). 1990. *Reworking the Past: Hitler, the Holocaust, and the Historians' Debate.* Boston: Beacon.

Bankier, David. 1990a. "Four-Year Plan." In I. Gutman (ed.), *Encyclopedia of the Holocaust.* New York: Macmillan.

Bankier, David. 1990b. "Mischlinge." In I. Gutman (ed.), *Encyclopedia of the Holocaust.* New York: Macmillan.

Barkai, Avraham. 1989. *From Boycott to Annihilation.* Hanover, MA: University Press of New England.

Baron, Lawrence. 1988. "The Historical Context of Rescue." In S. Oliner & P. Oliner, *The Altruistic Personality.* New York: Free Press.

Baron, Lawrence. 1992. "The Dutchness of Dutch Rescuers: The National Dimension of Altruism." In P. Oliner et al. (eds.), *Embracing the Other.* New York: New York University Press.

Bartov, Omer. 1993. "Intellectuals on Auschwitz: Memory, History and Truth." *History and Memory* 5:87–117.

Bartov, Omer. 1997a. "German Soldiers and the Holocaust: Historiography, Research and Implications." *History and Memory* 9:162–88.

Bartov, Omer. 1997b. "Spielberg's Oskar: Hollywood Tries Evil." In Y. Loshitzky (ed.), *Spielberg's Holocaust.* Bloomington: Indiana University Press.

Bash, Harry H. 1995. *Social Problems and Social Movements: An Exploration into the Sociological Construction of Alternative Realities.* Atlantic Highlands, NJ: Humanities.

Batson, C. Daniel. 1991. *The Altruism Question: Toward a Social-Psychological Answer.* Hillsdale, NJ: Lawrence Erlbaum.

Bauer, Yehunda. 1987. "On the Place of the Holocaust in History." *Holocaust and Genocide Studies* 2:209–20.

Bauer, Yehunda. 1989. "Jewish Resistance and Passivity in the Face of the Holocaust." In F. Furet (ed.), *Unanswered Questions*. New York: Schocken.

Bauer, Yehunda. 1991. "Who Was Responsible and When? Some Well-known Documents Revisited." *Holocaust and Genocide Studies* 6:129–49.

Bauer, Yehunda. 1994. *Jews for Sale? Nazi-Jewish Negotiations, 1933–1945*. New Haven, CT: Yale University Press.

Bauer, Yehunda. 2001. *Rethinking the Holocaust*. New Haven, CT: Yale University Press.

Bauman, Zygmunt. 1989. *Modernity and the Holocaust*. Ithaca, NY: Cornell University Press.

Bell, James B. 1993. "Statue of Liberty." *World Book Encyclopedia*. Chicago: World Book.

Bell-Fialkoff, Andrew. 1999. *Ethnic Cleansing*. New York: St. Martin's Griffin.

Ben-Rafel, Eliezer. 1982. *The Emergence of Ethnicity: Cultural Groups and Social Conflict in Israel*. Westport, CT: Greenwood.

Benner, Patricia, Ethel Roskies, & Richard S. Lazarus. 1980. "Stress and Coping under Extreme Conditions." In J. Dimsdale (ed.), *Survivors, Victims, and Perpetrators*. New York: Hemisphere.

Benz, Wolfgang. 1994. "Auschwitz and the Germans: The Remembrance of the Genocide." *Holocaust and Genocide Studies* 8:94–106.

Benz, Wolfgang. 2001. "Death Marches." In W. Laqueur (ed.), *The Holocaust Encyclopedia*. New Haven, CT: Yale University Press.

Berbrier, Mitch. 2000. "Ethnicity in the Making: Ethnicity Work, the Ethnicity Industry, and a Constructionist Framework for Research." In J. Holstein & G. Miller (eds.), *Perspectives on Social Problems*, Vol. 12. Stamford, CT: JAI.

Berenbaum, Michael. 1987. "The Americanization of the Holocaust." In I. Levkov (ed.), *Bitburg and Beyond*. New York: Sure Sellers.

Berenbaum, Michael. 1993. *The World Must Know: The History of the Holocaust as Told in the United States Holocaust Memorial Museum*. Boston: Little, Brown.

Berenbaum, Michael. 2001. "Theological and Philosophical Responses." In W. Laqueur (ed.), *The Holocaust Encyclopedia*. New Haven, CT: Yale University Press.

Bergen, Doris L. 1998. "The Ecclesiastical Final Solution: The German Christian Movement and the Anti-Jewish Church." In M. Berenbaum & A. Peck (eds.), *The Holocaust and History*. Bloomington: Indiana University Press.

Berger, Peter L., & Thomas Luckmann. 1966. *The Social Construction of Reality*. Garden City, NY: Doubleday.

Berger, Ronald J. 1993. "The 'Banality of Evil' Reframed: The Social Construction of the 'Final Solution' to the 'Jewish Problem.'" *Sociological Quarterly* 34:597–618.

Berger, Ronald J. 1995. *Constructing a Collective Memory of the Holocaust: A Life History of Two Brothers' Survival.* Boulder: University Press of Colorado.

Berger, Ronald J. 1996. "The Politics of Collective Memory: The Holocaust in Israel and West Germany." In J. Holstein & G. Miller (eds.), *Perspectives on Social Problems,* Vol. 8. Greenwich, CT: JAI.

Berger, Ronald J., Charles S. Green, & Kristen E. Krieser. 1998. "Altruism Amidst the Holocaust: An Integrated Social Theory." In J. Holstein & G. Miller (eds.), *Perspectives on Social Problems,* Vol. 10. Greenwich, CT: JAI.

Berkovits, Eliezer. 1973. *Faith After the Holocaust.* New York: KTAV.

Berman, Paul (ed.). 1994. *Blacks and Jews: Alliances and Arguments.* New York: Delta.

Bernston, Marit A., & Brian Ault. 1998. "Gender and Nazism: Women as Joiners of the Pre-1933 Nazi Party." *American Behavioral Scientist* 41:1193–1218.

Bershtel, Sara, & Allen Graubard. 1992. *Saving Remnants: Feeling Jewish in America.* Berkeley: University of California Press.

Best, Joel. 1990. *Threatened Children: Rhetoric and Concern about Child-Victims.* Chicago: University of Chicago Press.

Best, Joel. 1993. "But Seriously Folks." In J. Holstein & G. Miller (eds.), *Reconsidering Social Constructionism.* Hawthorne, NY: Aldine de Gruyter.

Best, Joel (ed.). 1995. *Images of Issues: Typifying Contemporary Social Problems.* Hawthorne, NY: Aldine de Gruyter.

Best, Joel (ed.). 2001. *How Claims Spread: Cross-National Diffusion of Social Problems.* Hawthorne, NY: Aldine de Gruyter.

Bettleheim, Bruno. 1960. *The Informed Heart.* Glencoe, IL: Free Press.

Billstein, Reinhold, Karola Fings, Anita Kugler, & Nicholas Levis. 2001. *Working for the Enemy: Ford, General Motors, and Forced Labor in Germany during the Second World War.* New York: Berghahn.

Black, Edwin. 2001. *IBM and the Holocaust: The Strategic Alliance between Nazi Germany and America's Most Powerful Corporation.* New York: Crown.

Blau, Peter M. 1955. *The Dynamics of Bureaucracy.* Chicago: University of Chicago Press.

Blumer, Herbert. 1971. "Social Problems as Collective Behavior." *Social Problems* 18:298–306.

Bock, Gisela. 1983. "Racism and Sexism in Nazi Germany: Motherhood, Compulsory Sterilization, and the State." *Signs* 8:400–21.

Bondy, Ruth. 2001. "Thereisienstadt." In W. Laqueur (ed.), *The Holocaust Encyclopedia.* New Haven, CT: Yale University Press.

Botwinick, Rita Steinhardt. 1996. *A History of the Holocaust: From Ideology to Annihilation.* Upper Saddle River, NJ: Prentice-Hall.

Bower, Tom. 1997. *Nazi Gold: The Full Story of the Fifty-Year Swiss-Nazi Conspiracy to Steal Billions from Europe's Jews and Holocaust Survivors.* New York: HarperCollins.

Boyer, Paul. 2001. "Rapturous Tidings: The Holocaust, Bible Prophecy Belief, and Conservative American Christianity." *Dimensions* 15:3–8.

Brady, Robert A. 1937. *The Spirit and Structure of German Fascism*. London: Gollancz.

Braham, Randolph L. 1989. "The Jewish Councils: An Overview." In F. Furet (ed.), *Unanswered Questions*. New York: Schocken.

Braham, Randolph L. 1999. "Remembering and Forgetting: The Vatican, the German Catholic Hierarchy, and the Holocaust." *Holocaust and Genocide Studies* 13:222–51.

Brecher, Frank W. 1990. "David Wyman and the Historiography of America's Response to the Holocaust: Counter-Consideration." *Holocaust and Genocide Studies* 5:423–46.

Breitman, Richard. 1991. *The Architect of Genocide: Himmler and the Final Solution*. Hanover, NH: Brandeis University Press.

Breitman, Richard. 1998. *Official Secrets: What the Nazis Planned, What the British and Americans Knew*. New York: Hill & Wang.

Breitman, Richard, & Alan M. Kraut. 1987. *American Refugee Policy and European Jewry, 1933–1945*. Bloomington: Indiana University Press.

Brenner, Reeve Robert. 1980. *The Faith and Doubt of Holocaust Survivors*. New York: Free Press.

Bresheeth, Haim. 1997. "The Great Taboo Broken: Reflections on the Israeli Reception of *Schindler's List*." In Y. Loshitzky (ed.), *Spielberg's Holocaust*. Bloomington: Indiana University Press.

Brodkin, Karen. 1998. *How Jews Became White Folks and What That Says About Race in America*. New Brunswick, NJ: Rutgers University Press.

Browning, Christopher R. 1990a. "Deportations." In I. Gutman (ed.), *Encyclopedia of the Holocaust*. New York: Macmillan.

Browning, Christopher R. 1990b. "Nisko and Lublin Plan." In I. Gutman (ed.), *Encyclopedia of the Holocaust*. New York: Macmillan.

Browning, Christopher R. 1990c. "Final Solution." In I. Gutman (ed.), *Encyclopedia of the Holocaust*. New York: Macmillan.

Browning, Christopher R. 1992. *Ordinary Men: Reserve Police Battalion 101 and the Final Solution in Poland*. New York: Oxford University Press.

Browning, Christopher R. 1996. "A Final Hitler Decision for the 'Final Solution'? The Riegner Telegram Reconsidered." *Holocaust and Genocide Studies* 10:3–10.

Browning, Christopher R. 1998. "Afterword." *Ordinary Men: Reserve Police Battalion 101 and the Final Solution*. New York: Oxford University Press.

Browning, Christopher R. 2000. *Nazi Policy, Jewish Workers, German Killers*. Cambridge, UK: Cambridge University Press.

Brunner, José. 1997. "Pride and Memory: Nationalism, Narcissism and the Historians' Debates in Germany and Israel." *History and Memory* 9:256–300.

Brustein, William. 1996. *The Logic of Evil: The Social Origins of the Nazi Party, 1925–1933*. New Haven, CT: Yale University Press.

Brustein, William. 1998a. "The Nazi Party and the German New Middle Class, 1925–1933." *American Behavioral Scientist* 41:1237–61.

Brustein, William (ed.). 1998b. "Nazism as a Social Phenomenon." *American Behavioral Scientist* 41(9).

Buckley, William F., Jr. 1992. "In Pursuit of Anti-Semitism." *National Review,* March 16, p. S.2.

Burleigh, Michael, & Wolfgang Wipperman. 1991. *The Racial State: Germany, 1933–1945*. New York: Cambridge University Press.

Buscher, Frank, & Michael Phayer. 1988. "German Catholic Bishops and the Holocaust 1940–1953." *German Studies Review* 11:463–85.

Buszko, Jozef. 1990. "Auschwitz." In I. Gutman (ed.), *Encyclopedia of the Holocaust*. New York: Macmillan.

Calhoun, Craig. 1993. "Nationalism and Ethnicity." In J. Blake & J. Hagen (eds.), *Annual Review of Sociology,* Vol. 19. Palo Alto, CA: Annual Reviews.

Caracciolo, Nicola. 1995. *Uncertain Refuge: Italy and the Jews during the Holocaust*. Edited and translated by F. Rechnitz Koffler & R. Koffler. Urbana and Chicago: University of Illinois Press.

Cargas, Harry J. 1986. "An Interview with Elie Wiesel." *Holocaust and Genocide Studies* 1:5–10.

Carmody, Denise L., & John T. Carmody. 1993. *Ways to the Center: An Introduction to the World Religions*. Belmont, CA: Wadsworth.

Carpi, Daniel. 2001. "Italy." In W. Laqueur (ed.), *The Holocaust Encyclopedia*. New Haven, CT: Yale University Press.

Chalk, Frank, & Kurt Jonassohn (eds.). 1990. *The History and Sociology of Genocide: Analyses and Case Studies*. New Haven, CT: Yale University Press.

Chambliss, William J., & Robert Seidman. 1982. *Law, Order, and Power*. Reading, MA: Addison-Wesley.

Chesnoff, Richard Z. 1999. *Pack of Thieves: How Hitler and Europe Plundered the Jews and Committed the Greatest Theft in History*. New York: Doubleday.

Childers, Thomas. 1984. *The Nazi Voter: The Social Foundations of Fascism in Germany, 1919–1933*. Durham: University of North Carolina Press.

Clendinnen, Inga. 1999. *Reading the Holocaust*. Cambridge, UK: Cambridge University Press.

Cochavi, Yehoyakim. 1990. "Zentralstelle für Judische Auswanderung." In I. Gutman (ed.), *Encyclopedia of the Holocaust*. New York: Macmillan.

Coffman, Edward M. 1993. "World War I." *World Book Encyclopedia*. Chicago: World Book.

Cohen, Arthur. 1981. *The Tremendum: A Theological Interpretation of the Holocaust*. New York: Crossroad.

Cohen, Nava. 1990. "Medical Experiments." In I. Gutman (ed.), *Encyclopedia of the Holocaust*. New York: Macmillan.

Cohn, Norman. 1967. *Warrant for Genocide*. London: Eyre & Spottiswoode.

Cole, Tim. 1999. *Selling the Holocaust*. New York: Routledge.

Cooper, Abraham. 1996/1997. "Who Profited from the Nazi Genocide?" *Response* 17(3):2–4.

Cooper, Abraham. 1998. "Switzerland's Unwanted Guests." *Response* 19(1):2.

Cooper, Abraham. 2001. "Auschwitz Disco to Close?" *Response* 22(2):8.

Cornwell, John. 1999. *Hitler's Pope: The Secret History of Pius XII*. New York: Viking.

Coser, Lewis A. 1992. "Introduction: Maurice Halbachs 1877-1945." *On Collective Memory*. Edited and translated by L. Coser. Chicago: University of Chicago Press.

Crader, Kelly W., & William W. Wentworth. 1984. "A Structural Reinterpretation of Responsibility, Risk and Helping in Small Collectives of Children." *American Sociological Review* 49:611–19.

Davidson, Shamai. 1992. *Holding on to Humanity—The Message of Holocaust Survivors: The Shamai Davidson Papers*. I. Charny (ed.). New York: New York University Press.

De Beauvoir, Simone. 1985. "Preface." C. Lanzmann, *Shoah*. New York: Pantheon.

De Felice, Renzo. 2001. *The Jews in Fascist Italy: A History*. New York: Bartleby.

Deák, István. 1983. "What Was Fascism?" *New York Review of Books,* March 3, p. 13.

Deák, István. 1984. "How Guilty Were the Germans?" *New York Review of Books,* May 31, p. 37.

Deák, István. 2000a. "Introduction." In I. Deák et al. (eds.), *The Politics of Retribution in Europe*. Princeton, NJ: Princeton University Press.

Deák, István. 2000b. "The Pope, the Nazis and the Jews." *New York Review of Books,* March 23, p. 44.

Deák, István, Jan T. Gross, & Tony Judt (eds.). 2000. *The Politics of Retribution in Europe: World War II and Its Aftermath*. Princeton, NJ: Princeton University Press.

DellaPergola, Sergio. 1996. "Between Science and Fiction: Notes on the Demography of the Holocaust." *Holocaust and Genocide Studies* 10:34–51.

Dershowitz, Alan M. 1991. *Chutzpah*. New York: Touchstone.

Des Pres, Terrence. 1976. *The Survivor: An Anatomy of Life in the Death Camps*. New York: Oxford University Press.

Deutsch, Anthony. 2001. "U.N. Court Convicts Serb of Genocide." *Wisconsin State Journal,* August 3, p. A1.

Dimsdale, Joel E. 1980. "The Coping Behavior of Nazi Concentration Camp Survivors." In J. Dimsdale (ed.), *Survivors, Victims, and Perpetrators*. New York: Hemisphere.

Diner, Dan. 1990. "Negative Symbiosis: Germans and Jews After Auschwitz." In P. Baldwin (ed.), *Reworking the Past*. Boston: Beacon.

Domansky, Elisabeth. 1997. "A Lost War: World War II in Postwar German

Memory." In A. Rosenfeld (ed.), *Thinking About the Holocaust*. Bloomington: Indiana University Press.

Doneson, Judith E. 1987. "The American History of Anne Frank's Diary." *Holocaust and Genocide Studies* 2:149–60.

Doneson, Judith E. 1997. "The Image Lingers: The Feminization of the Jew in *Schindler's List*." In Y. Loshitzky (ed.), *Spielberg's Holocaust*. Bloomington: Indiana University Press.

Douglas, Mary. 1966. *Pollution and Danger: An Analysis of Concepts of Pollution and Taboo*. New York: Praeger.

Dov Kulka, Otto. 1990. "Theresienstadt." In I. Gutman (ed.), *Encyclopedia of the Holocaust*. New York: Macmillan.

Durkheim, Émile. [1893] 1964. *The Division of Labor in Society*. New York: Free Press.

Durkheim, Émile. [1912] 1965. *The Elementary Forms of Religious Life*. New York: Free Press.

Dutt, R. Palme. 1935. *Fascism and Social Revolution: A Study of the Economics and Politics of the Extreme Stages of Capitalism in Decay*. New York: International.

Eckardt, Alice L. 1997. "The Shoah-Road to a Revised/Revived Christianity." In C. Rittner & J. Roth (eds.), *From the Unthinkable to the Unavoidable*. Westport, CT: Praeger.

Edelman, Murray. 1977. *Political Language*. New York: Academic.

Ehmann, Annegret. 2001. "Mischlinge." In W. Laqueur (ed.), *The Holocaust Encyclopedia*. New Haven, CT: Yale University Press.

Ellison, Ralph. 1952. *Invisible Man*. New York: Random House.

Engelmann, Bernt. 1986. *In Hitler's Germany: Everyday Life in the Third Reich*. New York: Pantheon.

Evans, Richard J. 1989. *In Hitler's Shadow: West German Historians and the Attempt to Escape from the Nazi Past*. New York: Pantheon.

Evans, Richard J. 1991. "German Unification and the New Revisionism." *Dimensions* 6:10–14.

Fackenheim, Emil. 1969. "Transcendence in Contemporary Culture: Philosophical Reflections and a Jewish Theology." In H. Richardson & D. Cutler (eds.), *Transcendence*. Boston: Beacon.

Fackenheim, Emil. 1972. *God's Presence in History: Jewish Affirmations and Philosophical Reflections*. New York: Harper & Row.

Fein, Helen. 1979. *Accounting for Genocide: National Response and Jewish Victimization during the Holocaust*. New York: Free Press.

Fein, Helen. 1993. *Genocide: A Sociological Perspective*. Newbury Park, CA: Sage.

Felman, Shoshana. 1994. "Film as Witness: Claude Lanzmann's *Shoah*." In G. Hartman (ed.), *Holocaust Remembrance*. Cambridge, MA: Blackwell.

Fenyvesi, Charles. 2001. "Raoul Wallenberg." In W. Laqueur (ed.), *The Holocaust Encyclopedia*. New Haven, CT: Yale University Press.

Finkelstein, Norman. 2000. *The Holocaust Industry: Reflections on the Exploitation of Jewish Suffering*. New York: Verso.

Finkelstein, Norman, & Ruth Bettina Birn. 1998. *A Nation on Trial: The Goldhagen Thesis and Historical Truth*. New York: Metropolitan.

Fischer, Klaus P. 1995. *Nazi Germany: A New History*. New York: Continuum.

Fisher, Ronit. 2001. "Medical Experimentation." In W. Laqueur (ed.), *The Holocaust Encyclopedia*. New Haven, CT: Yale University Press.

Fleischner, Eva. 2001. "The Crucial Importance of the Holocaust for Christians." In J. Mitchell & H. Mitchell (eds.), *The Holocaust*. New York: McGraw-Hill/Dushkin.

Foer, Franklin. 2000. "Protected Frum." *New Republic,* August 21, p. 14.

Fogelman, Eva. 1994. *Conscience and Courage: Rescuers of Jews during the Holocaust*. New York: Anchor.

Foucault, Michel. 1977. *Language, Counter-Memory, Practice*. Ithaca, NY: Cornell University Press.

Fox, John P. 2001. "Holocaust Education in Europe." In W. Laqueur (ed.), *The Holocaust Encyclopedia*. New Haven, CT: Yale University Press.

Fraenkel, Daniel. 2001. "Nuremberg Laws." In W. Laqueur (ed.), *The Holocaust Encyclopedia*. New Haven, CT: Yale University Press.

Frank, Anne. 1952. *The Diary of Anne Frank*. New York: Simon & Schuster.

Freedman, Samuel G. 2000. *Jew vs. Jew: The Struggle for the Soul of American Jewry*. New York: Simon & Schuster.

Freeman, Michael. 1991. "The Theory and Prevention of Genocide." *Holocaust and Genocide Studies* 6:185–65.

Friedlander, Henry. 1998. "The T4 Killers: Berlin, Lublin, San Sabba." In M. Berenbaum & A. Peck (eds.), *The Holocaust and History*. Bloomington: Indiana University Press.

Friedlander, Henry. 2001. "Euthanasia." In W. Laqueur (ed.), *The Holocaust Encyclopedia*. New Haven, CT: Yale University Press.

Friedlander, Saul. 1989. "From Anti-Semitism to Extermination: A Historiographical Study and an Essay in Interpretation." In F. Francois (ed.), *Unanswered Questions*. New York: Shocken.

Friedlander, Saul. 1993. *Memory, History, and the Extermination of the Jews of Europe*. Bloomington: Indiana University Press.

Friedlander, Saul. 1997. *Nazi Germany and the Jews*. New York: HarperCollins.

Friedrich, Otto. 1994. *The Kingdom of Auschwitz*. New York: HarperPerennial.

Fuller, Richard, & Richard Myers. 1941. "The Natural History of a Social Problem." *American Sociological Review* 6:320–28.

Funkenstein, Amos. 1992. "History, Counterhistory, and Narrative." In S. Friedlander (ed.), *Probing the Limits of Representation*. Cambridge, MA: Harvard University Press.

Gamson, William A. 1992. "The Social Psychology of Collective Action." In A. Morris & C. Mueller (eds.), *Frontiers in Social Movement Theory*. New Haven, CT: Yale University Press.

Gamson, William A. 1995. "Hiroshima, the Holocaust, and the Politics of Exclusion." *American Sociological Review* 60:1–20.

Garber, Zev. 1994. *Shoah: The Paradigmatic Genocide*. Lanham, MD: University Press of America.

Gellately, Robert. 1988. "The Gestapo and German Society: Political Denunciation in the Gestapo Case Files." *Journal of Modern History* 60:654–94.

Gellately, Robert. 1997. "Denunciations in Twentieth-Century Germany: Aspects of Self-Policing in the Third Reich and the German Democratic Republic." In S. Fitzpatrick & R. Gellately (eds.), *Accusatory Practices*. Chicago: University of Chicago Press.

Gerth, Hans, & C. Wright Mills (eds.). 1946. *From Max Weber*. New York: Oxford University Press.

Geyer, Michael, & Miriam Hansen. 1994. "German-Jewish Memory and National Consciousness." In G. Hartman (ed.), *Holocaust Remembrance*. Cambridge, MA: Blackwell.

Gilbert, Gustave M. 1950. *The Psychology of Dictatorship*. New York: Ronald.

Gilbert, Martin. 2000. *Never Again: A History of the Holocaust*. New York: Universe.

Goldhagen, Daniel Jonah. 1996. *Hitler's Willing Executioners: Ordinary Germans and the Holocaust*. New York: Knopf.

Goldhagen, Daniel Jonah. 1998. "*Modell Bundesrepublik*: National History, Democracy, and Internationalization in Germany." In R. Shandley (ed.), *Unwilling Germans?* Minneapolis: University of Minnesota Press.

Gouri, Haim. 1994. "Facing the Glass Both." In G. Hartman (ed.), *Holocaust Remembrance*. Cambridge, MA Blackwell.

Greenberg, Irving. 1990. "History, Holocaust and Covenant." *Holocaust and Genocide Studies* 5:1–12.

Greif, Gideon. 2001. "Gas Chambers." In W. Laqueur (ed.), *The Holocaust Encyclopedia*. New Haven, CT: Yale University Press.

Greif, Mark. 2000. "The Banality of Irving." *American Prospect,* April 24, p. 32.

Gross, Jan T. 2000. "Themes for a Social History of War Experience and Collaboration." In I. Deák et al. (eds.), *The Politics of Retribution in Europe*. Princeton, NJ: Princeton University Press.

Gross, Jan T. 2001. *Neighbors: The Destruction of the Jewish Community in Jedwabne, Poland*. Princeton, NJ: Princeton University Press.

Gross, Michael L. 1994. "Jewish Rescue in Holland and France During the Second World War: Moral Cognition and Collective Action." *Social Forces* 73:463–96.

Gusfield, Joseph R. 1981. *The Culture of Public Problems*. Chicago: University of Chicago Press.

Gushee, David. 1994. *The Righteous Gentiles of the Holocaust: A Christian Interpretation*. Minneapolis: Fortress.

Gutman, Israel. 1990a. "Ghetto." In I. Gutman (ed.), *Encyclopedia of the Holocaust*. New York: Macmillan.

Gutman, Israel. 1990b. "Warsaw: Jews during the Holocaust" and "Warsaw Ghetto Uprising" in I. Gutman (ed.), *Encyclopedia of the Holocaust*. New York: Macmillan.

Gutman, Israel. 1990c. "Youth Movements: General Survey." In I. Gutman (ed.), *Encyclopedia of the Holocaust*. New York: Macmillan.

Gutman, Israel. 1990d. "Zyklon B." In I. Gutman (ed.), *Encyclopedia of the Holocaust*. New York: Macmillan.

Gutman, Israel, & Robert Rozett. 1990. "Estimated Jewish Losses in the Holocaust." In I. Gutman (ed.), *Encyclopedia of the Holocaust*. New York: Macmillan.

Gutman, Roy, & Rod Nordland. 2001. "Body of Evidence." *Newsweek,* July 23, p. 34.

Guttenplan, D. D. 2000. "The Holocaust on Trial." *Atlantic Monthly,* February, p. 45.

Habermas, Jürgen. 1998. "Goldhagen and the Public Use of History: Why a Democracy Prize for Daniel Goldhagen." In R. Shandley (ed.), *Unwilling Germans?* Minneapolis: University of Minnesota Press.

Hacking, Ian. 1986. "Making Up People." In T. Heller et al. (eds.), *Reconstructing Individualism*. Stanford, CA: Stanford University Press.

Hacking, Ian. 1999. *The Social Construction of What?* Cambridge, MA: Harvard University Press.

Halbachs, Maurice. 1950. *The Collective Memory*. New York: Harper-Colophon.

Halbachs, Maurice. 1992. *On Collective Memory.* Edited and translated by L. Coser. Chicago: University of Chicago Press.

Hall, John R. 1992. "Where History and Sociology Meet: Forms of Discourse and Sociohistorical Inquiry." *Sociological Theory* 10:164–93.

Hamilton, Richard F. 1982. *Who Voted for Hitler?* Princeton, NJ: Princeton University Press.

Hamm, Mark S. 1993. *American Skinheads: The Criminology and Control of Hate Crime*. Westport, CT: Praeger.

Hancock, Ian. 1996. "Responses to the Porrajmos: The Romani Holocaust." In A. Rosenbaum (ed.), *Is the Holocaust Unique?* Boulder, CO: Westview.

Handler, Joel. 1978. *Social Movements and the Legal System: A Theory of Law Reform and Social Change*. New York: Academic Pre.

Hartman, Geoffrey (ed.). 1986. *Bitburg in Moral and Political Perspective*. Bloomington: Indiana University Press.

Hass, Aaron. 1995. *The Aftermath: Living With the Holocaust*. Cambridge, MA: Cambridge University Press.

Hayes, Peter. 1987. *Industry and Ideology: IG Farben in the Nazi Era*. Cambridge: Cambridge University Press.

Hayes, Peter. 1998. "State Policy and Corporate Involvement in the Holocaust." In M. Berenbaum & A. Peck (eds.), *The Holocaust and History*. Bloomington: Indiana University Press.

Haynes, Stephen R. 1998. "Holocaust Education at American Colleges and Universities: A Report on the Current Situation." *Holocaust and Genocide Studies* 12:282–307.

Helmreich, William B. 1992. *Against All Odds: Holocaust Survivors and the Successful Lives They Made in America*. New York: Simon & Schuster.

Henry, Stuart, & Dragan Milovanovic. 1996. *Constitutive Criminology: Beyond Postmodernism*. London: Sage.

Herf, Jeffrey. 1984. *Reactionary Modernism: Technology, Culture, and Politics in Weimar and the Third Reich*. New York: Cambridge University Press.

Herf, Jeffrey. 1994. "German Communism, the Discourse of 'Antifascist Resistance,' and the Jewish Catastrophe." In M. Geyer & J. Boyer (eds.), *Resistance against the Third Reich 1933–1990*. Chicago: University of Chicago Press.

Herf, Jeffrey. 1997. *Divided Memory: The Nazi Past in the Two Germanys*. Cambridge, MA: Harvard University Press.

Herman, Burt. 1999. "Breakthrough: $5.2 Billion Settlement Reached in Nazi Slave Labor Case." Associated Press, Dec. 15 (www.abcnews.go.com).

Hertzberg, Arthur. 1968. *The French Enlightenment and the Jews: The Origins of Modern Anti-Semitism*. New York: Schocken.

Higham, Charles. 1983. *Trading with the Enemy: The Nazi-American Money Plot, 1933–1949*. New York: Barnes & Noble.

Hilberg, Raul. 1961. *The Destruction of European Jews*. Chicago: Quadrangle.

Hilberg, Raul. 1985. *The Destruction of European Jews*. Abridged ed. New York: Holmes & Meier.

Hilberg, Raul. 1986. "Bitburg as Symbol." In G. Hartman (ed.), *Bitburg in Moral and Political Perspective*. Bloomington: Indiana University Press.

Hilberg, Raul. 1989. "The Bureaucracy of Annihilation." In F. Furet (ed.), *Unanswered Questions*. New York: Schocken.

Hilberg, Raul. 1991. "The Discovery of the Holocaust." In P. Hayes (ed.), *Lessons and Legacies*. Evanston, IL: Northwestern University Press.

Hilberg, Raul. 1992. *Perpetrators, Victims, Bystanders: The Jewish Catastrophe, 1933–1945*. New York: HarperPerennial

Hilberg, Raul. 1996. *The Politics of Memory: The Journey of a Holocaust Historian*. Chicago: Ivan Dee.

Hilberg, Raul. 2001. "Auschwitz." In W. Laqueur (ed.), *The Holocaust Encyclopedia*. New Haven, CT: Yale University Press.

Hilgartner, Stephen, & Charles L. Bosk. 1988. "The Rise and Fall of Social Problems." *American Journal of Sociology* 94:53–78.

Hindley, Meredith. 1996. "Negotiating the Boundary of Unconditional Surrender: The War Refugee Board in Sweden and Nazi Proposals to Ransom Jews, 1944–1945." *Holocaust and Genocide Studies* 10:52–77.

Hirsch, Michael. 1999. "A Nazi-Era Bill Finally Comes Due." *Newsweek*, February 22, p. 40.

Hitchens, Christopher. 2001. "Wiesel Words." *Nation,* February 19, p. 9.

Hitler, Adolf. [1925] 1943. *Mein Kampf.* Translated by R. Manheim. Boston: Houghton Mifflin.

Hofstader, Richard. 1959. *Social Darwinism in American Social Thought.* Boston: Beacon.

Holstein, James A., & Gale Miller. 1990. "Rethinking Victimization: An Interactional Approach to Victimology." *Symbolic Interaction* 13:103–22.

Holstein, James A., & Gale Miller (eds.). 1993. *Reconsidering Social Constructionism: Debates in Social Problems Theory.* Hawthorne, NY: Aldine de Gruyter.

Horowitz, Irving Louis. 1976. *Genocide and State Power.* New Brunswick, NJ: Transaction.

Hughes, Everett C. 1962. "Good People and Dirty Work." *Social Problems* 10:3–10.

Ibarra, Peter, & John Kitsuse. 1993. "Vernacular Constituents of Moral Discourse: An Interactionist Proposal for the Study of Social Problems." In J. Holstein & G. Miller (eds.), *Reconsidering Social Constructionism.* Hawthorne, NY: Aldine de Gruyter.

Ignatieff, Michael. 2001. "Lemkin's Words." *New Republic,* February 26, p. 25.

Insdorf, Annette. 1989. *Indelible Shadows: Film and the Holocaust.* New York: Cambridge University Press.

Irving, David. 1977. *Hitler's War.* New York: Viking.

Isaac, Jules. 1959. *Jesus et Israel.* Paris: Pasquelle.

James, Harold. 2001. *The Deutsche Bank and the Nazi Economic War against the Jews.* Cambridge: Cambridge University Press.

Jay, Martin. 1993. "Postmodern Fascism? Reflections on the Return of the Oppressed." *Tikkun* 8:37–41.

Jelinek, Pauline. 2000. "Holocaust Glare Turns on U.S. Companies." *Wisconsin State Journal,* August 28, p. A1.

Joffe, Josef. 1998. "'The Killers Were Ordinary Germans, Ergo the Ordinary Germans Were Killers': The Logic, the Language, and the Meaning of a Book That Conquered Germany." In R. Shandley (ed.), *Unwilling Germans?* Minneapolis: University of Minnesota Press.

Johnson, Eric A. 1999. *Nazi Terror: The Gestapo, Jews, and Ordinary Germans.* New York: Basic.

Johnson, Paul. 1987. *A History of the Jews.* New York: Harper & Row.

Jonas, Hans. 2001. "The Concept of God: A Jewish Voice." In M. Morgan (ed.), *A Holocaust Reader.* New York: Oxford University Press.

Jones, Priscilla Dale. 1990. "Trials of War Criminals: General Survey." In Y. Gutman (ed.), *Encyclopedia of the Holocaust.* New York: MacMillan.

Judt, Tony. 2000. "The Past Is Another Country: Myth and Memory in Postwar Europe." In I. Deák et al. (eds.), *The Politics of Retribution in Europe.* Princeton, NJ: Princeton University Press.

Kaplan, Marion A. 1998. *Between Dignity and Despair: Jewish Life in Nazi Germany*. New York: Oxford University Press.

Kater, Michael. 1983. *The Nazi Party: A Social Profile of Members and Leaders 1919–1945*. Cambridge, MA: Harvard University Press.

Kater, Michael. 1984. "Everyday Antisemitism in Prewar Nazi Germany: The Popular Bases." *Yad Vashem Studies* 16:129–59.

Katz, Steven T. 1989. "Quantity and Interpretation: Issues in the Comparative Historical Analysis of the Holocaust." *Holocaust and Genocide Studies* 4:127–48.

Katz, Steven T. 2001. "Jewish Faith After the Holocaust: Four Approaches." In J. Mitchell & H. Mitchell (eds.), *The Holocaust*. New York: McGraw-Hill/Dushkin.

Kaufman, Jonathan. 1994. *Broken Alliance: The Turbulent Time between Blacks and Jews in America*. New York: Simon & Schuster.

Kelman, Herbert C., & V. Lee Hamilton. 1989. *Crimes of Obedience: Toward a Social Psychology of Authority and Responsibility*. New Haven, CT: Yale University Press.

Kershaw, Ian. 1998. *Hitler: 1889–1936 Hubris*. New York: Norton.

Kershaw, Ian. 2000. *Hitler: 1936–1945 Nemesis*. New York: Norton.

Kidder, Robert L. 1983. *Connecting Law and Society: An Introduction to Research and Theory*. Englewood Cliffs, NJ: Prentice-Hall.

Koch, Hansjoachim W. 2000. *The Hitler Youth: Origins and Development 1922–1945*. New York: Cooper Square.

Kochan, Lionel. 1990. "Alfred Rosenberg." In I. Gutman (ed.), *Encyclopedia of the Holocaust*. New York: Macmillan.

Koehl, Robert Lewis. 1983. *The Black Corps: The Structure and Power Struggles of the Nazi SS*. Madison: University of Wisconsin Press.

Koffler, Florette & Richard Koffler. 1995. "Introduction." In N. Caracciolo, *Uncertain Refuge: Italy and the Jews during the Holocaust*. Edited and translated by F. Rechnitz Koffler & R. Koffler. Urbana and Chicago: University of Illinois Press.

Kommers, Donald. 1989. *The Constitutional Jurisprudence of the Federal Republic of Germany*. Durham, NC: Duke University Press.

Koonz, Claudia. 1987. *Mothers in the Fatherland: Women, the Family and Nazi Politics*. New York: St. Martin's.

Koonz, Claudia. 1991. "Genocide and Eugenics: The Language of Power." In P. Hayes (ed.), *Lessons and Legacies*. Evanston, IL: Northwestern University Press.

Krakowski, Shmuel. 1990a. "Chelmno." In I. Gutman (ed.), *Encyclopedia of the Holocaust*. New York: Macmillan.

Krakowski, Shmuel. 1990b. "Death Marches." In I. Gutman (ed.), *Encyclopedia of the Holocaust*. New York: Macmillan.

Kreimeier, Klaus. 1996. *The Ufa Story: A History of Germany's Greatest Film Company, 1918–1945*. New York: Hill & Wang.

Krondorfer, Bjorn. 1995. *Remembrance and Reconciliation: Encounters between Young Jews and Germans*. New Haven, CT: Yale University Press.

Kuper, Leo. 1990. "The United States Ratifies the Genocide Convention." In F. Chalk & K. Jonassohn (eds.), *The History and Sociology of Genocide*. New Haven, CT: Yale University Press.

Kurek-Lesik, Ewa. 1992. "The Role of Polish Nuns in the Rescue of Jews." In P. Oliner et al. (eds.), *Embracing the Other*. New York: New York University Press.

Kushner, Harold S. 1981. *When Bad Things Happen to Good People*. New York: Schocken.

Langer, Lawrence L. 1991. *Holocaust Testimonies: The Ruins of Memory*. New Haven, CT: Yale University Press.

Lanzmann, Claude. 1985. *Shoah: An Oral History of the Holocaust*. New York: Pantheon.

Laqueur, Walter. 1980. *The Terrible Secret: Suppression of the Truth about Hitler's "Final Solution."* Boston: Little, Brown.

Laqueur, Walter. 2000. "Auschwitz." In M. Neufeld & M. Berenbaum (eds.), *The Bombing of Auschwitz*. New York: St. Martin's.

Large, David Clay. 1994. "'A Beacon in the German Darkness': The Anti-Nazi Resistance Legacy in West German Politics." In M. Geyer & J. Boyer (eds.), *Resistance against the Third Reich 1933–1990*. Chicago: University of Chicago Press.

Lempkin, Raphael. 1944. *Axis Rule in Occupied Europe*. Washington, DC: Carnegie Endowment for International Peace.

Lerner, Gerda. 1994. "In the Footsteps of the Cathars." *Progressive,* March, p. 18.

Levi, Primo. 1986. *The Drowned and the Saved*. London: Michael Joseph.

Levine, Paul. 1998. "Bureaucracy, Resistance, and the Holocaust: Understanding the Success of Swedish Diplomacy in Budapest, 1944–1945." In M. Berenbaum & A. Peck (eds.), *The Holocaust and History*. Bloomington: Indiana University Press.

Lewy, Guenter. 1999. "Gypsies and Jews under the Nazis." *Holocaust and Genocide Studies* 13:383–404.

Linenthal, Edward T. 1995. *Preserving Memory: The Struggle to Create America's Holocaust Museum*. New York: Viking.

Lipset, Seymour Martin. 1960. *Political Man: The Social Basis of Politics*. Garden City, NY: Doubleday.

Lipset, Seymour Martin, & Earl Raab. 1995. *Jews and the American Scene*. Cambridge, MA: Harvard University Press.

Lipstadt, Deborah. 1993. *Denying the Holocaust: The Growing Assault on Truth and Memory*. New York: Free Press.

Lipstadt, Deborah. 2000. "The Failure to Rescue and Contemporary American Jewish Historiography of the Holocaust: Judging from a Distance." In

M. Neufeld & M. Berenbaum (eds.), *The Bombing of Auschwitz*. New York: St. Martin's.

Lipton, Robert Jay. 1986. *The Nazi Doctors: Medical Killing and the Psychology of Genocide*. New York: Basic.

Litvak, Meir. 1994. "A Palestinian Past: National Construction and Reconstruction." *History and Memory* 6:24–56.

Loseke, Donileen R. 1999. *Teaching about Social Problems*. Hawthorne, NY: Aldine de Gruyter.

Loshitzky, Yosefa (ed.). 1997. *Spielberg's Holocaust: Critical Perspectives on Schindler's List*. Bloomington: Indiana University Press.

Lubetkin, Zivia. 1981. *In the Days of Destruction and Revolt*. Tel Aviv: Hakibbutz Hameuchad.

Maier, Charles S. 1988. *The Unmasterable Past: History, Holocaust, and German National Identity*. Cambridge, MA: Harvard University Press.

Marcuse, Harold. 2001. *Legacies of Dachau: The Uses and Abuses of a Concentration Camp, 1933–2001*. New York: Cambridge University Press.

Markle, Gerald E. 1995. *Meditations of a Holocaust Traveler*. New York: SUNY Press.

Markovitz, Andrei S. 1990. "Coping with the Past: The West German Labor Movement and the Left." In P. Baldwin (ed.), *Reworking the Past*. Boston: Beacon.

Markovitz, Andrei S. 1998. "Discomposure in History's Final Resting Place." In R. Shandley (ed.), *Unwilling Germans?* Minneapolis: University of Minnesota Press.

Marrus, Michael. 1987. *The Holocaust in History*. New York: New American Library.

Marrus, Michael. 1991. "The Use and Abuse of the Holocaust." In P. Hayes (ed.), *Lessons and Legacies*. Evanston, IL: Northwestern University Press.

Marrus, Michael. 1997. *The Nuremberg War Crimes Trial 1945–46: A Documentary History*. Boston: Bedford.

Marrus, Michael, & Robert O. Paxton. 1981. *Vichy France and the Jews*. New York: Stanford University Press.

Marrus, Michael, & Robert O. Paxton. 1989. "The Nazis and the Jews in Occupied Western Europe, 1940–1944." In F. Furet (ed.), *Unanswered Questions*. New York: Shocken.

Marx, Karl. [1852] 1963. *The Eighteenth Brumaire of Louis Bonaparte*. New York: International.

Marx, Karl, & Friedrich Engels. [1848] 1948. *Manifesto of the Communist Party*. New York: International.

Mauss, Armand L. 1975. *Social Problems as Social Movements*. Philadelphia: Lippincott.

Maybaum, Ignaz. 1965. *The Face of God after Auschwitz*. Amsterdam: Polak & Van Gennep.

Mayer, Arno J. 1989. *Why Did the Heavens Not Darken? The "Final Solution" in History.* New York: Pantheon.

McCright, Aaron M., & Riley E. Dunlap. 2000. "Challenging Global Warming as a Social Problem: An Analysis of the Conservative Movement's Counter Claims." *Social Problems* 47:499–522.

Mendes-Flohr, Paul, & Jehuda Reinharz (eds.). 1995. *The Jew in the Modern World: A Documentary History.* New York: Oxford University Press.

Mierzejewski, Alfred C. 2001. "A Public Enterprise in the Service of Mass Murder: The Deutsche Reichsbahn and the Holocaust." *Holocaust and Genocide Studies* 15:33–46.

Miller, Gale, & James A. Holstein. 1989. "On the Sociology of Social Problems." In J. Holstein & G. Miller (eds.), *Perspectives on Social Problems,* Vol. 1. Greenwich, CT: JAI.

Miller, Gale, & James A. Holstein. 1993. "Reconsidering Social Constructionism." In J. Holstein & G. Miller (eds.), *Reconsidering Social Constructionism.* Hawthorne, NY: Aldine de Gruyter.

Miller, Ingo. 1991. *Hitler's Justice: The Courts of the Third Reich.* Cambridge, MA: Harvard University Press.

Miller, Judith. 1990. *One, by One, by One: Facing the Holocaust.* New York: Touchstone.

Milton, Sybil. 1990. "The Context of the Holocaust." *German Studies Review* 13:269–83.

Mitchell, Joseph R., & Helen Buss Mitchell (eds.). 2001. *The Holocaust: Readings and Interpretations.* New York: McGraw-Hill/Dushkin.

Moll, Christiane. 1994. "Acts of Resistance: The White Rose in the Light of New Archival Evidence." In M. Geyer & J. Boyer (eds.), *Resistance against the Third Reich 1933–1990.* Chicago: University of Chicago Press.

Mommsen, Hans. 1986. "The Realization of the Unthinkable: The 'Final Solution of the Jewish Question' in the Third Reich." In G. Hirschfeld (ed.), *The Politics of Genocide.* London: Allen & Unwin.

Mommsen, Hans. 1998a. "The Civil Service and the Implementation of the Holocaust: From Passive to Active Complicity." In M. Berenbaum & A. Peck (eds.), *The Holocaust and History.* Bloomington: Indiana University Press.

Mommsen, Hans. 1998b. "The Thin Patina of Civilization: Anti-Semitism Was a Necessary, but by No Means a Sufficient, Condition for the Holocaust." In R. Shandley (ed.), *Unwilling Germans?* Minneapolis: University of Minnesota Press.

Monroe, Kristen R. 1996. *The Heart of Altruism: Perceptions of a Common Humanity.* Princeton, NJ: Princeton University Press.

Muller-Hill, Benno. 1998. "Human Genetics and the Mass Murder of Jews, Gypsies, and Others." In M. Berenbaum & A. Peck (eds.), *The Holocaust and History.* Bloomington: Indiana University Press.

Murray, Williamson. 2000. "Monday-Morning Quarterbacking and the Bombing of Auschwitz." In M. Neufeld & M. Berenbaum (eds.), *The Bombing of Auschwitz*. New York: St. Martin's.

Mushkat, Marian. 1990. "Trials of War Criminals: Nuremberg Trial." In I. Gutman (ed.), *Encyclopedia of the Holocaust*. New York: Macmillan.

Nagel, Joane. 1994. "Constructing Ethnicity: Creating and Recreating Ethnic Identity and Culture." *Social Problems* 41:152–76.

Nesaule, Agate. 1995. *A Woman in Amber: Healing the Trauma of War and Exile*. New York: Soho.

Neufeld, Michael J., & Michael Berenbaum (eds.). 2000. *The Bombing of Auschwitz: Should the Allies Have Attempted It?* New York: St. Martin's.

Neuman, W. Lawrence. 1998. "Negotiated Meanings and State Transformation: The Trust Issue in the Progressive Era." *Social Problems* 45:315–35.

Nichols, Lawrence T. 1990. "Reconceptualizing Accounts: An Agenda for Theory Building and Empirical Research." In S. McNall (ed.), *Current Perspectives on Social Theory,* Vol. 10. Greenwich, CT: JAI.

Nichols, Lawrence T. 1995. "Cold Wars, Evil Empires, Treacherous Japanese: Effects of International Context on Problem Construction." In J. Best (ed.), *Images of Issues*. Hawthorne, NY: Aldine de Gruyter.

Nichols, Lawrence T. 2000. "Dialogical Constructionism: Toward Holistic Understanding of Social Problems Discourse." In J. Holstein & G. Miller (eds.), *Perspectives on Social Problems,* Vol. 12. Stamford, CT: JAI.

Nolte, Ernst. 1965. *Three Faces of Fascism*. New York: Holt, Rinehart & Winston.

Nora, Pierre. 1986. *Les Lieux de Memoire, La Nation*. Paris: Gallimard.

Novick, Peter. 1999. *The Holocaust in American Life*. Boston: Houghton Mifflin.

Olick, Jeffrey K., & Daniel Levy. 1997. "Collective Memory and Cultural Constraint: Holocaust Myth and Rationality in German Politics." *American Sociological Review* 62:921–36.

Oliner, Pearl M., et al. (eds.). 1992. *Embracing the Other: Philosophical, Psychological, and Historical Perspectives on Altruism*. New York: New York University Press.

Oliner, Samuel P., & Pearl M. Oliner. 1988. *The Altruistic Personality: Rescuers of Jews in Nazi Europe*. New York: Free Press.

Osiel, Mark. 1997. *Mass Atrocity, Collective Memory, and the Law*. New Brunswick, NJ: Transaction.

Paldiel, Mordecai. 1996. *Sheltering the Jews: Stories of Holocaust Rescuers*. Minneapolis: Fortress.

Parrillo, Vincent N. 1997. *Strangers to These Shores: Race and Ethnic Relations in the United States*. Boston: Allyn & Bacon.

Patterson, Orlando. 1991. *Freedom in the Making of Western Culture*. New York: Basic.

Pawełczynska, Anna. 1979. *Values and Violence in Auschwitz: A Sociological Analysis*. Berkeley: University of California Press.

Pawlikowski, John T. 1997. "Penetrating Barriers: A Holocaust Retrospective." In C. Rittner & J. Roth (eds.), *From the Unthinkable to the Unavoidable*. Westport, CT: Praeger.

Pawlikowski, John T. 1998. "The Catholic Response to the Holocaust: Institutional Perspectives." In M. Berenbaum & A. Peck (eds.), *The Holocaust and History*. Bloomington: Indiana University Press.

Payne, Stanley G. 1980. *Fascism: Comparison and Definition*. Madison: University of Wisconsin Press.

Payne, Stanley G. 2001. "Fascism in Western Europe." In W. Laqueur (ed.), *The Holocaust Encyclopedia*. New Haven, CT: Yale University Press.

Penslar, Derek Jonathan. 1995. "Innovation and Revisionism in Israeli Historiography." *History and Memory* 7:125–46.

Petropoulos, Jonathan. 1997. "Co-Opting Nazi Germany: Neutrality in Europe during World War II." *Dimensions* 11:15–21.

Petropoulos, Jonathan. 2001. "The Roller Coaster of Restitution: The United States Government's Involvement with Holocaust Victims' Assets." *Dimensions* 15:9–18.

Peyrot, Mark. 1984. "Cycles of Social Problem Development: The Case of Drug Abuse." *Sociological Quarterly* 25:83–96.

Peyser, Marc. 2001. "Out of the Attic, At Last." *Newsweek*, May 21, p. 57.

Phayer, Michael. 2000. *The Catholic Church and the Holocaust, 1930–1965*. Bloomington: Indiana University Press.

Piliavin, Jane, & Hong-Wen Charng. 1990. "Altruism: A Review of Recent Theory and Research." *Annual Review of Sociology* 16:27–65. Palo Alto, CA: Annual Reviews.

Pingel, Falk. 1990. "Concentration Camps." In I. Gutman (ed.), *Encyclopedia of the Holocaust*. New York: Macmillan.

Podeh, Elie. 2000. "History and Memory in the Israeli Educational System: The Portrayal of the Arab-Israeli Conflict in History Textbooks (1948–2000)." *History and Memory* 12:65–100.

Poole, James. 1997a. *Hitler and His Secret Partners: Contributions, Loot and Rewards, 1933–1945*. New York: Pocket Books.

Poole, James. 1997b. *Who Financed Hitler: The Secret Funding of Hitler's Rise to Power, 1919–1933*. New York: Pocket Books.

Popora, Douglas. 1990. *How Holocausts Happen: The United States in Central America*. Philadelphia: Temple University Press.

Prekerowa, Teresa. 1990. "Zegota." In I. Gutman (ed.), *Encyclopedia of the Holocaust*. New York: Macmillan.

Proctor. 1988. *Racial Hygiene: Medicine under the Nazis*. Cambridge, MA: Harvard University Press.

Prosono, Marvin. 1994. "Symbolic Territoriality and the Holocaust: The Controversy over the Carmelite Convent at Auschwitz." In J. Holstein & G. Miller (eds.), in *Perspectives on Social Problems,* Vol. 5. Greenwich, CT: JAI.

Prosono, Marvin, & Gary Brock. 1996. "The Holocaust and the Construction of the Sacred: The Emerging Mythos of the 'Crucified Clan.'" In J. Holstein & G. Miller (eds.), *Perspectives on Social Problems,* Vol. 8. Greenwich, CT: JAI.

Public Broadcasting Corporation. 1995. "Nazi Designers of Death." NOVA.

Rabinbach, Anson. 1997. "From Explosion to Erosion: Holocaust Memorialization in America Since Bitburg." *History and Memory* 9:226–55.

Rafter, Nicole. 1992a. "Claims-Making and Socio-Cultural Context in the First U.S. Eugenics Campaign." *Social Problems* 39:17–34.

Rafter, Nicole. 1992b. "Some Consequences of Strict Constructionism." *Social Problems* 39:38–39.

Ram, Uri. 1995. "Zionist Historiography and the Invention of Modern Jewish Nationhood: The Case of Ben Zion Dinur." *History and Memory* 7:91–124.

Reemtsma, Jan Philipp. 1998. "Turning Away from Denial: *Hitler's Willing Executioners* as a Counterforce to 'Historical Explanation.'" In R. Shandley (ed.), *Unwilling Germans?* Minneapolis: University of Minnesota Press.

Reinharz, Jehuda, & Evyatar Friesel. 1997. "The Zionist Leadership between the Holocaust and the Creation of the State of Israel." In A. Rosenfeld (ed.), *Thinking about the Holocaust.* Bloomington: Indiana University Press.

Reiss, Albert J., Jr. 1971. *The Police and the Public.* New Haven, CT: Yale University Press.

Rempel, Gerhard. 1989. *Hitler's Children: The Hitler Youth and the SS.* Chapel Hill: University of North Carolina Press.

Reynaud, Michel, & Sylvie Graffard. 2001. *The Jehovah's Witnesses and the Nazis: Persecution, Deportation, and Murder, 1933–1945.* New York: Cooper Square.

Riemer, Jeremiah H. 1998. "Burdens of Proof." In R. Shandley (ed.), *Unwilling Germans?* Minneapolis: University of Minnesota Press.

Ritzer, George. 1992. *Classical Sociological Theory.* New York: McGraw–Hill.

Roiphe, Anne. 1988. *A Season for Healing: Reflections on the Holocaust.* New York: Summit.

Rose, Paul L. 1990. *Revolutionary Antisemitism in Germany: From Kant to Wagner.* Princeton, NJ: Princeton University Press.

Rosenbaum, Alan S. 1993. *Prosecuting Nazi War Criminals.* Boulder, CO: Westview.

Rosenbaum, Alan S. (ed.). 1996. *Is the Holocaust Unique? Perspectives on Comparative Genocide.* Boulder, CO: Westview.

Rosenbaum, Ron. 1998. *Explaining Hitler: The Search for the Origins of Evil.* New York: Random House.

Rosenfeld, Alvin H. 1985. *Imagining Hitler.* Bloomington: Indiana University Press.

Rosenfeld, Alvin H. 1991. "Popularization and Memory: The Case of Anne

Frank." In P. Hayes (ed.). *Lessons and Legacies*. Evanston, IL: Northwestern University Press.

Rosenfeld, Alvin H. 1997. "The Americanization of the Holocaust." In A. Rosenfeld (ed.), *Thinking About the Holocaust*. Bloomington: Indiana University Press.

Rosenfeld, Gavriel D. 1999. "The Politics of Uniqueness: Reflections on the Recent Polemical Turn in Holocaust and Genocide Scholarship." *Holocaust and Genocide Studies* 13:28–61.

Roth, Michael. 1993. "Politics, Piety, and Transformation." *Tikkun* 8:79–81.

Rubenstein, Richard L., & John K. Roth. 1987. *Approaches to Auschwitz: The Holocaust and Its Legacy*. Atlanta: John Knox.

Rubenstein, William D. 1997. *The Myth of Rescue: Why the Democracies Could Not Have Saved More Jews*. New York: Routledge.

Ruckerl, Adalbert. 1990a. "Denazification." In I. Gutman (ed.), *Encyclopedia of the Holocaust*. New York: Macmillan.

Ruckerl, Adalbert. 1990b. "Trials of War Criminals: West Germany." In I. Gutman (ed.), *Encyclopedia of the Holocaust*. New York: Macmillan.

Sachar, Howard M. 1992. *A History of Jews in America*. New York: Vintage.

Salzman, Jack (ed.). 1992. *Bridges and Boundaries: African Americans and American Jews*. New York: Braziller.

Santner, Eric. L. 1990. "On the Difficulty of Saying 'We': The 'Historians' Debate' and Edgard Reitz's *Heimat*." *History and Memory* 2:276–96.

Schleunes, Karl A. 1970. *The Twisted Road to Auschwitz: Nazi Policy toward German Jews, 1933–1939*. Urbana: University of Illinois Press.

Schmitt, Raymond L. 1989. "Sharing the Holocaust: Bitburg as Emotional Reminder." In N. Denzin (ed.), *Studies in Symbolic Interaction,* Vol. 10. Greenwich, CT: JAI.

Schoeps, Julius H. 1998. "From Character Assassination to Murder." In R. Shandley (ed.), *Unwilling Germans?* Minneapolis: University of Minnesota Press.

Schuman, Howard, & Jacqueline Scott. 1989. "Generations and Collective Memories." *American Sociological Review* 54:359–81.

Schutz, Alfred. 1962. *Collected Papers I: The Problem of Social Reality*. The Hague: Martinus Nijhoff.

Schwartz, Barry. 1991. "Iconography and Collective Memory: Lincoln's Image in the American Mind." *Sociological Quarterly* 32:301–19.

Schwartz, Barry. 1996. "Memory as a Cultural System: Abraham Lincoln in World War II." *American Sociological Review* 61:908–27.

Segev, Tom. 1993. *The Seventh Million: The Israelis and the Holocaust*. New York: Hill & Wang.

Sen, Amartya. 2000. "Other People." *New Republic,* December 18, p. 23.

Sewell, William H., Jr. 1992. "A Theory of Structure: Duality, Agency, and Transformation." *American Journal of Sociology* 98:1–29.

Shandler, Jeffrey. 1997. "Schindler's Discourse: America Discusses the Holocaust and Its Mediation, from NBC's Miniseries to Spielberg's Film." In Y. Loshitzky (ed.), *Spielberg's Holocaust*. Bloomington: Indiana University Press.

Shandley, Robert R. (ed.). 1998. *Unwilling Germans? The Goldhagen Debate*. Minneapolis: University of Minnesota Press.

Shapira, Anita. 1995. "Politics and Collective Memory: The Debate over the 'New Historians' in Israel." *History and Memory* 7:9–40.

Shapira, Anita. 1997. "The Holocaust and World War II as Elements of the Yishuv Psyche until 1948." In A. Rosenfeld (ed.), *Thinking about the Holocaust*. Bloomington: Indiana University Press.

Sheehan, James J. 1993. "Germany." *World Book Encyclopedia*. Chicago: World Book.

Sherman, Franklin, & Helmut T. Lehman (eds.). 1971. *Luther's Works*. Philadelphia: Fortress.

Shermer, Michael, & Alex Grobman. 2000. *Denying History: Who Says the Holocaust Never Happened and Why Do They Say It?* Berkeley: University of California Press.

Shirer, William. 1960. *The Rise and Fall of the Third Reich: A History of Nazi Germany*. New York: Simon & Schuster.

Simmons, Robert G. 1991. "Altruism and Sociology." *Sociological Quarterly* 32:1–22.

Simpson, Christopher. 1988. *Blowback: America's Recruitment of Nazi War Criminals and Its Effects on the Cold War*. New York: Weidenfeld & Nicolson.

Simpson, Christopher. 1993. *The Splendid Blond Beast: Money, Law, and Genocide in the Twentieth Century*. New York: Grove.

Snow, David A., & Robert D. Benford. 1992. "Master Frames and Cycles of Protest." In A. Morris & Carol Mueller (eds.), *Frontiers in Social Movement Theory*. New Haven, CT: Yale University Press.

Snow, David A., E. Burke Rochford, Steven K. Worden, & Robert D. Benford. 1986. "Frame Alignment Processes, Micromobilization, and Movement Participation." *American Sociological Review* 51:464–81.

Spector, Malcolm, & John I. Kitsuse. 1987. *Constructing Social Problems*. Hawthorne, NY: Aldine de Gruyter.

Spector, Shmuel. 1990a. "Einsatzgruppen." In I. Gutman (ed.), *Encyclopedia of the Holocaust*. New York: Macmillan.

Spector, Shmuel. 1990b. "Railways, German." In I. Gutman (ed.), *Encyclopedia of the Holocaust*. New York: Macmillan.

Spector, Shmuel. 1990c. "Yad Vashem." In I. Gutman (ed.), *Encyclopedia of the Holocaust*. New York: Macmillan.

Speier, Hans. 1986. *German White-Collar Workers and the Rise of Hitler*. New Haven, CT: Yale University Press.

Spielvogel, Jackson J. 1996. *Hitler and Nazi Germany: A History.* Upper Saddle River, NJ: Prentice-Hall.

Stein, Eric. 1986. "History against Free Speech: The New German Law against 'Auschwitz'—and Other—'Lies.'" *Michigan Law Review* 85:277–324.

Steinweis, Alan E. 2001. "The Holocaust and American Culture: An Assessment of Recent Scholarship." *Holocaust and Genocide Studies* 15:296–310.

Stylinski, Andrzej. 2001. "Polish Bishops Plan Major Apology to Jews." *Wisconsin State Journal,* May 26, p. A6.

Tal, Uriel. 1975. *Christians and Jews in Germany: Religion, Politics and Ideology in the Second Reich, 1870–1914.* Ithaca, NY: Cornell University Press.

Taraki, Lisa. 1990. "The Development of Political Consciousness Among Palestinians in the Occupied Territories, 1967–1987." In J. Nassar & R. Heacock (eds.), *Intifada: Palestine at the Crossroads.* New York: Greenwood.

Taylor, James, & Warren Shaw. 1987. *The Third Reich Almanac.* New York: World Almanac.

Tec, Nechama. 1986. *When Light Pierced the Darkness: Christian Rescue of Jews in Nazi-Occupied Poland.* New York: Oxford University Press.

Tec, Nechama. 1993. *Defiance: The Bielski Partisans.* New York: Oxford University Press.

Teveth, Shabtai. 1996. *Ben-Gurion and the Holocaust.* New York: Harcourt Brace.

Tiryakian, Edward A. 1993. "American Religious Exceptionalism: A Reconsideration." *Annals of the American Academy of Political and Social Science* 527:40–54.

Todorov, Tzvetan. 2001a. *The Fragility of Goodness: Why Bulgaria's Jews Survived the Holocaust.* Princeton, NJ: Princeton University Press.

Todorov, Tzvetan. 2001b. "In Search of Lost Crime." *New Republic,* January 29, p. 29.

Troyer, Ronald J. 1992. "Some Consequences of Contextual Constructionism." *Social Problems* 39:35–37.

Turner, Henry Ashby, Jr. (ed.). 1975. *Reappraisals of Fascism.* New York: New Viewpoints.

Turner, Henry Ashby, Jr. 1985. *German Big Business and the Rise of Hitler.* New York Oxford University Press.

Turque, Bill. 1991. "The Real David Duke." *Newsweek,* November 18, p. 24.

U.S. Census Bureau. 2001. *Statistical Abstract of the United States.* Washington, DC: U.S. Census Bureau.

Vago, Bela. 1989. "The Reaction to Nazi Anti-Jewish Policy in East-Central Europe and in the Balkans." In F. Furet (ed.), *Unanswered Questions.* New York: Schocken.

Van Buren, Paul. 1980. *Discerning the Way: A Theology of the Jewish Christian Reality.* New York: Seabury.

Vidal-Naquet, Pierre. 1992. *Assassins of Memory: Essays on the Denial of the Holocaust*. New York: Columbia University Press.

Vital, David. 1991. "After the Catastrophe: Aspects of Contemporary Jewry." In P. Hayes (ed.), *Lessons and Legacies*. Evanston, IL: Northwestern University Press.

Volkov, Shulamit. 1989. "The Written Matter and the Spoken Word: On the Gap between Pre-1914 and Nazi Anti-Semitism." In F. Furet (ed.), *Unanswered Questions*. New York: Schocken.

Walker, Kizer. 1994. "The Persian Gulf War and the Germans' 'Jewish Question?'" In S. Gilman & K. Remmler (eds.), *Reemerging Jewish Culture in Germany*. New York: New York University Press.

Webster, Ronald. 2001. "Opposing 'Victors' Justice': German Protestant Churchmen and Convicted Criminals in Western Europe after 1945." *Holocaust and Genocide Studies* 15:47–69.

Wehler, Hans-Ulbrich. 1998. "Like a Thorn in the Flesh." In R. Shandley (ed.), *Unwilling Germans?* Minneapolis: University of Minnesota Press.

Weinberg, Daniel. 2001. "France." In W. Laqueur (ed.), *The Holocaust Encyclopedia*. New Haven, CT: Yale University Press.

Weinberg, Gerhard L. 1998. "The Allies and the Holocaust." In M. Berenbaum & A. Peck (eds.), *The Holocaust and History*. Bloomington: Indiana University Press.

Weissberg, Liliane. 1997. "The Tale of a Good German: Reflections on the German Reception of *Schindler's List*." In Y. Loshitzky (ed.), *Spielberg's Holocaust*. Bloomington: Indiana University Press.

Weitz, Yechiam. 1994. "The Herut Movement and the Kasztner Trial." *Holocaust and Genocide Studies* 8:349–71.

Welch, David. 1993. *The Third Reich: Politics and Propaganda*. New York: Routledge.

Wendell, Susan. 1996. *The Rejected Body: Feminist Philosophical Reflections on Disability*. New York: Routledge.

Wiesel Elie. 1960. *Night*. New York: Bantam.

Wiesel Elie. 1978. *A Jew Today*. New York: Random House.

Wiesel Elie. 1995. Interview on "The Oprah Winfrey Show." CBS.

Wiesenthal, Simon. 1998. *The Sunflower: On the Possibilities and Limits of Forgiveness*. New York: Schocken.

Will, George. 2001. "July 10, 1941, in Jedwabne." *Newsweek,* July 9, p. 68.

Willis, Ellen. 2001. "Freedom from Religion." *Nation,* February 19, p. 11.

Wistrich, Robert S. 1995. *Who's Who in Nazi Germany*. New York: Routledge.

Wolffsohn, Michael. 1993. *External Guilt? Forty Years of German-Jewish-Israeli Relations*. New York: Columbia University Press.

Wolin, Richard. 1996. "The Ambivalences of German-Jewish Identity: Hannah Arendt in Jerusalem." *History and Memory* 8:9–34.

World Almanac. 2001. *The World Book Almanac of Facts*. Mahwah, NJ: World Almanac.

Wright, Erik O. 1978. *Class, Crisis, and the State*. New York: Schocken.

Wyman, David S. 1984. *The Abandonment of the Jews: America and the Holocaust, 1941–1945*. New York: Pantheon.

Wyman, David S. 1990. "Evian Conference." In I. Gutman (ed.), *Encyclopedia of the Holocaust*. New York: Macmillan.

Yahil, Leni. 1990. *The Holocaust: The Fate of European Jewry*. New York: Oxford University Press.

Young, James E. 1993. *The Texture of Memory: Holocaust Memorials and Meanings in Europe, Israel, and America*. New Haven, CT: Yale University Press.

Zahn, Gordon C. 1962. *German Catholics and Hitler's Wars*. New York: Sheed & Ward.

Zald, Mayer N., & Bert Useem. 1987. "Movement and Countermovement Interaction: Mobilization, Tactics, and State Involvement." In M. Zald & J. McCarthy (eds.), *Social Movements in an Organizational Society*. New Brunswick, NJ: Transaction.

Zeitlan, Irving. 1990. *Ideology and the Development of Sociological Theory*. Englewood Cliffs, NJ: Prentice-Hall.

Zuccotti, Susan. 1987. *The Italians and the Holocaust: Persecution, Rescue, and Survival*. New York: Basic.

Index